DEMOSTHENES, SPEECHES 20–22

THE ORATORY OF CLASSICAL GREECE

Translated with Notes • *Michael Gagarin, Series Editor*

VOLUME 12

DEMOSTHENES, SPEECHES 20–22

Translated with introduction and notes by

Edward M. Harris

 UNIVERSITY OF TEXAS PRESS, AUSTIN

First edition, 2008

Requests for permission to reproduce material from this work should be
sent to: Permissions, University of Texas Press, P.O. Box 7819, Austin, TX
78713-7819. www.utexas.edu/utpress/about/bpermission.html

⊚ The paper used in this book meets the minimum requirements of
ANSI/NISO z39.48-1992 (R1997) (Permanence of Paper).

Library of Congress Cataloging-in-Publication Data
Demosthenes.
    [Adversus Leptinem. English]
    Demosthenes, speeches 20–22 / translated with introduction and notes
by Edward M. Harris.
        p.   cm. — (The oratory of classical greece)
    Includes bibliographical references and index.
    ISBN 978-0-292-71783-1 (cloth : alk. paper) — ISBN 978-0-292-71784-8
(pbk. : alk. paper)
    1. Demosthenes—Translations into English.   2. Speeches, addresses,
etc., Greek—Translations into English. 3. Athens (Greece)—Politics
and government—Early works to 1800.   I. Harris, Edward Monroe.
II. Demosthenes. Against Midias. English.   III. Demosthenes. Kat'
Androtionos. English.   IV. Title.   V. Series.
    PA3951.E5 2008
    885'.01—dc22

                                                          2007052241

To the memory of
Marion Stevens Harris

CONTENTS

SERIES EDITOR'S PREFACE

This is the twelfth volume in a series of translations of *The Oratory of Classical Greece*. The aim of the series is to make available primarily for those who do not read Greek up-to-date, accurate, and readable translations with introductions and explanatory notes of all the surviving works and major fragments of the Attic orators of the classical period (*ca.* 420–320 BC): Aeschines, Andocides, Antiphon, Demosthenes, Dinarchus, Hyperides, Isaeus, Isocrates, Lycurgus, and Lysias. This volume contains speeches from three of Demosthenes' best known and most important public cases. They mark the beginning of his public career, which he advanced in part by the prosecution of other high-profile public figures, and they established Demosthenes as a major force in Athenian public life.

This volume, like the others in the series, has benefited greatly from the careful attention of many at the University of Texas Press, including Director Joanna Hitchcock, Humanities Editor Jim Burr, production editor Lynne Chapman, and copy editor Nancy Moore. As always, they have been a pleasure to work with.

—M. G.

TRANSLATOR'S ACKNOWLEDGMENTS

I would like to express my gratitude to several scholars who were kind enough to help me at various stages in the preparation of this book. Fred Naiden read over some early drafts of the translations, pointed out errors and omissions, and offered suggestions for improvement. At a later stage, Peter J. Rhodes scrutinized the introductions, translations, and notes of *Against Leptines* and *Against Androtion,* corrected errors, and supplied valuable information about Athenian laws and institutions. Michael Gagarin read the penultimate draft of the entire manuscript for the press. He not only removed several errors but also helped to make the translation more concise and readable. He also made perceptive comments about points of interpretation, some of which I have quoted in the notes. Alan Boegehold acted as second reader for the press and offered some brief comments. Robert Pitt gave the final draft a very careful reading, checked it for consistency, and caught several small mistakes.

For the translations of *Against Leptines* and *Against Androtion* I have used the Oxford Classical Text edited by my friend Mervin Dilts, who kindly sent me a copy of his text soon after it was published. For the text of *Against Meidias* I have used the text edited by D. M. MacDowell in 1990. Even though Professor MacDowell did not help in the preparation of this book, I have learned an enormous amount from his splendid introduction and commentary to this speech. My debt to his work is acknowledged in the notes.

In other volumes in this series the Greek word *dikastes* is normally translated with the English word "juror," which is both misleading and anachronistic. The Common Law distinction between judges, who decide questions of law, and jurors, who decide questions of fact (guilt or innocence), did not exist in the Athenian courts, in which the *dikastai* decided both questions of law and questions of fact (see Harris 2000, 2004a). *Dikastai* were also unlike modern jurors because they normally heard many cases and acquired some legal expertise by serving in the courts for many years. Moreover, the noun *dikastes* is formed from the verb *dikazein,* which means "to judge," and should therefore be translated as "one who judges" or "judge."

The draft of this book was submitted to the press in the middle of 2006. Aside from a few items, I have therefore not been able to take account of work published in that year or later.

—E. H.

SERIES INTRODUCTION
Greek Oratory

〰〰〰〰〰〰〰〰〰〰〰〰〰〰〰〰〰〰〰〰〰〰〰〰〰〰〰〰〰〰〰〰〰〰〰〰〰

By Michael Gagarin

ORATORY IN CLASSICAL ATHENS

From as early as Homer (and undoubtedly much earlier) the Greeks placed a high value on effective speaking. Even Achilles, whose greatness was primarily established on the battlefield, was brought up to be "a speaker of words and a doer of deeds" (*Iliad* 9.443); and Athenian leaders of the sixth and fifth centuries,[1] such as Solon, Themistocles, and Pericles, were all accomplished orators. Most Greek literary genres—notably epic, tragedy, and history—underscore the importance of oratory by their inclusion of set speeches. The formal pleadings of the envoys to Achilles in the *Iliad,* the messenger speeches in tragedy reporting events like the battle of Salamis in Aeschylus' *Persians* or the gruesome death of Pentheus in Euripides' *Bacchae,* and the powerful political oratory of Pericles' funeral oration in Thucydides are but a few of the most notable examples of the Greeks' never-ending fascination with formal public speaking, which was to reach its height in the public oratory of the fourth century.

In early times, oratory was not a specialized subject of study but was learned by practice and example. The formal study of rhetoric as an "art" (*technē*) began, we are told, in the middle of the fifth century in Sicily with the work of Corax and his pupil Tisias.[2] These two are

---

[1] All dates in this volume are BC unless the contrary is either indicated or obvious.

[2] See Kennedy 1963: 26–51. Cole 1991 has challenged this traditional picture, arguing that the term "rhetoric" was coined by Plato to designate and denigrate an activity he strongly opposed. Cole's own reconstruction is not without problems,

scarcely more than names to us, but another famous Sicilian, Gorgias of Leontini (ca. 490–390), developed a new style of argument and is reported to have dazzled the Athenians with a speech delivered when he visited Athens in 427. Gorgias initiated the practice, which continued into the early fourth century, of composing speeches for mythical or imaginary occasions. The surviving examples reveal a lively intellectual climate in the late fifth and early fourth centuries, in which oratory served to display new ideas, new forms of expression, and new methods of argument.[3] This tradition of "intellectual" oratory was continued by the fourth-century educator Isocrates and played a large role in later Greek and Roman education.

In addition to this intellectual oratory, at about the same time the practice also began of writing speeches for real occasions in public life, which we may designate "practical" oratory. For centuries Athenians had been delivering speeches in public settings (primarily the courts and the Assembly), but these had always been composed and delivered impromptu, without being written down and thus without being preserved. The practice of writing speeches began in the courts and then expanded to include the Assembly and other settings. Athens was one of the leading cities of Greece in the fifth and fourth centuries, and its political and legal systems depended on direct participation by a large number of citizens; all important decisions were made by these large bodies, and the primary means of influencing these decisions was oratory.[4] Thus, it is not surprising that oratory flourished in Athens,[5] but it may not be immediately obvious why it should be written down.

The pivotal figure in this development was Antiphon, one of the fifth-century intellectuals who are often grouped together under the

---

but he does well to remind us how thoroughly the traditional view of rhetoric depends on one of its most ardent opponents.

[3] Of these only Antiphon's Tetralogies are included in this series. Gorgias' *Helen* and *Palamedes,* Alcidamas' *Odysseus,* and Antisthenes' *Ajax* and *Odysseus* are translated in Gagarin and Woodruff 1995.

[4] Yunis 1996 has a good treatment of political oratory from Pericles to Demosthenes.

[5] All our evidence for practical oratory comes from Athens, with the exception of Isocrates 19, written for a trial in Aegina. Many speeches were undoubtedly delivered in courts and political forums in other Greek cities, but it may be that such speeches were written down only in Athens.

name "Sophists."[6] Like some of the other sophists he contributed to the intellectual oratory of the period, but he also had a strong practical interest in law. At the same time, Antiphon had an aversion to public speaking and did not directly involve himself in legal or political affairs (Thucydides 8.68). However, he began giving general advice to other citizens who were engaged in litigation and were thus expected to address the court themselves. As this practice grew, Antiphon went further, and around 430 he began writing out whole speeches for others to memorize and deliver. Thus began the practice of "logography," which continued through the next century and beyond.[7] Logography particularly appealed to men like Lysias, who were metics, or noncitizen residents of Athens. Since they were not Athenian citizens, they were barred from direct participation in public life, but they could contribute by writing speeches for others.

Antiphon was also the first (to our knowledge) to write down a speech he would himself deliver, writing the speech for his own defense at his trial for treason in 411. His motive was probably to publicize and preserve his views, and others continued this practice of writing down speeches they would themselves deliver in the courts and (more rarely) the Assembly.[8] Finally, one other type of practical oratory was the special tribute delivered on certain important public occasions, the best known of which is the funeral oration. It is convenient to designate these three types of oratory by the terms Aristotle later uses: forensic (for the courts), deliberative (for the Assembly), and epideictic (for display).[9]

---

[6] The term "sophist" was loosely used through the fifth and fourth centuries to designate various intellectuals and orators, but under the influence of Plato, who attacked certain figures under this name, the term is now used of a specific group of thinkers; see Kerferd 1981.

[7] For Antiphon as the first to write speeches, see Photius, *Bibliotheca* 486a7–11 and [Plut.], *Moralia* 832c–d. The latest extant speech can be dated to 320, but we know that at least one orator, Dinarchus, continued the practice after that date.

[8] Unlike forensic speeches, speeches for delivery in the Assembly were usually not composed beforehand in writing, since the speaker could not know exactly when or in what context he would be speaking; see further Trevett 1996.

[9] *Rhetoric* 1.3. Intellectual orations, like Gorgias' *Helen,* do not easily fit into Aristotle's classification. For a fuller (but still brief) introduction to Attic oratory and the orators, see Edwards 1994.

THE ORATORS

In the century from about 420 to 320, dozens—perhaps even hundreds—of now unknown orators and logographers must have composed speeches that are now lost, but only ten of these men were selected for preservation and study by ancient scholars, and only works collected under the names of these ten have been preserved. Some of these works are undoubtedly spurious, though in most cases they are fourth-century works by a different author rather than later "forgeries." Indeed, modern scholars suspect that as many as seven of the speeches attributed to Demosthenes may have been written by Apollodorus, son of Pasion, who is sometimes called "the eleventh orator."[10] Including these speeches among the works of Demosthenes may have been an honest mistake, or perhaps a bookseller felt he could sell more copies of these speeches if they were attributed to a more famous orator.

In alphabetical order the Ten Orators are as follows:[11]

- AESCHINES (ca. 390–ca. 322) rose from obscure origins to become an important Athenian political figure, first an ally, then a bitter enemy of Demosthenes. His three speeches all concern major public issues. The best known of these (Aes. 3) was delivered at the trial in 330, when Demosthenes responded with *On the Crown* (Dem. 18). Aeschines lost the case and was forced to leave Athens and live the rest of his life in exile.

- ANDOCIDES (ca. 440–ca. 390) is best known for his role in the scandal of 415, when just before the departure of the fateful Athenian expedition to Sicily during the Peloponnesian War (431–404), a band of young men mutilated statues of Hermes, and at the same time information was revealed about the secret rites of Demeter. Andocides was exiled but later returned. Two of the four speeches

---

[10] See Trevett 1992.

[11] The Loeb volumes of *Minor Attic Orators* also include the prominent Athenian political figure Demades (ca. 385–319), who was not one of the Ten; but the only speech that has come down to us under his name is a later forgery. It is possible that Demades and other fourth-century politicians who had a high reputation for public speaking did not put any speeches in writing, especially if they rarely spoke in the courts (see above n. 8).

in his name give us a contemporary view of the scandal: one pleads for his return, the other argues against a second period of exile.

• ANTIPHON (ca. 480–411), as already noted, wrote forensic speeches for others and only once spoke himself. In 411 he participated in an oligarchic coup by a group of 400, and when the democrats regained power he was tried for treason and executed. His six surviving speeches include three for delivery in court and the three Tetralogies—imaginary intellectual exercises for display or teaching that consist of four speeches each, two on each side. All six of Antiphon's speeches concern homicide, probably because these stood at the beginning of the collection of his works. Fragments of some thirty other speeches cover many different topics.

• DEMOSTHENES (384–322) is generally considered the best of the Attic orators. Although his nationalistic message is less highly regarded today, his powerful mastery of and ability to combine many different rhetorical styles continues to impress readers. Demosthenes was still a child when his wealthy father died. The trustees of the estate apparently misappropriated much of it, and when he came of age, he sued them in a series of cases (27–31), regaining some of his fortune and making a name as a powerful speaker. He then wrote speeches for others in a variety of cases, public and private, and for his own use in court (where many cases involved major public issues), and in the Assembly, where he opposed the growing power of Philip of Macedon. The triumph of Philip and his son Alexander the Great eventually put an end to Demosthenes' career. Some sixty speeches have come down under his name, about a third of them of questionable authenticity.

• DINARCHUS (ca. 360–ca. 290) was born in Corinth but spent much of his life in Athens as a metic (a noncitizen resident). His public fame came primarily from writing speeches for the prosecutions surrounding the Harpalus affair in 324, when several prominent figures (including Demosthenes) were accused of bribery. After 322 he had a profitable career as a logographer.

• HYPERIDES (389/8–322) was a political leader and logographer of so many different talents that he was called the pentathlete of orators. He was a leader of the Athenian resistance to Philip and

Alexander and (like Demosthenes) was condemned to death after Athens' final surrender. One speech and substantial fragments of five others have been recovered from papyrus remains; otherwise, only fragments survive.

* ISAEUS (ca. 415–ca. 340) wrote speeches on a wide range of topics, but the eleven complete speeches that survive, dating from ca. 390 to ca. 344, all concern inheritance. As with Antiphon, the survival of these particular speeches may have been the result of the later ordering of his speeches by subject; we have part of a twelfth speech and fragments and titles of some forty other works. Isaeus is said to have been a pupil of Isocrates and the teacher of Demosthenes.

* ISOCRATES (436–338) considered himself a philosopher and educator, not an orator or rhetorician. He came from a wealthy Athenian family but lost most of his property in the Peloponnesian War, and in 403 he took up logography. About 390 he abandoned this practice and turned to writing and teaching, setting forth his educational, philosophical, and political views in essays that took the form of speeches but were not meant for oral delivery. He favored accommodation with the growing power of Philip of Macedon and panhellenic unity. His school was based on a broad concept of rhetoric and applied philosophy; it attracted pupils from the entire Greek world (including Isaeus, Lycurgus, and Hyperides) and became the main rival of Plato's Academy. Isocrates greatly influenced education and rhetoric in the Hellenistic, Roman, and modern periods until the eighteenth century.

* LYCURGUS (ca. 390–ca. 324) was a leading public official who restored the financial condition of Athens after 338 and played a large role in the city for the next dozen years. He brought charges of corruption or treason against many other officials, usually with success. Only one speech survives.

* LYSIAS (ca. 445–ca. 380) was a metic—an official resident of Athens but not a citizen. Much of his property was seized by the Thirty during their short-lived oligarchic coup in 404–403. Perhaps as a result he turned to logography. More than thirty speeches survive in whole or in part, though the authenticity of some is doubted. We also have fragments or know the titles of more than a hundred

others. The speeches cover a wide range of cases, and he may have delivered one himself (Lys. 12), on the death of his brother at the hands of the Thirty. Lysias is particularly known for his vivid narratives, his *ēthopoiia,* or "creation of character," and his prose style, which became a model of clarity and vividness.

THE WORKS OF THE ORATORS

As soon as speeches began to be written down, they could be preserved. We know little about the conditions of book "publication" (i.e., making copies for distribution) in the fourth century, but there was an active market for books in Athens, and some of the speeches may have achieved wide circulation.[12] An orator (or his family) may have preserved his own speeches, perhaps to advertise his ability or demonstrate his success, or booksellers may have collected and copied them in order to make money.

We do not know how closely the preserved text of these speeches corresponded to the version actually delivered in court or in the Assembly. Speakers undoubtedly extemporized or varied from their text on occasion, but there is no good evidence that deliberative speeches were substantially revised for publication.[13] In forensic oratory a logographer's reputation would derive first and foremost from his success with jurors. If a forensic speech was victorious, there would be no reason to alter it for publication, and if it lost, alteration would probably not deceive potential clients. Thus, the published texts of forensic speeches were probably quite faithful to the texts that were provided to clients, and we have little reason to suspect substantial alteration in the century or so before they were collected by scholars in Alexandria (see below).

In addition to the speaker's text, most forensic speeches have breaks for the inclusion of documents. The logographer inserted a notation in his text—such as *nomos* ("law") or *martyria* ("testimony")—and the

---

[12] Dover's discussion (1968) of the preservation and transmission of the works of Lysias (and perhaps others under his name) is useful not just for Lysias but for the other orators too. His theory of shared authorship between logographer and litigant, however, is unconvincing (see Usher 1976).

[13] See further Trevett 1996: 437–439.

speaker would pause while the clerk read out the text of a law or the testimony of witnesses. Many speeches survive with only a notation that a *nomos* or *martyria* was read at that point, but in some cases the text of the document is included. It used to be thought that these documents were all creations of later scholars, but many (though not all) are now accepted as genuine.[14]

With the foundation of the famous library in Alexandria early in the third century, scholars began to collect and catalogue texts of the orators, along with many other classical authors. Only the best orators were preserved in the library, many of them represented by over 100 speeches each (some undoubtedly spurious). Only some of these works survived in manuscript form to the modern era; more recently a few others have been discovered on ancient sheets of papyrus, so that today the corpus of Attic Oratory consists of about 150 speeches, together with a few letters and other works. The subject matter ranges from important public issues and serious crimes to business affairs, lovers' quarrels, inheritance disputes, and other personal or family matters.

In the centuries after these works were collected, ancient scholars gathered biographical facts about their authors, produced grammatical and lexicographic notes, and used some of the speeches as evidence for Athenian political history. But the ancient scholars who were most interested in the orators were those who studied prose style, the most notable of these being Dionysius of Halicarnassus (first century BC), who wrote treatises on several of the orators,[15] and Hermogenes of Tarsus (second century AD), who wrote several literary studies, including *On Types of Style*.[16] But relative to epic or tragedy, oratory was little studied; and even scholars of rhetoric whose interests were broader than style, like Cicero and Quintilian, paid little attention to the orators, except for the acknowledged master, Demosthenes.

Most modern scholars until the second half of the twentieth century continued to treat the orators primarily as prose stylists.[17] The

[14] See MacDowell 1990: 43–47; Todd 1993: 44–45.

[15] Dionysius' literary studies are collected and translated in Usher 1974–1985.

[16] Wooten 1987. Stylistic considerations probably also influenced the selection of the "canon" of ten orators; see Worthington 1994.

[17] For example, the most popular and influential book ever written on the orators, Jebb's *The Attic Orators* (1875) was presented as an "attempt to aid in giving Attic Oratory its due place in the history of Attic Prose" (I.xiii). This modern focus

reevaluation of Athenian democracy by George Grote and others in the nineteenth century stimulated renewed interest in Greek oratory among historians; and increasing interest in Athenian law during that century led a few legal scholars to read the orators. But in comparison with the interest shown in the other literary genres—epic, lyric, tragedy, comedy, and even history—Attic oratory has been relatively neglected until the last third of the twentieth century. More recently, however, scholars have discovered the value of the orators for the broader study of Athenian culture and society. Since Dover's groundbreaking works on popular morality and homosexuality,[18] interest in the orators has been increasing rapidly, and they are now seen as primary representatives of Athenian moral and social values, and as evidence for social and economic conditions, political and social ideology, and in general those aspects of Athenian culture that in the past were commonly ignored by historians of ancient Greece but are of increasing interest and importance today, including women and the family, slavery, and the economy.

GOVERNMENT AND LAW IN CLASSICAL ATHENS

The hallmark of the Athenian political and legal systems was its amateurism. Most public officials, including those who supervised the courts, were selected by lot and held office for a limited period, typically a year. Thus a great many citizens held public office at some point in their lives, but almost none served for an extended period of time or developed the experience or expertise that would make them professionals. All significant policy decisions were debated and voted on in the Assembly, where the quorum was 6,000 citizens, and all significant legal cases were judged by bodies of 200 to 500 jurors or more. Public prominence was not achieved by election (or selection) to public office but depended rather on a man's ability to sway the majority of citizens in the Assembly or jurors in court to vote in favor of a pro-

---

on prose style can plausibly be connected to the large role played by prose composition (translation of English prose into Greek, usually in imitation of specific authors or styles) in the Classics curriculum, especially in Britain.

[18] Dover (1974, 1978). Dover recently commented (1994: 157), "When I began to mine the riches of Attic forensic oratory I was astonished to discover that the mine had never been exploited."

posed course of action or for one of the litigants in a trial. Success was never permanent, and a victory on one policy issue or a verdict in one case could be quickly reversed in another.[19] In such a system the value of public oratory is obvious, and in the fourth century, oratory became the most important cultural institution in Athens, replacing drama as the forum where major ideological concerns were displayed and debated.

Several recent books give good detailed accounts of Athenian government and law,[20] and so a brief sketch can suffice here. The main policy-making body was the Assembly, open to all adult male citizens; a small payment for attendance enabled at least some of the poor to attend along with the leisured rich. In addition, a Council of 500 citizens, selected each year by lot with no one allowed to serve more than two years, prepared material for and made recommendations to the Assembly; a rotating subgroup of this Council served as an executive committee, the Prytaneis. Finally, numerous officials, most of them selected by lot for one-year terms, supervised different areas of administration and finance. The most important of these were the nine Archons (lit. "rulers"): the eponymous Archon after whom the year was named, the Basileus ("king"),[21] the Polemarch, and the six Thesmothetae. Councilors and almost all these officials underwent a preliminary examination (*dokimasia*) before taking office, and officials submitted to a final accounting (*euthynai*) upon leaving; at these times any citizen who wished could challenge a person's fitness for his new position or his performance in his recent position.

---

[19] In the Assembly this could be accomplished by a reconsideration of the question, as in the famous Mytilenean debate (Thuc. 3.36–50); in court a verdict was final, but its practical effects could be thwarted or reversed by later litigation on a related issue.

[20] For government, see Sinclair 1988, Hansen 1991; for law, MacDowell 1978, Todd 1993, and Boegehold 1995 (Bonner 1927 is still helpful). Much of our information about the legal and political systems comes from a work attributed to Aristotle but perhaps written by a pupil of his, *The Athenian Constitution* (*Ath. Pol.*—conveniently translated with notes by Rhodes 1984). The discovery of this work on a papyrus in Egypt in 1890 caused a major resurgence of interest in Athenian government.

[21] Modern scholars often use the term *archōn basileus* or "king archon," but Athenian sources (e.g., *Ath. Pol.* 57) simply call him the *basileus*.

There was no general taxation of Athenian citizens. Sources of public funding included the annual tax levied on metics, various fees and import duties, and (in the fifth century) tribute from allied cities; but the source that figures most prominently in the orators is the Athenian system of liturgies (*leitourgiai*), by which in a regular rotation the rich provided funding for certain special public needs. The main liturgies were the *chorēgia,* in which a sponsor (*chorēgos*) supervised and paid for the training and performance of a chorus which sang and danced at a public festival,[22] and the trierarchy, in which a sponsor (trierarch) paid to equip and usually commanded a trireme, or warship, for a year. Some of these liturgies required substantial expenditures, but even so, some men spent far more than required in order to promote themselves and their public careers, and litigants often tried to impress the jurors by referring to liturgies they had undertaken (see, e.g., Lys. 21.1–n5). A further twist on this system was that if a man thought he had been assigned a liturgy that should have gone to someone else who was richer than he, he could propose an exchange of property (*antidosis*), giving the other man a choice of either taking over the liturgy or exchanging property with him. Finally, the rich were also subject to special taxes (*eisphorai*) levied as a percentage of their property in times of need.

The Athenian legal system remained similarly resistant to professionalization. Trials and the procedures leading up to them were supervised by officials, primarily the nine Archons, but their role was purely administrative, and they were in no way equivalent to modern judges. All significant questions about what we would call points of law were presented to the jurors, who considered them together with all other issues when they delivered their verdict at the end of the trial.[23] Trials were "contests" (*agōnes*) between two litigants, each of whom presented his own case to the jurors in a speech, plaintiff first, then de-

---

[22] These included the productions of tragedy and comedy, for which the main expense was for the chorus.

[23] Certain religious "interpreters" (*exēgētai*) were occasionally asked to give their opinion on a legal matter that had a religious dimension (such as the prosecution of a homicide), but although these opinions could be reported in court (e.g., Dem. 47.68–73), they had no official legal standing. The most significant administrative decision we hear of is the refusal of the Basileus to accept the case in Antiphon 6 (see 6.37–46).

fendant; in some cases each party then spoke again, probably in rebuttal. Since a litigant had only one or two speeches in which to present his entire case, and no issue was decided separately by a judge, all the necessary factual information and every important argument on substance or procedure, fact or law, had to be presented together. A single speech might thus combine narrative, argument, emotional appeal, and various digressions, all with the goal of obtaining a favorable verdict. Even more than today, a litigant's primary task was to control the issue—to determine which issues the jurors would consider most important and which questions they would have in their minds as they cast their votes. We only rarely have both speeches from a trial,[24] and we usually have little or no external evidence for the facts of a case or the verdict. We must thus infer both the facts and the opponent's strategy from the speech we have, and any assessment of the overall effectiveness of a speech and of the logographer's strategy is to some extent speculative.

Before a trial there were usually several preliminary hearings for presenting evidence; arbitration, public and private, was available and sometimes required. These hearings and arbitration sessions allowed each side to become familiar with the other side's case, so that discussions of "what my opponent will say" could be included in one's speech. Normally a litigant presented his own case, but he was often assisted by family or friends. If he wished (and could afford it), he could enlist the services of a logographer, who presumably gave strategic advice in addition to writing a speech. The speeches were timed to ensure an equal hearing for both sides,[25] and all trials were completed within a day. Two hundred or more jurors decided each case in the popular courts, which met in the Agora.[26] Homicide cases and certain other religious trials (e.g., Lys. 7) were heard by the Council of the Areopagus or an associated group of fifty-one Ephetae. The Areopagus was composed of all former Archons—perhaps 150–200 members at most

[24] The exceptions are Demosthenes 19 and Aeschines 2, Aeschines 3 and Demosthenes 18, and Lysias 6 (one of several prosecution speeches) and Andocides 1; all were written for major public cases.

[25] Timing was done by means of a water-clock, which in most cases was stopped during the reading of documents.

[26] See Boegehold 1995.

times. It met on a hill called the Areopagus ("rock of Ares") near the Acropolis.

Jurors for the regular courts were selected by lot from those citizens who registered each year and who appeared for duty that day; as with the Assembly, a small payment allowed the poor to serve. After the speakers had finished, the jurors voted immediately without any formal discussion. The side with the majority won; a tie vote decided the case for the defendant. In some cases where the penalty was not fixed, after a conviction the jurors voted again on the penalty, choosing between penalties proposed by each side. Even when we know the verdict, we cannot know which of the speaker's arguments contributed most to his success or failure. However, a logographer could probably learn from jurors which points had or had not been successful, so that arguments that are found repeatedly in speeches probably were known to be effective in most cases.

The first written laws in Athens were enacted by Draco (ca. 620) and Solon (ca. 590), and new laws were regularly added. At the end of the fifth century the existing laws were reorganized, and a new procedure for enacting laws was instituted; thereafter a group of Law-Givers (*nomothetai*) had to certify that a proposed law did not conflict with any existing laws. There was no attempt, however, to organize legislation systematically, and although Plato, Aristotle, and other philosophers wrote various works on law and law-giving, these were either theoretical or descriptive and had no apparent influence on legislation. Written statutes generally used ordinary language rather than precise legal definitions in designating offenses, and questions concerning precisely what constituted a specific offense or what was the correct interpretation of a written statute were decided (together with other issues) by the jurors in each case. A litigant might, of course, assert a certain definition or interpretation as "something you all know" or "what the lawgiver intended," but such remarks are evidently tendentious and cannot be taken as authoritative.

The result of these procedural and substantive features was that the verdict depended largely on each litigant's speech (or speeches). As one speaker puts it (Ant. 6.18), "When there are no witnesses, you (jurors) are forced to reach a verdict about the case on the basis of the prosecutor's and defendant's words alone; you must be suspicious and examine their accounts in detail, and your vote will necessarily be cast on the basis of likelihood rather than clear knowledge." Even the testimony of witnesses (usually on both sides) is rarely decisive. On the other hand, most speakers make a considerable effort to establish facts and provide legitimate arguments in conformity with established law. Plato's view of rhetoric as a clever technique for persuading an ignorant crowd that the false is true is not borne out by the speeches, and the legal system does not appear to have produced many arbitrary or clearly unjust results.

The main form of legal procedure was a *dikē* ("suit") in which the injured party (or his relatives in a case of homicide) brought suit against the offender. Suits for injuries to slaves would be brought by the slave's master, and injuries to women would be prosecuted by a male relative. Strictly speaking, a *dikē* was a private matter between individuals, though like all cases, *dikai* often had public dimensions. The other major form of procedure was a *graphē* ("writing" or "indictment") in which "anyone who wished" (i.e., any citizen) could bring a prosecution for wrongdoing. *Graphai* were instituted by Solon, probably in order to allow prosecution of offenses where the victim was unable or unlikely to bring suit himself, such as selling a dependent into slavery; but the number of areas covered by *graphai* increased to cover many types of public offenses as well as some apparently private crimes, such as *hybris.*

The system of prosecution by "anyone who wished" also extended to several other more specialized forms of prosecution, like *eisangelia* ("impeachment"), used in cases of treason. Another specialized prosecution was *apagōgē* ("summary arrest"), in which someone could arrest a common criminal (*kakourgos,* lit. "evil-doer"), or have him arrested, on the spot. The reliance on private initiative meant that Athenians never developed a system of public prosecution; rather, they presumed that everyone would keep an eye on the behavior of his political enemies and bring suit as soon as he suspected a crime, both to harm his opponents and to advance his own career. In this way all public officials would be watched by someone. There was no disgrace in admitting that a prosecution was motivated by private enmity.

By the end of the fifth century the system of prosecution by "anyone who wished" was apparently being abused by so-called sykophants (*sykophantai*), who allegedly brought or threatened to bring false suits against rich men, either to gain part of the fine that would be levied or to induce an out-of-court settlement in which the accused would pay to have the matter dropped. We cannot gauge the true extent of this problem, since speakers usually provide little evidence to support their claims that their opponents are sykophants, but the Athenians did make sykophancy a crime. They also specified that in many public procedures a plaintiff who either dropped the case or failed to obtain one-fifth of the votes would have to pay a heavy fine of 1,000 drachmas. Despite this, it appears that litigation was common in Athens and was seen by some as excessive.

Over the course of time, the Athenian legal and political systems have more often been judged negatively than positively. Philosophers and political theorists have generally followed the lead of Plato (427–347), who lived and worked in Athens his entire life while severely criticizing its system of government as well as many other aspects of its culture. For Plato, democracy amounted to the tyranny of the masses over the educated elite and was destined to collapse from its own instability. The legal system was capricious and depended entirely on the rhetorical ability of litigants with no regard for truth or justice. These criticisms have often been echoed by modern scholars, who particularly complain that law was much too closely interwoven with politics and did not have the autonomous status it achieved in Roman law and continues to have, at least in theory, in modern legal systems.

Plato's judgments are valid if one accepts the underlying presuppositions, that the aim of law is absolute truth and abstract justice and that achieving the highest good of the state requires thorough and systematic organization. Most Athenians do not seem to have subscribed to either the criticisms or the presuppositions, and most scholars now accept the long-ignored fact that despite major external disruptions in the form of wars and two short-lived coups brought about by one of these wars, the Athenian legal and political systems remained remarkably stable for almost two hundred years (508–320). Moreover, like all other Greek cities at the time, whatever their form of government, Athenian democracy was brought to an end not by internal forces but by the external power of Philip of Macedon and his son Alexander. The legal system never became autonomous, and the rich sometimes complained that they were victims of unscrupulous litigants, but there is no indication that the people wanted to yield control of the legal process to a professional class, as Plato recommended. For most Athenians—Plato being an exception in this and many other matters—one purpose of the legal system was to give everyone the opportunity to have his case heard by other citizens and have it heard quickly and cheaply; and in this it clearly succeeded.

Indeed, the Athenian legal system also served the interests of the rich, even the very rich, as well as the common people, in that it provided a forum for the competition that since Homer had been an important part of aristocratic life. In this competition, the rich used the courts as battlegrounds, though their main weapon was the rhetoric of popular ideology, which hailed the rule of law and promoted the ideal of moderation and restraint.[27] But those who aspired to political leadership and the honor and status that accompanied it repeatedly entered the legal arena, bringing suit against their political enemies whenever possible and defending themselves against suits brought by others whenever necessary. The ultimate judges of these public competitions were the common people, who seem to have relished the dramatic clash of individuals and ideologies. In this respect fourth-century oratory was the cultural heir of fifth-century drama and was similarly appreciated by the citizens. Despite the disapproval of intellectuals like Plato, most Athenians legitimately considered their legal system a hallmark of their democracy and a vital presence in their culture.

THE TRANSLATION OF GREEK ORATORY

The purpose of this series is to provide students and scholars in all fields with accurate, readable translations of all surviving classical Attic oratory, including speeches whose authenticity is disputed, as well as the substantial surviving fragments. In keeping with the originals, the language is for the most part nontechnical. Names of persons and places are given in the (generally more familiar) Latinized forms, and names of officials or legal procedures have been translated into English equivalents, where possible. Notes are intended to provide the necessary historical and cultural background; scholarly controversies are generally not discussed. The notes and introductions refer to scholarly treatments in addition to those listed below, which the reader may consult for further information.

---

[27] Ober 1989 is fundamental; see also Cohen 1995.

Cross-references to other speeches follow the standard numbering system, which is now well established except in the case of Hyperides (for whom the numbering of the Oxford Classical Text is used).[28] References are by work and section (e.g., Dem. 24.73); spurious works are not specially marked; when no author is named (e.g., 24.73), the reference is to the same author as the annotated passage.

ABBREVIATIONS

Aes.   = Aeschines
And.   = Andocides
Ant.   = Antiphon
Arist.   = Aristotle
Aristoph. = Aristophanes
Ath. Pol. = *The Athenian Constitution*
Dem.   = Demosthenes
Din.   = Dinarchus
Herod.   = Herodotus
Hyp.   = Hyperides
Is.   = Isaeus
Isoc.   = Isocrates
Lyc.   = Lycurgus
Lys.   = Lysias
Plut.   = Plutarch
Thuc.   = Thucydides
Xen.   = Xenophon

NOTE: The main unit of Athenian currency was the drachma; this was divided into obols and larger amounts were designated minas and talents.

1 drachma = 6 obols
1 mina   = 100 drachmas
1 talent   = 60 minas (6,000 drachmas)

It is impossible to give an accurate equivalence in terms of modern currency, but it may be helpful to remember that the daily wage of

---

[28] For a listing of all the orators and their works, with classifications (forensic, deliberative, epideictic) and rough dates, see Edwards 1994: 74–79.

some skilled workers was a drachma in the mid-fifth century and 2–2½ drachmas in the later fourth century. Thus it may not be too misleading to think of a drachma as worth about $50 or £33 and a talent as about $300,000 or £200,000 in 1997 currency.

BIBLIOGRAPHY OF WORKS CITED

Boegehold, Alan L., 1995: *The Lawcourts at Athens: Sites, Buildings, Equipment, Procedure, and Testimonia.* Princeton.
Bonner, Robert J., 1927: *Lawyers and Litigants in Ancient Athens.* Chicago.
Carey, Christopher, 1997: *Trials from Classical Athens.* London.
Cohen, David, 1995: *Law, Violence and Community in Classical Athens.* Cambridge.
Cole, Thomas, 1991: *The Origins of Rhetoric in Ancient Greece.* Baltimore.
Dover, Kenneth J., 1968: *Lysias and the Corpus Lysiacum.* Berkeley.
———, 1974: *Greek Popular Morality in the Time of Plato and Aristotle.* Oxford.
———, 1978: *Greek Homosexuality.* London.
———, 1994: *Marginal Comment.* London.
Edwards, Michael, 1994: *The Attic Orators.* London.
Gagarin, Michael, and Paul Woodruff, 1995: *Early Greek Political Thought from Homer to the Sophists.* Cambridge.
Hansen, Mogens Herman, 1991: *The Athenian Democracy in the Age of Demosthenes.* Oxford.
Jebb, Richard, 1875: *The Attic Orators,* 2 vols. London.
Kennedy, George A., 1963: *The Art of Persuasion in Greece.* Princeton.
Kerferd, G. B., 1981: *The Sophistic Movement.* Cambridge.
MacDowell, Douglas M., 1978: *The Law in Classical Athens.* London.
———, ed. 1990: *Demosthenes, Against Meidias.* Oxford.
Ober, Josiah, 1989: *Mass and Elite in Democratic Athens.* Princeton.
Rhodes, P. J., trans., 1984: *Aristotle, The Athenian Constitution.* Penguin Books.
Sinclair, R. K., 1988: *Democracy and Participation in Athens.* Cambridge.
Todd, Stephen, 1993: *The Shape of Athenian Law.* Oxford.
Trevett, Jeremy, 1992: *Apollodoros the Son of Pasion.* Oxford.

————, 1996: "Did Demosthenes Publish His Deliberative Speeches?" *Hermes* 124: 425–441.

Usher, Stephen, 1976: "Lysias and His Clients," *Greek, Roman and Byzantine Studies* 17: 31–40.

————, trans., 1974–1985: *Dionysius of Halicarnassus, Critical Essays.* 2 vols. Loeb Classical Library. Cambridge, MA.

————, 1999: *Greek Oratory: Tradition and Originality.* Oxford.

Wooten, Cecil W., trans., 1987: *Hermogenes' On Types of Style.* Chapel Hill, NC.

Worthington, Ian, 1994: "The Canon of the Ten Attic Orators," in *Persuasion: Greek Rhetoric in Action,* ed. Ian Worthington. London: 244–263.

Yunis, Harvey, 1996: *Taming Democracy: Models of Political Rhetoric in Classical Athens.* Ithaca, NY.

DEMOSTHENES, SPEECHES 20–22

INTRODUCTION TO DEMOSTHENES

By Michael Gagarin

Since antiquity Demosthenes (384–322 BC) has usually been judged the greatest of the Attic orators. Although the patriotic and nationalistic tenor of his message has been more highly regarded in some periods of history than in others, he is unique in his mastery of so many different rhetorical styles and his ability to blend them into a powerful ensemble.

LIFE

Demosthenes was born into an old wealthy Athenian family. His father Demosthenes owned workshops that made swords and furniture. His maternal grandfather, Gylon, had been exiled from Athens and lived in the Crimea, where his mother Cleobule was born (perhaps to a Scythian mother). When Demosthenes was seven, his father died leaving his estate in the trust of several guardians. According to Demosthenes' own account, the guardians mismanaged and defrauded the estate to the point that when he turned eighteen, the age of majority, he received almost nothing. He devoted the next several years to recovering his property, first studying forensic pleading and then bringing a series of suits against the guardians to recover his patrimony (speeches 27–31). He won the first case (27, *Against Aphobus I*), but then had to bring several more suits in order to collect the amount awarded him by the court. In the course of these trials he gained a reputation as a successful speaker, became sought after by others, and began to write speeches for a wide range of private suits, including inheritance, shipping loans, assault, and trespass. His clients included one of the richest men in Athens, the banker Phormio; the speech *For Phormio* (36) involves a dispute over twenty talents (equivalent to several million dollars today). Demosthenes' vivid characterization of the honest, hard-working Phormio and his malicious and extravagant opponent proved so convincing that the jurors reportedly refused to listen to the other side and took the highly unusual step of voting immediately for Phormio.

In 355 Demosthenes became involved in his first major public case (22, *Against Androtion*). By this time it was common for ambitious or influential citizens to bring legal charges against their political opponents on matters of public interest. Charges of proposing an illegal decree (the *graphē paranomōn*) were particularly common; these involved the indictment of the proposer of a decree on the ground that it conflicted with existing law.[1] Although these speeches addressed the specific issue of a conflict between laws, it was generally accepted that the merits of the decree, and of its proposer, were also relevant factors, and these cases formed a major arena for the ongoing political struggles between leading figures in the city.

About the same time Demosthenes also began to publish speeches on public issues which he delivered in the assembly, and after 350, although he continued from time to time to write speeches for private disputes, he turned his attention primarily to public policy, especially relations between Athens and the growing power of Macedon under King Philip. Demosthenes' strategy throughout was to increase Athens' military readiness, to oppose Philip's expansion and to support other Greek cities in their resistance to it. Most notable in support of these objectives were the three *Olynthiacs* (1–3) in 349 unsuccessfully urging support for the city of Olynthus (which soon afterwards fell to Philip) and the four *Philippics* (4, 6, 9, 10) in 351–341 urging greater opposition to Philip. But Philip continued to extend his power into Greece, and in 338 he defeated a combined Greek force (including Athens) at the battle of Chaeronea in Boeotia, north of Attica. This

---

[1] One might compare the U.S. procedure of challenging the constitutionality of a law in court. Differences include the fact that today no charge is brought against the proposer of the law and that the case is heard by a small panel of professional judges, not the hundreds of untrained jurors who would have heard the case in Athens.

battle is usually taken to mark the end of the Greek cities' struggle to remain independent.

After Chaeronea Demosthenes continued to urge resistance to Philip, but his efforts were largely ineffectual and his successes and failures are more a matter of internal Athenian politics. His most prominent opponent during this period was Aeschines, who had been acquitted earlier (343) when Demosthenes brought a suit against him in connection with a delegation to Philip on which both men had served (19, cf. Aeschines 2). After Chaeronea, when a minor ally of Demosthenes named Ctesiphon proposed a decree awarding a crown to Demosthenes in recognition of his service to the city, Aeschines brought a *graphē paranomōn* against Ctesiphon (Aeschines 3). The suit, which was not tried until 330, raised legal objections to the proposed decree but also attacked the person and career of Demosthenes at considerable length. Demosthenes responded with his most famous speech *On the Crown* (18), often known by its Latin name *De Corona*. The verdict was so one-sided that Aeschines was fined for not receiving one-fifth of the votes and went into exile. This was Demosthenes' greatest triumph. The last years of his life, however, resulted in notable defeats, first in the rather shadowy Harpalus affair (324–323), from which no speech of his survives (but see Dinarchus 1). Shortly afterwards he was condemned to death at the instigation of pro-Macedonian forces and committed suicide.

WORKS

Sixty-one speeches and some miscellaneous works, including a collection of letters, have come down to us under Demosthenes' name. The authenticity of many of these has been challenged, often because of the allegedly poor quality of the work; but this reason is less often accepted today, and most of the public speeches and many of the private speeches are now thought to be authentic. Among the main exceptions are a group of private speeches (45, 46, 49, 50, 52, 53, 59 and possibly 47 and 51) that were delivered by Apollodorus and are now commonly thought to have been composed by him (Trevett 1992).

Apart from a funeral oration (60) and collections of proems and letters, Demosthenes' works fall into two groups, the assembly speeches (1–17) and the court speeches (18–59); the latter can be further divided into public and private speeches, though these are not formal legal categories. Notable among the public forensic speeches are *Against Meidias* (21), which has recently drawn attention for its pronouncements on Athenian public values, and his last surviving speech, *On the Crown* (18), generally recognized as his masterpiece. In this speech he uses his entire repertory of rhetorical strategies to defend his life and political career. He treats the legal issues of the case briefly, as being of minor concern, and then defends his conduct during the past three decades of Athenian history, arguing that even when his policy did not succeed, on each occasion it was the best policy for the city, in contrast to Aeschines' policies, which, when he ventured to propose any, were disastrous. Demosthenes' extensive personal attack on Aeschines' life and family may be too harsh for modern taste, but the blending of facts, innuendoes, sarcasm, rhetorical questions, and other devices is undeniably effective.

Demosthenes' private speeches have recently begun to attract more interest from scholars, who draw from them insight into Athenian social, political, and economic life. Only the speeches concerned with recovering his inheritance (27–31) were delivered by Demosthenes himself; the rest were written for delivery by other litigants. We have already noted *For Phormio*, which is one of several having to do with banking. *Against Conon* (54) alleges an assault by several young rowdies spurred on by their father, and *Against Neaera* (59), delivered and probably written by Apollodorus, recounts the life of a former slave woman and her affairs with different Athenian men.

STYLE

Demosthenes is a master of Greek prose style; he paid careful attention to style, and to the oral delivery of his speeches. His Roman counterpart, Cicero, modeled his oratorical style (and some other features of his work) in part on Demosthenes' Greek. Although Demosthenes' style varied considerably over the course of time and among the different types of speeches, later assessments of his style are based primarily on the public forensic speeches, and especially the last of these, *On the Crown*. Long and sometimes elaborate sentences are one feature of his style, but Demosthenes' true greatness is his ability to write in many styles and to vary his style, mixing different features together both to suit the topic and to give variety and vigor to his speeches. The final product required great skill and practice to deliver effectively, and the stories about Demosthenes' rigorous training in delivery (see in general Plutarch, *Life of Demosthenes* 6–7), even if not literally true, accurately reflect his priorities. Indeed, only by reading aloud sections of *On the Crown* in Greek can one truly appreciate the power and authority of his prose.

SIGNIFICANCE

Demosthenes played a vital role in Athenian public affairs for some thirty years. His advocacy of the vigilant defense of Greece against foreign invaders, though ultimately unsuccessful in preserving Greek freedom, inspired his fellow Athenians with patriotic loyalty, and has similarly inspired many others in later times. In recent times political rhetoric has not been so widely admired as in the past, and Demosthenes is less read today than he used to be. But he still represents the greatest achievement of Greek oratory and stands as one of the greatest orators of any age.

INTRODUCTION TO THIS VOLUME

By Edward M. Harris

The three speeches in this volume were delivered at trials during the decade following the Social War (357–355 BCE). This period marked an important transition in the history of Athenian democracy. Earlier in the fourth century the Athenians attempted to regain the hegemony that they had lost by their defeat in the Peloponnesian War.[1] In 378 the Athenians created a league of allies and portrayed themselves as the champions of Greek freedom against Spartan oppression. The new league got off to a promising start: in 376 Chabrias defeated the Spartan fleet off Naxos, freeing Athens from a Spartan blockade. Many Greek city-states in Ionia and Central Greece joined the new league, and in 375 Timotheus won allies in Western Greece and defeated another Spartan fleet at Alyzia.[2] But the alliance was weakened by the defection of Thebes in 371. After the Thebans defeated the Spartans at Leuctra later that year and invaded the Peloponnese, the Athenians voted to conclude an alliance with Sparta and destroyed the main rationale for the new league. The Athenians further undermined their claim of protecting Greek liberty when they revived their territorial ambitions in Northern Greece.[3] Between 368 and 359, first Iphicrates, then Timotheus commanded Athenian forces that subdued many cities in the Chalcidice and Chersonnese, but they failed to capture Amphipolis.[4]

---

[1] For the revival of Athenian ambitions to regain leadership, see Seager 1967.

[2] For Chabrias' victory at Naxos, see Xen. *Hellenica* 5.4.61; Diodorus 15.34–35. For Timotheus' victory at Alyzia, see Xen. *Hellenica* 5.4.62–66.

[3] For an analysis of the reasons for the failure of the Second Athenian League, see Cawkwell 1981.

[4] For a brief summary of these campaigns, see E. M. Harris 1995: 41–43. For the chronology of Timotheus' campaigns, see also E. M. Harris 2006a: 355–364.

By 357 the city of Byzantium and the powerful islands of Chios and Rhodes no longer saw any reason to accept Athenian leadership, and they started a revolt with the encouragement of Mausolus, the Carian dynast.[5] The Athenians sent the general Chares with a fleet to blockade Chios, but it was defeated in late 356.[6] The Chians, Rhodians, and Byzantines then attacked Athenian possessions at Imbros and Lemnos and laid siege to Samos. The Athenians responded by sending a fleet of sixty ships under Iphicrates and Menestheus to join Chabrias and attack Byzantium. The rebels struck a decisive blow against this force in 355 at the battle of Embata near Erythrae.[7] The Athenians were now short of funds, and Chares attempted to raise funds by hiring out Athenian troops to the rebellious satrap Artabazus. But this strategy ran aground when the Persian King sent a protest to Athens and threatened to take the side of their enemies.[8] Isolated and without resources, the Athenians were forced to make peace in 355 and accept the withdrawal of their most powerful allies from the league.

The defeat exposed the weaknesses of the Athenian military and sparked a vigorous debate about Athenian foreign policy and financial administration. According to Isocrates (8.61–81), the lesson to be learned from the debacle in the Social War was that the Athenians should abandon their ambitions to regain their naval empire. In his work *The Ways and Means,* Xenophon advised the Athenians to give up their dreams of conquest and acquire wealth by encouraging commerce and exploitation of the silver mines at Laurion. Several politicians took practical steps to address the crisis. During the Social War Periander enacted a reform of the trierarchy.[9] Androtion and Satyrus may have been assigned to collect arrears of the war tax at this time.[10] Eubulus may have created or reorganized the Theoric Fund during this period and used its resources to embark on an ambitious building program (Aes. 3.25). Demosthenes too joined in the debate. In an early speech to the Assembly, Demosthenes (14.16–23) made a proposal to increase the number of contributors in the symmories. In his *Olynthiacs*

---

[5] For the role of Mausolus, see Dem. 15.3; Diodorus 15.7.

[6] On the defeat at Chios, see Diodorus 16.7; Plut. *Phocion* 6; Dem. 20.81.

[7] For the battle of Embata, see Nepos *Timotheus* 3; Polyaenus 3.9.29.

[8] Diodorus 16.22.1–2; Dem. 15.26; Isoc. 8.16.

[9] See Dem. 21.155n.

[10] See Dem. 22.47–58nn.

delivered in 349/8, Demosthenes (1.19–20, 3.10–13) attacks the habit of taking money from the Military Fund for festivals instead of using it for soldiers' pay and equipment.[11]

One of the proposals to improve Athenian finances during the Social War was a law passed by Leptines in 356 to abolish exemptions from liturgies. These exemptions had been awarded to citizens and foreigners for outstanding public service. Two years later, in 355/4, a man named Apsephion brought a charge against this law on the grounds that it was inexpedient. Demosthenes delivered *Against Leptines* in support of Apsephion's prosecution; it was his first speech in a public case. Demosthenes not only deals with the central legal charges in the case but also addresses the larger issues of the nature of democracy, the rule of law, and relations between the wealthy and the rest of the community. Demosthenes (20.2–6; cf. 102–103) attacks Leptines' law because it violates basic democratic principles. In particular, it deprives the Assembly of its power to reward its benefactors, whether they be citizens or foreigners (Dem. 20.29–87).

Demosthenes (20.120–124, 134–142) urges the Athenians to maintain their awards to powerful men at home and abroad to show their appreciation for public service and to avoid appearing ungrateful.[12] In a period when Athens was losing power, it was important to maintain good relations with powerful leaders like Leucon, the ruler of the Crimean Bosporus. Athens was dependent on imported grain and could not afford to alienate Leucon, who granted exemptions from export duties for Athenian merchants (Dem. 20.29–40). Athenian foreign policy also relied on the cooperation of friends in the Greek city-states. If these men could not trust the Athenians to respect and maintain the privileges granted to them, the Athenians would find it difficult to encourage others to promote their interests (Dem. 20.41–56). Demosthenes also stresses the need for the Assembly to reciprocate by showing gratitude to wealthy Athenians who are willing

---

[11] There is no evidence that Demosthenes was opposed to Eubulus' policies or hostile to the Theoric Fund. In the *Fourth Philippic,* Demosthenes (10.35–42) defends the fund against criticism, and after the battle of Chaeronea he was elected supervisor of the fund (Aes. 3.24). See E. M. Harris 2006a: 120–139.

[12] On the Athenian view about the need to show gratitude toward the wealthy for their generosity, see Fisher 2003.

to spend their own money on liturgies, trierarchies, and public subscriptions. These arguments show that Demosthenes had a firm grasp of the realities of Athens' position in the Greek world after its defeat in the Social War.[13]

Besides inhibiting the power of the people to reward its benefactors, the law of Leptines also violated basic legal principles. The Athenians believed that their laws should be consistent and not contradict one another. This principle is well illustrated in a law dated to 374, which orders that all other statutes in conflict with this law be destroyed.[14] The Athenian courts did not make ad hoc decisions when rendering verdicts; they voted in accordance with general principles contained in the laws. For the courts to do their work, therefore, the laws passed by the Assembly had to be clear and consistent. Demosthenes points out that Leptines' law violates the law that all awards granted by the Assembly are to remain valid (Dem. 20.95–97). Apsephion, by contrast, respects the need for consistency in Athenian statutes by indicting Leptines' law about exemptions before proposing a measure of his own on the same topic (Dem. 20.102–104). The court evidently found the arguments of Apsephion, Phormio, and Demosthenes convincing because Leptines' law was overturned.

During the previous year, Demosthenes wrote a speech for an accuser Diodorus, who was speaking in support of the politician Euctemon for his prosecution of Androtion in 355/4. It is impossible to know to what extent the arguments in the speech reflect the views of Demosthenes. Much of the personal slander directed at Androtion probably owes more to Diodorus' desire to retaliate against him because Androtion had had his associate Euctemon removed from office and prosecuted his uncle (Dem. 22.2) than to Demosthenes' personal views (Dem. 22.27, 48). The general points made in the speech about Athenian democracy and public policy, however, bear some similarity

---

[13] There is no need to accept the view of Badian (2000: 36) that in this period Demosthenes "had no basic policy of his own, no assessment of political and strategic priorities." On the contrary, Demosthenes reveals a shrewd understanding of the balance of power in his early speeches. See, for example, his application of this principle to Athenian relations with Sparta and Thebes in Dem. 16 and to relations with the Thracian kings at Dem. 23.10–103.

[14] For this point, see Dem. 24.34–36.

to statements made in his other speeches from this period. One of the legal charges against Androtion's proposal was that it granted honors to those serving in the Council during 356/5 when they had not had triremes built. Demosthenes uses this charge as an opportunity to remind the court about the key role of the fleet in maintaining Athenian power and prestige, a timely issue after the Athenian defeat in the Social War (Dem. 22.12–16). At the same time he warns the Athenians that the drive to increase revenues does not give officials the power to trample on the legal rights of individual citizens (Dem. 22.47–58).

Demosthenes delivered his speech *Against Meidias* at a trial on a charge of outrage (*hybris*) in early 346. By this time, Demosthenes had given many speeches in the Assembly, performed many liturgies,[15] and become a member of the Council. Despite his efforts, he was still struggling to acquire a position of influence. Part of the reason may have been that he lacked powerful friends and had gained many enemies who stood in his way.[16] One of these enemies was the wealthy politician Meidias. The tension between the two men erupted into violence when Meidias attempted to destroy the costumes for Demosthenes' chorus and then punched him during the Dionysia of 348 (Dem. 21.13–18). Demosthenes immediately brought a charge of committing an offence against the festival at a subsequent meeting of the Assembly, which voted to censure Meidias.[17] He could have let the matter end there, but Meidias continued to harass him. This left him no choice but to proceed against Meidias in court.

The speech Demosthenes composed for the trial is a *tour de force,* which attempts to transform a single punch into a dangerous assault on democracy and the rule of law. It also sheds valuable light on the intense competition for honors and prestige in Athenian life and on Athenian attitudes towards wealth. The Athenians held many dramatic and choral competitions and assigned affluent men to finance

---

[15] For his liturgies, see Dem. 21.154–157nn.

[16] See Sealey 1993: 97–98 and Dem. 21.205–218 for his opponents. Demosthenes (21.20, 112, 136–140) also complains about how difficult it was for him to find people to support his charge. This may be an attempt to cover up a weakness in his case but may also be an indication of his lack of political support.

[17] See Dem. 21.1–2, 19. On the procedure followed by Demosthenes, see the Introduction to *Against Meidias.*

the performances. There was no requirement to spend a certain amount of money.[18] To provide incentives, therefore, the democracy offered prizes for the best performances.[19] Judges were appointed to choose the winners, and the victorious performers were allowed to erect monuments to commemorate their victories.[20] The prestige gained in these contests was a major source of political capital, which could prove useful during elections and at meetings of the Assembly.[21] Because the rewards of victory were so great, the competition for prizes could become very intense.

To ensure fairness, the Athenians passed and enforced several laws regulating these contests.[22] Demosthenes (21.58–66) reminds the court how other rich men respected these rules even when competing against personal enemies. By contrast Meidias showed nothing but contempt for these democratic rules (Dem. 21.67–69). In *Against Leptines* Demosthenes urged the average Athenian to show gratitude toward their benefactors by not withdrawing the exemptions voted to them. In *Against Meidias* he contrasts Meidias with other law-abiding Athenians to illustrate the right and wrong ways to perform liturgies and other kinds of public service. The two speeches are thus complementary in their approaches to the issue of reciprocity in the relationship between the rich and the rest of the Athenian people. Although those Athenians who spend their money to benefit the people are entitled to honor and respect, they should not become arrogant and feel that they deserve the right to treat others with contempt.

The speech contains several attacks on Meidias' character, but they should not be viewed as irrelevant to the legal issue. To prove the charge of *hybris,* Demosthenes had to show not only that Meidias had assaulted him but also that he struck him with the intent to humiliate

---

[18] For Athenian attitudes about wealth and liturgies, see Makres 1994: 172–245.

[19] For the use of competition to stimulate generosity, see Xen. *Hipparchikos* 1.25–26.

[20] For the tripods erected to commemorate victories, see Dem. 21.5n.

[21] For the benefits of victories in choral contests, see Xen. *Memorabilia* 3.4.3–6 and Makres 1994: 189. For Meidias' boasts about his liturgies at meetings of the Assembly, see Dem. 21.152–153.

[22] For the laws about choruses, see MacDowell 1989a.

him. He must therefore demonstrate that his opponent did not act on the spur of the moment but as part of a deliberate plan (Dem. 21.38–42).[23] This requires that Demosthenes recount all his previous relations with Meidias, which reveal a consistent pattern of repeated attempts to harm his reputation. For this reason he recalls Meidias' efforts to thwart his charge of slander (Dem. 21.81–101), which resulted in the disenfranchisement of Strato, his plot to have Euctemon bring a charge of desertion against him (Dem. 21.103, 110), and his attempt to have him charged with the murder of Nicodemus (Dem. 21.104, 116–122).

Demosthenes also shows that Meidias uses his wealth for his own pleasure and not for public benefit (Dem. 21.143–174). For instance, his contribution of a trireme was only a ruse to avoid military duty (Dem. 21.160–167). This material is also relevant to the legal charge of *hybris* because the Athenians believed that the unbridled pursuit of pleasure and excessive wealth were two of the sources of *hybris*.[24] To strengthen his case, Demosthenes describes several cases in which Meidias acted abusively toward other citizens (21.123–142). This evidence supports the charge of *hybris* by proving that Meidias' character makes him predisposed to committing this crime. If Meidias has treated other people this way, the court should conclude that his actions toward Demosthenes were done in the same way.

The speech is also valuable for the light it sheds on Athenian views about the rule of law. In fact, Demosthenes uses *nomos,* the Greek word for "law," roughly one hundred times in the speech and often discusses its role in protecting the safety of average citizens. The role of the court is not to rehabilitate the defendant's status or to assuage his anger but to enforce the law when it has been violated (Dem. 21.25, 57). Demosthenes often reminds judges of their oath to follow the laws (Dem. 21.4, 21, 24, 34, 177, 188, 211–212).[25] The purpose of the court's verdict is to provide a deterrent against future crimes (Dem. 21.4, 9, 227). If the law is not vigorously enforced, similar crimes will occur in the future, and average citizens will not be safe (Dem. 21.21, 37, 79). In particular, no one will be willing to perform liturgies for

---

[23] For the role of intent in Athenian law, see Dem. 21.42–45.

[24] For wealth as a cause of *hybris,* see Dem. 21.138 and MacDowell 1976.

[25] On the terms of the judicial oath and its importance, see E. M. Harris 2007b.

the public if Meidias is not punished for breaking the law (Dem. 21.66). Each of the judges on his own is not strong enough to restrain Meidias, but their collective verdict can put an end to his abuse (Dem. 21.121, 140, 222–225). If Demosthenes did not physically retaliate when Meidias struck him, it is because he trusts in the laws and the protection granted by the legal process (Dem. 21.76). Although Meidias has performed public service, he has already received adequate gratitude from the people (Dem. 21.171). In this case, the judges should not take his wealth or social status into account but punish him for breaking the law (Dem. 21.98, 143, 183, 210). Demosthenes sees no conflict between democratic values and the rule of law. On the contrary, the two ideals go hand in hand (Dem. 21.63, 142, 150, 207).

20. AGAINST LEPTINES

〰〰〰〰〰〰〰〰〰〰〰〰〰〰〰〰〰〰〰〰〰〰〰〰〰〰〰〰〰〰〰〰〰〰〰〰〰〰

INTRODUCTION

The Athenians assigned many public duties called liturgies to wealthy citizens and metics (resident aliens). These were divided into military (e.g., the trierarchy) and festival liturgies. The festival liturgies were quite numerous: there were normally over 97 every year, but this number could rise to over 118 once every four years when the Panathenaic festival was celebrated.[1] They fell into four general categories. The most important was the *choregia* for dramatic festivals. The person assigned to this duty was responsible for paying the expenses of a chorus and for hiring an instructor to train its members (see also the Introduction to *Against Meidias*).[2] The second was the *gymnasiarchia*, which involved providing financial support for various athletic competitions such as the festival for Prometheus, Pan, and Hephaestus. The third was the *hestiasis* ("giving a feast") for one of the ten Attic tribes.[3] The final type of liturgy was the *architheoria* or the responsibility for leading a sacred embassy to one of the Panhellenic festivals such as the Olympic games or to the temple of Apollo at Delphi. These liturgies were distinguished from duties such as the trierarchy and the property tax (*eisphora*), which were imposed on the richest citizens during wartime. Those who had performed outstanding public service might, however, receive exemptions from liturgies (but not from the trierarchy—see 26) and other public duties and

---

[1] For the number of liturgies, see Davies 1967.
[2] On the *choregia*, see Makres 1994 and Wilson 2000.
[3] On the *hestiasis*, see Schmitt Pantel 1992: 121–131.

taxes.[4] Famous generals such as Conon and Chabrias had been given exemptions for their military victories, and several foreigners who had acted in Athenian interests had also received them.

During the Social War (357–355) the Athenians found themselves in dire financial straits and passed several measures to increase public revenues. Aristophon proposed a decree calling for the appointment of a commission to collect all money owed to the treasury (see the Introduction to *Against Androtion*). There was also a reform of the trierarchy by Periander in 357.[5] In 356 a politician named Leptines passed a law abolishing all exemptions from liturgies.[6] The main provisions of the law can be reconstructed from Demosthenes' speech.[7] Its aim was to ensure that the wealthiest men performed liturgies, and it provided that no one, whether citizen, metic, or foreigner, be exempt except the descendants of Harmodius and Aristogeiton.[8] Henceforth it was illegal for the people to grant an exemption (2, 55, 160); if anyone were to ask for an exemption, the punishment was loss of rights (*atimia*) and confiscation of property. All those convicted of this crime were to be subject to denunciation (*endeixis*) and arrest (*apagoge*) if they tried to hold public office and subject to the same law that applied to public debtors (156).

Soon after the law was passed, it was attacked by a man named Bathippus, who died before he could bring his case to trial. Two other men also brought charges, but were persuaded to drop their cases (145).

---

[4] For the different types of exemptions, see Sandys 1890: xi–xviii and MacDowell 2004: 127–128.

[5] Demosthenes alludes to this reform at 23.

[6] Little is known about Leptines. He may be the person of this name who spoke in support of the Spartan appeal for help during the Theban invasion of the Peloponnese in 369 and declared that "he would not allow the Athenians to stand aside while Greece lost one of its two eyes" (Arist. *Rhetoric* 3.10.7). He may also be the Leptines of Koile mentioned at Dem. 20.60.

[7] That Leptines' measure was a law (*nomos*) and not a decree (*psephisma*) is made clear at 26, 92.

[8] 29, 127, 160. Although the stated intent of the law gives the impression that it covered only exemptions for liturgies, 29 shows that it extended to all types of exemptions, though this may have been "owing to careless drafting" (Sandys 1890: xvii–xviii).

The prosecution was then taken up by Bathippus' son Apsephion, who brought a public charge against the law on the grounds that it was inexpedient (*graphē nomon mē epitēdeion theinai*).[9] Because the case was brought two years after the law was passed, Leptines was no longer subject to prosecution, and so the case was aimed solely at repealing his law (89–98). At the same time, Apsephion proposed a law of his own to take the place of Leptines' law. This measure would confirm all exemptions granted by the Athenian people but would create a legal procedure for removing exemptions that had been illegally obtained. At the preliminary hearing (*anakrisis*), Leptines claimed that this proposal was only a ruse designed at persuading the court to rescind his own law and charged that Apsephion had no intention of actually passing his law (98). In reply to this objection, Apsephion and his supporters made a public declaration promising to carry through their alternative proposal should Leptines' law be rejected (100).

The case came to court in the year 355/4.[10] Demosthenes participated at the trial as one of the two supporting speakers (*synegoroi*) for Apsephion; the other was Phormio.[11] It was the first time that Demosthenes appeared in a public case; all his earlier experience had been acquired in pleading private cases. Demosthenes says that he decided to join the prosecution for two reasons: first, he was convinced that Athens would gain by the repeal of Leptines' law and, second, that he wished to help Chabrias' son Ctesippus, whose exemption was threatened by the law.[12] Demosthenes does not mention any personal

---

[9] On this action, see Hansen 1974: 44–48. Sandys 1890: xxiii and Badian 2000: 27 mistakenly think that the charge was a *graphē paranomōn*.

[10] Dionysius of Halicarnassus *Letter to Ammaeus* 1.4 places the speech in the archonship of Callistratus (355/4). As Schaefer 1885–1887, Vol. I: 415–417, showed, this dating is in accord with all the historical events alluded to in the speech.

[11] I, 51, 97, 100, 159. On the identity of Phormio, see Rubinstein 2000: 50 n. 69.

[12] Plutarch (*Demosthenes* 15) relates that "some say" that Demosthenes agreed to speak against the law because he was wooing Chabrias' widow, but the story may have been invented by one of Demosthenes' numerous detractors. Plutarch himself appears skeptical of the story because he observes that Demosthenes did not marry her and adds that Demetrius of Magnesia wrote that he lived with a Samian woman.

or political ties with Apsephion and Phormio in the speech, and he is not known to have had any political ties to Phocion, who was Ctesippus' guardian (Plut. *Phocion* 7.3–4). Nor is there any reason to think that he was acting out of personal enmity toward Leptines: on the contrary, he generally avoids attacking his opponent's character.[13] In short, there is no reason to doubt that Demosthenes was acting primarily on his conviction that Leptines' law was harmful to the city.[14]

Because Apsephion and Phormio had already discussed the main objections to Leptines' law, Demosthenes limits himself to developing their points at greater length and to anticipating the arguments of their opponents. He begins with the main substantive issue: because the charge against the law was that it was inexpedient, Demosthenes must show that its provisions will bring major disadvantages and that its repeal will benefit the community (1). To begin with, the law is undemocratic: it weakens the power of the Assembly by abolishing its right to award honors (2–6; cf. 102–103). Demosthenes also predicts that Leptines will argue that the law will increase the number of men eligible to perform liturgies and thus make more money available for community and distribute the burden of this duty more equitably (7–17). Demosthenes responds that this advantage is nugatory: the number of men added to those eligible to perform liturgies will not be very large and will not compensate for the damage done to the city's reputation (18–28).

One of the most serious disadvantages of the law is that it risks alienating Leucon, the ruler of the Bosporus. Leucon has received an exemption along with other awards in return for privileges granted to Athenian merchants. If the Athenians revoke his exemption, Leucon might retaliate by canceling these privileges, which would threaten Athens' grain supply (29–40). It would also be unfair to Epicerdes, who helped Athens during the Peloponnesian War and whose sons now benefit from his exemption (41–47) and to other foreigners,

---

[13] At 102 Demosthenes claims he is not disparaging Leptines, and his criticisms at 143–144 are very mild in comparison to his attacks on Meidias, Androtion, and Aeschines.

[14] On Demosthenes' motivation, see Rubinstein 2000: 138–140.

some of whom were driven into exile for promoting Athenian interests (51–66). Demosthenes then turns to the achievements of two Athenians who were given exemptions, Conon (68–74) and Chabrias (75–87). Although the style of this section often resembles panegyric, the arguments are not rhetorical in the superficial sense, but directly relevant to the legal issue. All parts of the section are designed to show that the recipients of the exemptions deserve their honors and that it would therefore be unjust to take them away. By reminding the court of the advantages gained by awarding exemptions, Demosthenes uncovers the disadvantage of Leptines' law and shows that it is indeed inexpedient.

In the next section, Demosthenes moves on to the procedural issues (88–101). He discusses the law that requires anyone wishing to propose a new law first to repeal any opposing statutes. He charges Leptines with having violated this law by failing to repeal the law that made all awards granted by the people irrevocable before enacting his own law abolishing the exemptions (95–97). He then contrasts the way in which Apsephion and his supporters have proceeded in the correct fashion by first indicting Leptines' law before submitting their proposal. Apsephion's law permits deserving recipients to keep their exemptions while providing a legal action to remove those exemptions that have been illegally obtained (98–101). He then accuses Leptines of violating the spirit of Solon's laws by depriving the people of their right to grant honors to whomever they wish (102–104).

The rest of the speech adds more arguments and replies to points that the prosecutors expect their opponents to make. In response to the objection that the Spartans and the Thebans do not grant similar honors to their citizens, he observes that the Spartans and the Thebans do not practice democracy, and so their customs are inappropriate for Athens. Besides, the Thebans are cruel and dishonest and therefore do not provide an example to follow (105–111). It is not true that the Athenians did not grant generous rewards in the past; Demosthenes cites the example of Lysimachus, who received land and money (112–117). The oath that the judges have sworn binds them to vote in accordance with the laws that conferred the exemptions, not those of Sparta, Thebes, or their ancestors (118–119). Leptines may claim that his law does not take away other kinds of honors and leaves many rewards intact, but that does not matter, because it destroys confidence in the reliability of the Athenian people (120–124). The argument that granting exemptions from liturgies bars men from sacred rites is specious (125–130). If they claim that many dishonest foreigners have obtained exemptions as *proxenoi,* they must produce evidence to prove it (131–133). Even if Leptines can demonstrate that his law contains advantages, it will still give the Athenians a reputation for deceiving their benefactors (134–135). The law proposed to replace it avoids damaging Athens' image (136–142). Leptines will not be punished if he loses the case, but his reputation will suffer if he wins (143–144).

Demosthenes then criticizes each of the men who will defend the law and accuses them of violating the rules about speaking in public cases (146–153). Next, he denounces the law's penalties as harsh and illegal (155–159). The law may help Athens in the short run but threatens to deprive the city of benefactors in the future (160–162). In the final section, Demosthenes invites the judges to compare Leptines' law with Apsephion's alternative proposal and the consequences of each measure (163–167).

Dio Chrysostom (31.128) reports that the prosecution was successful and the law was repealed.[15] There is no reason to doubt this evidence because it is confirmed by a decree dated to 346 granting to Spartocus and Berisades, the sons of Leucon, the same privileges that their father enjoyed.[16] Because these privileges included an exemption from liturgies, the sons must have also received one.[17] Some

---

[15] The verdict in the trial refutes the view of Burke 2002: 178 that Leptines' law was "popular with the dicasts" and shows that Demosthenes' arguments in the speech do not contain an elite bias that would have offended average Athenians. The verdict also undermines the view of Hesk (2000: 40–51), who claims that Leptines' law was egalitarian and democratic and that Demosthenes upholds aristocratic values in the speech. But Demosthenes bases his arguments on the democratic principles of popular sovereignty (2–6, 102–103) and democratic attitudes toward rewards for benefactors (15–17, 105–111). For good criticisms of Hesk's narrow conception of democratic values, see Fisher 2003.

[16] For the inscription, see Rhodes and Osborne 2003: no. 64.

[17] This was first noted by Schaefer 1885–1887, Vol. I: 416–417, but appears to have escaped the notice of Badian 2000: 28 and Sealey 1993: 127 ("The outcome

scholars have pointed out that Chabrias' son Ctesippus, who inherited his father's exemption, appears to have performed a liturgy for the tribe Cecropis, and they have argued that this indicates that Leptines' law remained in effect. But Ctesippus could have performed the liturgy voluntarily. Alternatively, he may have lost his exemption because Apsephion's law was passed after Leptines' law was repealed. This law made it possible to take away exemptions from those who did not deserve them.[18] In short, there is no reason to doubt the evidence of Dio Chrysostom, which is confirmed by contemporary sources.

The speech was highly regarded in antiquity. The Stoic philosopher Panaetius praised it for persuading the Athenians to choose what was just and honorable instead of what was profitable and pleasant.[19] Dionysius of Halicarnassus (*Letter to Ammaeus* 1.4) calls it "most graceful and precise" (*chariestatos . . . graphikotatos*). Cicero (*Orator* 11) cited the speech as a model of the plain style (*oratio subtilis*). Aelius Aristides paid it the compliment of composing two declamations (53 and 54) on the law of Leptines in the style of Demosthenes. The style of the speech is relatively simple and aims for clarity of argument. The language is restrained and contains few vivid metaphors or striking expressions. The structure of the speech is loose, with many of the arguments introduced by the same Greek particle (*toinun* "well, now"). Though logical and effective, the style lacks the emotional power and confidence of Demosthenes' later speeches.

---

of the trial is not known"). Sandys 1890: xxxi doubts Schaefer's argument on the grounds that exemption is not explicitly mentioned in the decree, but the wording of the award makes it clear that the sons were to gain all the privileges granted to their father. If the exemption was not among them, the decree would have had to exclude it explicitly. Schaefer's argument is confirmed by two other decrees dated after the trial containing grants of exemption. The first is *IG* ii² 237, lines 25–26, which is dated to 338/7; the phrase is restored, but the restoration is confirmed by the parallel found in *IG* ii² 545, line 12 [after 318]. The second is *IG* ii² 286, lines 4–5 [352–336] with Walbank 1990: 442, who dates the decree to the third quarter of the fourth century. I would like to thank Dr. Stephen Lambert for help with this note.

[18] For Ctesippus' reputation, see Plut. *Phocion* 7.3.

[19] Plut. *Demosthenes* 13.

20. AGAINST LEPTINES

[**1**] Judges, it is mainly because I think that the city will benefit by annulling the law and then also for the sake of Chabrias' young child [20] that I have agreed to speak to the best of my ability in support of these men.[21] It is no secret, men of Athens, that Leptines and anyone else who defends the law will not say anything honest about it, but will claim that certain men have avoided performing liturgies by obtaining an exemption that they do not deserve.[22] In fact, he will devote most of his speech to this argument. [**2**] In my opinion, taking away an award from everyone on the basis of an accusation against a mere handful is the wrong way to act, but I will not dwell on this. After all, this point has already been made in a way, and I presume you already know about it. But what I would like to ask Leptines is this: even if we grant that in the worst case not just some but all men do not deserve an award, why did he think that you deserve to be treated the same way that they are? By writing "no one is exempt," Leptines took away the exemption from those who have it, but by adding a clause "in the future it is not permitted to grant an exemption," he took away your power to grant it. Certainly he cannot argue that his contention that the men who have received exemptions do not deserve them rests on the same grounds as his view that the people do not deserve to have the power to grant them to whomever they wish. [**3**] No, by Zeus, but he might perhaps reply to this point by arguing that the people are easily misled and that this is the reason why he framed the law in this way.[23] But according to

---

[20] Chabrias died during the siege of Chios two years before, in 357, leaving his young son Ctesippus an orphan. See 75. Although Demosthenes speaks partly to help Ctesippus, he does not stress the relationship.

[21] Apsephion brought the charge against Leptines and spoke first, followed by Phormio. Demosthenes spoke third and, like Phormio, was a *synegoros* or supporting speaker. Because others had preceded him, there was no need for a lengthy *prooemium* (introductory section) or narrative laying out the facts of the case. See Chremmydas 2005: 51.

[22] Demosthenes anticipates what he predicts his opponents' main argument will be. Cf. 7, 18, 56, 113, 131–133. On anticipation of arguments, see Dorjahn 1935.

[23] Athenian orators often say that the people never made mistakes but are only misled by dishonest leaders. See Aes. 3.35; Dem. 19.29–30, 23.97; Isoc. 8.10.

this line of reasoning, what then prevents him from taking everything away from you, even your entire form of government? There is not a single area out of all in which this has not happened to you. On the contrary, you have often been misled when passing decrees, and sometimes you have been persuaded to choose weaker allies rather than more powerful ones. In fact, you have so much business to deal with that I think it is quite inevitable that something like this will happen. [4] Will we then for this reason establish a law that "in the future it is no longer permitted for the Council to hold prior deliberation or for the Assembly to hold a vote"?[24] I certainly do not think so. The right thing for us to do is not to abolish our power to decide about any issues where we are misled but to learn how to prevent this from happening and not to pass a law that undermines our sovereignty but one that gives us the power to punish the person who deceives us.[25]

[5] Now let us suppose that someone were to grant this point and were to consider just the following question: is it better for you to retain the power to grant the award even though you might be misled into giving it to an unworthy candidate or for you not to have any power at all to grant honors to someone even if you know that he deserves them? He would find the former the better choice. For what reason? Because if you grant honors to more people than you should, you encourage a large number of men to perform public service, whereas if you do not grant honors to anyone even if someone deserves it, you will discourage everyone from being ambitious.[26] [6] In addition, there is also this reason: those who honor an unworthy person may gain a reputation for being naïve, but those who do

---

[24] A decree could not be passed by the Assembly unless the matter received prior consideration by the Council. See Dem. 22.5 and *Ath. Pol.* 45.4 with Rhodes 1972: 52–81.

[25] Demosthenes alludes to the law proposed by Apsephion, which he discusses later. See 95–101.

[26] Lit. "to love honor." "Love of honor" (*philotimia*) might be criticized if it harmed the community (e.g., Thuc. 2.65.7, 3.82.8; Euripides *Iphigenia at Aulis* 337–342, 527). As Whitehead 1983: 59–60 notes, however, "As far as the *polis* was concerned, *philotimia* (. . .) could be not merely accommodated, but actively welcomed, provided always that the community itself was acknowledged to be the only proper source of *time* and thus the only proper object of the energy and (in particular) the expense that the *philotimos* sought to lay out."

not repay their benefactors in full acquire one for dishonesty.[27] In the same way that it is better to appear naïve than to be dishonest, it is also better to annul this law than to put it into effect.

[7] Well, now, as I think about it, men of Athens, it strikes me as irrational to take honors away from men who have proved to be helpful because of criticisms against the awards that a few now possess. If there are some who are worthless and do not deserve the honors that they have (as our opponents claim), what must we expect to happen in the future when there will be no advantage at all to be gained from being a good citizen? [8] Next, you must certainly bear this point in mind: according to the laws that exist now and have been in effect for a long time (not even this man can deny that they are excellent),[28] each man performs liturgies every other year so that he is exempt half of the time.[29] Everyone enjoys this half exemption, even those who have done nothing good for you at all; should we then take away this additional exemption we have granted from men who have actually helped us? Not at all! In general that would not be honorable, and it would not be right for you. [9] You have enacted a law that prohibits making false statements in the marketplace, although this does not harm the public interest;[30] how would it not be disgraceful, men of Athens, if the city, after issuing this order to individuals, were not to follow this law itself when conducting public business but were to deceive those who have performed some service, especially when the harm that will result is far from inconsiderable?[31] [10] The question is not just whether you are losing money but whether you are losing your good reputation, which you care about more than money—and not only you but also your ancestors. Here is the proof: at the time of

---

[27] The duty to repay benefactors was one of the "unwritten laws" (Xen. *Memorabilia* 4.4.24). For their relationship to the written laws of the city, see E. M. Harris 2006a: 51–57.

[28] For the idea that the antiquity of a law is a sign of its excellence, see Ant. 5.14, 6.2.

[29] For this rule, see *Ath. Pol.* 56.3 with Rhodes 1981: 625.

[30] This law is also mentioned at Hyp. *Athenogenes* 14. See Whitehead 2000: 307–309.

[31] The Athenians generally maintained that the same standards applied in private and public life and that one should follow the same rules in both spheres. Cf. 136 and see, for example, Sophocles *Antigone* 661–662; Aes. 1.30, 3.78.

their greatest prosperity they spent all their money on the pursuit of honor and shirked no danger to defend their reputation; they never stopped spending even their private fortunes.[32] Now this law covers the city with disgrace rather than a good reputation, something that is not worthy either of your ancestors or of you. The city incurs three very serious grounds for censure: we look as if we are spiteful, untrustworthy, and ungrateful.

[11] Putting a law like this into effect is completely contrary to your character, men of Athens. I will try to demonstrate this in a few words by describing one event in the city's history. The story goes that the Thirty borrowed money from the Spartans to fight against the men of the Piraeus.[33] After the city was reunited and that conflict was over, the Spartans sent ambassadors and asked for this money back. [12] During the debate, some demanded that the borrowers, that is, the men from the city, pay it back, while others thought that the repayment of the debt from public funds should be the first sign of unity.[34] They say that the Assembly chose to make the payments on its own and to take responsibility for the expense so as to avoid breaking any of the agreements.[35] So, then, since in the past you were willing to pay money to men who had wronged you to avoid defaulting on your loan, how would it not be terrible, men of Athens, now when it is possible for you to do the right thing for your benefactors by annul-

---

[32] Orators in the fourth century often claimed that in the past the Athenians were more public spirited. See Dem. 3.25–26.

[33] After the surrender of Athens to Sparta in 404, a group called the Thirty seized power and set up a narrow oligarchy. Many democrats fled, and a small but growing number seized Phyle in the Attic countryside where they organized a force to resist the Thirty. After defeating the oligarchs in a battle, the democratic forces captured the Piraeus (thus becoming "the men of the Piraeus") and attacked the oligarchs who still controlled the city ("the men of the city"). For an account of this period, see Krentz 1982.

[34] After the end of the civil war in 403 both sides pledged to observe an amnesty to restore unity. See Xen. *Hellenica* 2.4.38; *Ath. Pol.* 39.

[35] This incident is also mentioned at *Ath. Pol.* 40.3 and Isoc. 7.67–69 and is alluded to at Lys. 30.22. The loan is mentioned at Plut. *Lysander* 21 and Xen. *Hellenica* 2.4.28. A scholion on the passage denies that the Athenians repaid under pressure, but Lys. 30.22 alludes to Spartan threats made at the time. On the question of when a *polis* should repay its debts, see Arist. *Politics* 3.1.10.1276a.

ling the law without spending any money, for you to choose to default instead on your obligation? I do not consider this right.

[13] One might observe the city's character both in this case that I have just described and in many others: it is honest and virtuous, concerned not with what is most profitable in terms of money, but what is the really honorable thing to do. As for the character of the man who wrote this law, I know nothing about it in other respects—I have nothing derogatory to say, nor am I aware of anything. But when I look at this law, I find that it is far removed from the city's character. [14] So I say that it is better for him to follow you in annulling the law than for you to follow him in enacting it and that it is more advantageous both to you and to Leptines for the city to persuade him to adopt its ways than for it to be persuaded by this man to adopt his ways. Even if he is a thoroughly good person—as far as I am concerned, let us assume that he is[36]—he is not morally superior to the city.

[15] Judges, I think that you will make a better decision about the issue before you if you bear the following in mind: the only advantage that awards granted by a democracy have over those granted by other forms of government is now being removed by this law. In terms of the material benefits enjoyed by those who receive awards, tyrants and oligarchic regimes are in the best position to grant honors: they make anyone whom they want wealthy right away.[37] But in terms of honor and reliability, you will find the awards granted by democracies superior. [16] Instead of accepting a shameful reward for flattery, what is honorable is to receive honors because one is thought to deserve them where there is freedom of speech.[38] The unforced admiration of one's peers is recognized to be more valuable than any favor accepted from a tyrant.[39] Under a tyranny, fear of the future outweighs any enjoyment

---

[36] Since the main issue involves the public interest, Demosthenes carefully avoids personal slander.

[37] That is, they do not have to obtain approval from the community.

[38] For the equal right to free speech in Athenian democracy, see e.g., Euripides *Suppliants* 434–441; Aes. 1.27; Dem. 60.28.

[39] The word used here is *despotes,* which literally means "master" and is normally applied to a master of slaves, but it is used here in a metaphorical sense instead of the word *tyrannos.* For the meaning of the term, see E. M. Harris 2006a: 272–273, 278–279.

in the present; in your city, by contrast, the person who receives an award has had nothing to worry about, at least until now.[40] [17] Well, by destroying the confidence in our awards, this law destroys the only advantage that makes your awards more valuable. Take any form of government in the world: surely if you abolish the practice of showing gratitude to its supporters, you will have destroyed an important means of protecting it.

[18] Well, perhaps Leptines might possibly try to distract you from this point by making the following argument: liturgies are now falling on poor men, but as a result of this law, the richest men will perform liturgies. When expressed in this way, his point seems reasonable. But if someone should study it closely, its fallacy would become obvious. As you know, we have some liturgies that are performed by metics and some by citizens.[41] Men from both of these groups have received the exemption that this man is removing. In regard to the property taxes for war and defense of the city and to the trierarchy the old laws rightly and correctly do not allow for any exemption, not even for the descendants of Harmodius and Aristogeiton,[42] for whom Leptines has made an exception. [19] Let us take a look at the men whom he is adding to the list of those eligible to perform liturgies and at the number of men who will be released from duty if we do not follow his advice. Well, the wealthiest men are always exempt from producing choruses when they serve as trierarchs,[43] and the men who possess less than the required amount receive a mandatory exemption and are not subject to this duty.[44] Thanks to this law you will not add one more person from either of these groups to produce choruses.

---

[40] For a similar contrast between fear under a tyranny and security under democracy, see Aes. 1.4–5.

[41] On liturgies performed by metics, see Whitehead 1977: 77–82.

[42] Harmodius and Aristogeiton were killed after assassinating Hipparchus, the younger brother of the tyrant Hippias, in 514. See Herod. 5.55; Thuc. 1.20, 6.54–59; *Ath. Pol.* 18. On the tradition that they put an end to the tyranny, see Thomas 1989: 238–261. On the tyrannicides, see also Chremmydas 2005: 89–90.

[43] For the rule that no one could be required to perform more than one duty at once, see Dem. 21.155, 50.9.

[44] Only those with fortunes above about three talents were eligible for liturgies. See Is. 3.80, 11.40–41 with Davies 1971: xxiii–xxiv.

[**20**] "No, by Zeus, he is adding many people to the list of metics eligible to perform liturgies." If he comes up with five, I admit I am talking nonsense.[45] Let us assume that I am, that more than that number of metics will perform liturgies if the law is enacted and that no citizen will be exempt for serving as trierarch. Let us consider what benefit will accrue to the city if all these men perform liturgies: it will clearly not compensate (far from it!) for the dishonor that will result. [**21**] Look at it in this way. Some foreigners are exempt—I will put it at ten. But, by the gods, as I was just saying, I do not think there are five. In fact, there are not more than five or six citizens with exemptions. Certainly sixteen from both groups. Let us make it twenty, or if you wish, thirty. How many are there who perform the regular liturgies every year, the chorus producers, and gymnasiarchs, and feast-givers? There are perhaps sixty or a few more all together.[46] [**22**] In order to have thirty more men to perform liturgies for the rest of time, are we to make everyone lose confidence in us? But this we know for certain, that many men will perform liturgies if the city continues to exist and will never be in short supply. But no one will wish to do us any favors, if he sees that those who have done so before are treated unjustly. [**23**] Very good; but if in the worst case there was a shortage of men capable of producing choruses, by Zeus, would it be better to organize the production of choruses into groups of contributors as is done with the trierarchies or to deprive our benefactors of what has been given to them?[47] The former, in my opinion. As things are, each man in this group[48] provides relief to them only while he is performing a liturgy, but afterwards each man in that

---

[45]The number of metics may have been very low after the Social War. See Xen. *Poroi* 2–3; Isoc. 8.21 with Whitehead 1977: 159–160.

[46]Demosthenes has lowered the actual number to give the impression that the burden was not very great. As Davies 1967 has shown, there were over 97 in a normal year and 118 in a Panathenaic year.

[47]For the system of symmories for sharing the cost of a trierarchy, which was introduced by Periander in 358/7, see Dem. 21.121n. Demosthenes is suggesting that the same system be used for liturgies if there are not enough wealthy men to perform this duty. Such a shortage of qualified candidates was not an imaginary possibility, but actually occurred in 348; see Dem. 21.13.

[48]The thirty men who were exempt before Leptines' law was passed.

group [49] will spend no less than before. In the other case, were each man to make a small contribution from his property, nothing terrible would happen to anyone, even if his assets were quite small.

[24] Well, now, some speakers are so completely unreasonable that they will not try to reply to this point but resort to other arguments such as this: it will be a dreadful situation if the city has no funds at all for public use, but some private individuals will get an exemption and grow rich. It is not right to make both of these claims. If someone has a great deal of money and has done you no wrong, one should certainly not hold a grudge against him. If, on the other hand, they are going to charge that someone has obtained money stealthily or in some other unjust way, there are laws that one must follow to punish this person. [50] When our opponents do not do this, they must not use this argument either. [25] Then, as for the argument that the city has no money for public use, you should keep this in mind: you will not be any better off if you get rid of the exemptions. These expenses have nothing in common with public revenues and the surplus from the budget. Apart from this, of the two possible advantages that the city can now possess, wealth and a sense of trust among all its citizens, the one it now has is trust. If someone thinks that there is no need to maintain our good reputation when we are short of money, he is mistaken. My most fervent prayer to the gods is that we be well supplied with money, but if we are not, that we at least maintain our reputation for being trustworthy and reliable.

[26] Come, then, let me show you that the wealth that they are going to claim some men will enjoy if they are relieved of these duties will serve your needs. You are certainly aware that no one is exempt from the trierarchy nor from the property tax levied for war. Indeed, the man who possesses a great deal of money, this man will contribute a great deal to these taxes no matter who he is. He has no choice. Now certainly everyone would agree that the city should keep a very large supply of money available for these duties. For although the pleasure that we as spectators enjoy from the money spent on liturgies for festivals lasts for a small part of a day, the security that the entire city gains

---

[49] The sixty men who regularly perform liturgies mentioned in 21.
[50] On the range of actions for theft, see Dem. 22.25–27.

from an abundant supply of military equipment lasts for all time. [27] As a result, everything that you give up here, you will recoup there. Besides, you are also granting in the form of an honor those things that men whose wealth qualifies them for the trierarchy have a right to, even if they have not received an exemption. Even though I think that all of you know that no one is exempt from the trierarchy, the clerk will also read to you the actual law. Take the law about trierarchies and read just this passage.

[LAW]

No one is to be exempt from the trierarchy except the nine Archons.[51]

[28] You see, men of Athens, that the law clearly has stated that no one is exempt except the nine Archons. Whereas those who have less than the amount needed to qualify for the trierarchy contribute the property tax for war, those who do qualify will benefit you in both ways, by serving as trierarchs and by paying the property tax. What relief does your law afford the majority if it creates another *choregos* for every one or two tribes,[52] who, once he has performed his duty in place of someone else, will be scot-free? I see none. Yet it infects the entire city with shame and dishonesty. Because this will do far more harm than good, is it not right for this court to annul it? I would say so.

[29] Furthermore, judges, he writes explicitly in his law that "no citizen or person with equal rights[53] or foreigner is to be exempt," but he does not specify the duty from which he is exempt, whether it be

---

[51] The text of this law "is almost certainly a later forgery. There is nothing in it which can not be deduced from the actual text of the speech immediately following it" (Chremmydas 2005: 108).

[52] In 20–22 Demosthenes calculates that Leptines' law will add only five or ten men qualified to perform liturgies, that is, either one for every two of ten tribes or one for each tribe.

[53] A person with equal obligations (*isoteles*) had many of the legal rights of a citizen but none of the political rights.

a festival liturgy or some other obligation.[54] But he simply states "no one is exempt except the descendants of Harmodius and Aristogeiton," including everyone else with the phrase "no one," and in the category "foreigners" does not add the qualifying phrase "resident in Athens."[55] He therefore takes away from Leucon, ruler of the Bosporus, and his children the award that you gave them.[56] [30] Although Leucon is of course a foreigner by birth, you have made him a citizen by adoption.[57] In either respect he cannot hold an exemption as a result of this law. Yet whereas each of our other benefactors has proven helpful to us for some period of time, if you study the matter, you will see that this man constantly helps us, especially in that area where the city needs it most. [31] You are certainly aware that we rely on imported grain more than any other community. In fact, the grain that is shipped from the Black Sea is equivalent to all the grain imported from other regions.[58] Rightly so, for not only does this region supply the largest amount of grain, but Leucon, who controls the region, has granted an exemption to those who transport grain to Athens and commands that those sailing to your port be the first to load their cargoes. This

---

[54] Despite Leptines' failure to specify what type of obligations the exemption applied to, the previous clause of the decree, quoted at 127, makes it clear the law was aimed at exemptions from liturgies. For the different types of exemptions, see MacDowell 2004: 127–128.

[55] This phrase was sometimes added in decrees. See *IG* ii[2] 109b, lines 15–16; 237, lines 25–26.

[56] Leucon is called a "ruler" (*archōn*) here, but elsewhere the kings of the Bosporus are called tyrants (Aes. 3.171; Din. 1.43). The Bosporan kingdom consisted of the eastern part of the Crimea and the neighboring part of the Caucasus. See Werner 1955. Leucon reigned from around 390 to around 350. Leucon's sons were Spartocus, Paerisades, and Apollonius; see Rhodes and Osborne 2003: no. 64.

[57] The Athenians sometimes granted citizenship as an honor to foreigners who had acted in Athenian interests. For Athenian grants of citizenship, see Osborne 1981–1983.

[58] This statement combined with the figure for Leucon's imports reported below would give a total of 800,000 *medimnoi* imported each year. Strabo (7.4.6) says that Leucon sent 2,100,000 *medimnoi* from Theudosia, but he does not indicate whether this was a single shipment or the total sent over several years.

man has given all of you an exemption because he possesses one for himself and his children. [32] Consider how extensive this exemption is. This man collects a duty of one-thirtieth from those who export grain from his territory.[59] The amount of grain that reaches us from his territory is about 400,000 *medimnoi*.[60] One can find this figure in the records kept by the Grain Supervisors.[61] For 300,000 Leucon gives us an extra 10,000 *medimnoi,* and for the other 100,000 he gives as a gift as it were 3,000.[62] [33] So far is he from depriving us of this gift that he made Theudosia[63] available as a trading post (merchants who sail there say it is just as good as Bosporus)[64] and gave us an exemption there. I will not discuss all the other benefits that this man and his ancestors have provided you, although I could list many. But two years ago[65] when the whole world was experiencing a grain shortage, Leucon sent you not only a sufficient amount of grain but such a large amount that there was an additional profit of fifteen talents of silver, which Callisthenes administered.[66] [34] How then do you think this man, who has treated you like this, will react when he hears that you have passed a law taking away his exemption and have voted to abol-

---

[59] Athens was not the only city to receive special treatment; Leucon also gave Mytilene a reduced rate (Tod 1947: no. 163).

[60] Garnsey 1988: 183–195 claims that this figure was exceptional and that the amount in a normal year would have been lower, but see Whitby 1998.

[61] The Grain Supervisors (*sitophylakes*) exercised jurisdiction over the import of grain and kept records of the amounts imported. See *Ath. Pol.* 51.3 with Rhodes 1981: 577–579 and Rhodes and Osborne 2003: no. 25, lines 18–23.

[62] "The orator breaks up the whole sum (. . .) to enable his audience to follow his calculation more readily" (Sandys 1890: 36).

[63] Theudosia was situated at the tip of the Crimea. Strabo (7.4.4) says that its harbor could hold 100 ships. This kind of trading post (*emporion*) was a place within a kingdom where foreign traders were permitted to carry on business with the ruler's permission. For the nature of the *emporion*, see Bresson 1993.

[64] This is Panticapaeum in the Crimea.

[65] I.e., in 357.

[66] Demosthenes does not make it clear where the fifteen talents came from. There are two possibilities: Leucon either made a gift of grain, part of which was given to the people, the rest of it sold by Callisthenes (see Whitby 1998: 125), or sold at a discount a large amount that was then sold by Callisthenes at a slight markup to make a profit (Bresson 2000: 209–210).

ish the power to grant one, even if you change your mind? Don't you realize that this same law, if it goes into effect, will deprive him of an exemption and you of men to transport grain from his kingdom? [35] Certainly, no one has assumed that this man will put up with having the privileges that he received from you canceled while allowing those you received from him to remain. Besides the many disadvantages that the law will apparently create, it will also remove one of the advantages that you already possess. Are you still considering whether it is necessary to repeal this law? Haven't you made up your minds long ago? Take and read the decrees regarding Leucon.

[DECREES]

[36] Judges, you have heard from the decrees that Leucon has rightly and justly obtained his exemption from you. You and he have set up *stelai* inscribed with copies of all these decrees, one at Bosporus, one at the Piraeus, and another at Hieron.[67] Just think how extremely disreputable a position the law puts you in when it makes our democracy less trustworthy than a single individual. [37] You should not think that you have set up these *stelai* for any other purpose than to serve as an agreement regarding all these privileges that you enjoy or have granted. Everyone will see that Leucon has kept to this agreement and is always treating you well, whereas you have made them null and void while they were still standing. This is much worse than tearing them down because if someone wishes to speak ill of the city, these *stelai* will stand as evidence that he is speaking the truth. [38] Come let us imagine that Leucon sends a message to us asking on the basis of what charge or complaint you have taken away his exemption. By the gods, what are we going to say? What will the man who draws up the decree for you write down? That some people, by Zeus, who have received exemptions do not deserve them? [39] What if Leucon replies to this by saying: "Yes and perhaps some Athenians are scoundrels, but I did not deprive honest people of the exemption for that reason. Because I think that the people as a whole are good, I allow everyone to keep it"? Won't his argument be more just than ours? I for one think so. There

---

[67] Hieron was located near Byzantium at the entrance to the Black Sea.

is a custom throughout the world that on account of benefactors, it is better also to do favors to other men who have not been helpful than on account of scoundrels to take away favors given to those who are agreed to deserve them. [40] Indeed, as I think about it, I cannot figure out why someone, if he wishes, would not challenge Leucon to an exchange of property.[68] This man always keeps money in your city,[69] yet by virtue of this law, if anyone tries to lay hold of his money, Leucon will either lose it or be forced to perform a liturgy. What is most important for him is not the amount of the expense but his impression that you have taken away his privilege.

[41] Making sure that Leucon is not treated unfairly is not the only thing you should consider. For him this privilege is more a question of honor than a matter of need. But there may also be someone else who brought you help when he was prosperous, but who now stands in need of the exemption that you granted him in the past. Who is this person? Epicerdes of Cyrene. If any person has justly deserved to receive this honor, it was this man, not so much because his services were large or impressive but because they came at a crucial moment when, out of all those who had received favors from us, it was hard to find one who was willing to recall the good that we did for him. [42] Yet as the decree proposed on his behalf demonstrates,[70] this man contributed a hundred minas for the citizens who were taken prisoner in Sicily during that infamous debacle there[71] and was the person most responsible for preventing all of them from dying of

---

[68] Because Leucon would be eligible to perform liturgies if he were to lose his exemption, he could be challenged to an exchange of property (*antidosis*). In this procedure a person who was ordered to perform a liturgy could challenge another person on the grounds of being more wealthy either to perform the liturgy or to exchange property. For the procedure, see *Ath. Pol.* 56.3 with Rhodes 1981: 624–625.

[69] Possibly on deposit in a private bank. For foreigners maintaining accounts in Athenian banks, see, for example, Isoc. 17; Dem. 52.

[70] Fragments of this decree, dated to 405/4, have been found in the Athenian Agora; see Meritt 1970 and *IG* i³ 125. The extant portions of the inscription confirm Demosthenes' summary of its contents. Benseler suggested emending the text to read "Decrees," because the next sentence says that several were read out.

[71] An allusion to the defeat at Syracuse in 413.

hunger.[72] And later, after having received an exemption from you for these services, he contributed a talent on his own initiative when he saw that the people were short of money during the war.[73] **[43]** By Zeus and the gods, just think about it, men of Athens: how could a person provide clearer evidence that he is loyal to you and does not deserve to be treated unjustly? First, when he was present at the city's defeat, he chose to take the side of the losers and to count on their potential gratitude in the future rather than that of the victors, in whose city he was residing at the time. Second, when he saw that the city was again in need of help, he demonstrated his generosity not in order to save his own property but to make sure as best he could that none of your needs would go unmet. **[44]** Here is a man who by his actions shared his wealth with the people during their greatest crises and received in return an exemption consisting only of honorific words. Are you going to take away not only his award (he clearly does not even use it) but also his trust in you? What could be more damaging to your reputation? Well, now, the clerk will read the actual decree that was voted for him at the time. Just consider how many decrees this law will nullify and how many people it will treat unjustly and also the seriousness of the crises during which these men rendered their services. You will discover that it harms those men who least deserve it.

[DECREE]

[45] Judges, you have heard from these decrees about the services that earned Epicerdes his exemption. Do not pay attention so much to his gift of a hundred minas and later a talent (I do not think that the men who received the money were impressed by the amount), as to his loyalty, his willingness to act on his own initiative, and the circumstances in which he acted. **[46]** All men who take the initiative in

---

[72] Meritt 1970 suggests that the money was used to ransom Athenian prisoners held in the quarries at Syracuse, but Pritchett 1991: 272–273 notes that 30 minas would not have paid the ransom of many men. It is more likely the money bought food to prevent starvation. See Chremmydas 2005: 134–136.

[73] The manuscripts read "a little before the Thirty came to power," but this phrase is deleted by Weil, followed by Dilts.

doing good deserve to receive an equal amount of gratitude in return, especially those who act in times of need. Epicerdes certainly belongs in this group. Are we not ashamed, men of Athens, if we are seen to forget completely about what he did and to take away his award, even though we have no complaint to make against the children of such a man?[74] [47] Even if it was one set of men who were saved and granted the exemption, but you, who are the ones now taking it away, constitute a different group, that does not remove the stain on your reputation. No, in fact, this is precisely what is shocking. If the men who witnessed and received his help thought his services merited rewards, but we, who owe our knowledge of these events to hearsay, are about to take these rewards away as if his services did not merit them, how are we not about to do something that is truly horrendous? [48] One could apply the same argument to the men who overthrew the Four Hundred[75] and to the men who proved their worth when the democrats were in exile.[76] If any of the privileges granted to them at the time were to be abolished, I think that it would be a terrible way to treat these men.

[49] Well, now, if someone among you has convinced himself that there is little chance that the city will need such help, let him say a prayer to the gods, and I will join him. Yet let him also bear in mind, first, that he is going to cast his vote about a law that he will have to follow if it is not annulled and, second, that bad laws harm even those communities where men believe their lives are safe. The fortunes of a community do not change in one direction or the other unless either noble actions, good laws, and honest men combine with careful administration to put a city threatened by danger in a better position, or the neglect of all these factors undermines little by little the position of men who think they are living at the height of prosperity. [50] Most people acquire wealth by careful planning and by spurning no opportunity, but they do not tend to preserve it by the same methods.

---

[74] As noted by MacDowell 2004, the exemption awarded to Epicerdes must have been hereditary, like the one given to Chabrias.

[75] The Four Hundred attempted to seize power in 411 BCE during an attempted reform of the democratic constitution. On this period, see E. M. Harris 1990.

[76] Under the rule of the Thirty, the exiled democrats began to assemble at Phyle and organized forces to overthrow the oligarchy.

Do not let this happen to you: do not think that you must put a law like this into effect, one that will taint our city with shame during a time of prosperity and, if something should happen, will deprive it of men who are willing to help.

[51] Certainly, the men who decided to help you and provided their services during the kinds of crises that Phormio described a little earlier and that I have just discussed are not the only people whom you should avoid mistreating. There are also many others who during the war with Sparta have brought entire communities, their native lands, over to your side, men who advanced the city's interests both by their words and by their actions.[77] [52] Several of these men are without a country because of their loyalty to you. The first group that strikes me as worth considering are the exiles from Corinth. In describing these events to you, I am obliged to rely on what I have heard from the older men among you. I am not going to mention all the other times they provided help, but I will recall the important battle against the Spartans that took place at Corinth.[78] After the battle, the men inside the city decided not to receive our troops within their walls, but to open negotiations with the Spartans. [53] These men,[79] when they saw our city defeated and the Spartans barring our path of retreat, did not betray us or take their personal safety into account. Even though all the Peloponnesian forces were nearby and under arms,[80] they defied the majority and opened their gates for you.[81] They chose to share if necessary the fate of those of you serving in the army at the time rather

---

[77] Demosthenes is referring to the Corinthian War (395–387), in which the Athenians, Boeotians, Argives, and Corinthians fought against the Spartans and their allies.

[78] This battle took place in the summer of 394 near the Nemean river between Corinth and Sicyon (Diodorus 14.83; Xen. *Hellenica* 4.2.14–23; Plut. *Agesilaus* 16.4).

[79] Those sympathetic to Athens who were later driven into exile.

[80] Xenophon (*Hellenica* 4.2.16) reports that the Spartans were joined by soldiers from Elis, Sicyon, Epidaurus, Troezen, Hermione, Halieis, and several other cities.

[81] This version does not agree with the account of Xenophon (*Hellenica* 4.2.23), who says that the Athenians and their allies returned to their camp after being shut out of Corinth.

than to save themselves and avoid danger by abandoning you. They led your army in and saved both you and their allies. [54] Later when peace was concluded with Sparta, that is, the Peace of Antalcidas,[82] they were driven into exile by the Spartans for what they did. When you took them in, you acted like honorable men: you voted them everything that they needed. Are we now going to decide whether those measures should remain valid? To begin with, even the question is disgraceful! Just imagine if someone were to hear that the Athenians are debating whether they must allow their benefactors to keep what they gave them! This question should have been discussed and settled a long time ago. Read this decree too for them.

[DECREE]

[55] These are the measures, judges, that you voted for the Corinthians who were in exile because of you. Imagine someone familiar with these events, because he either was present or learned about them from an eyewitness: if he should hear that this law is taking away the rewards that you granted at the time, think how bitterly he would condemn the authors of this law for their ingratitude! When we needed their help, we were so generous and accommodating, but when we achieved all that we prayed for, we were so ungrateful and mean-spirited that we deprived the recipients of their rewards and passed a law making it illegal to grant such awards in the future. [56] "But, by Zeus, some of the men who received these awards did not deserve them"—this will be their reply to every argument.[83] And then we will admit that we are forgetting the principle that one should decide whether someone deserves a reward when one gives it, not long afterwards. Refusing to give any reward in the first place is the way sensible people act, but taking a reward away from people who have received it is the way spiteful ones act. Do not give the impression that this is the way you feel. [57] In fact, I am not reluctant to discuss the question of worth. In my opinion, the city should not employ the

---

[82] The Peace of Antalcidas was concluded in 387/6 and gave the King of Persia control over the Greeks of Asia Minor (Xen. *Hellenica* 5.1.31).

[83] Cf. 1, where Demosthenes predicts that this will be his opponents' reply to all his points.

same criteria when judging a person's worth as a private individual does; the decision is not made on the same basis. In private life, each of us decides who is worthy to become his son-in-law or some other relation, and these questions are determined by certain laws and social attitudes. In public life, however, the people in the community decide who treats them well and protects their interests not on the basis of family or reputation but by their actions.[84] Are we going to allow any volunteer to help us when we need help, but then after we have received it, decide what this person deserves for his efforts? That is not the correct way for us to make decisions.

[58] "But, by Zeus, these are the only men who will suffer. I am going on and on so much about these men alone." Far from it. No, I could not even attempt to make a list of all the men who have helped you and will have their rewards taken away by this law if it is not repealed. I will cite one or two more decrees, and then I am finished with this topic. [59] Well, how are you going to avoid mistreating Ecphantus of Thasos and his followers if you take away their exemption?[85] These men turned over Thasos to you and forcibly expelled the Spartan garrison, then brought in Thrasybulus. By bringing their country over to your side, were they not responsible for turning the people in the area around Thrace into your allies? [60] What about Archebius and Heraclides,[86] who turned over Byzantium to Thrasybulus and placed the Hellespont under your con-

---

[84] In the Funeral Oration that Thucydides (2.37) attributes to Pericles, the Athenians are praised for granting honors to men not because of their membership in a class but on the basis of merit.

[85] Fragments of the decree granting exemption to Ecphantus and his followers has been found (*IG* ii² 33), and it appears to date to the early years of the fourth century. This honor may have been awarded for Ecphantus' help when Thrasybulus captured Thasos in 410 after a civil war in which the pro-Spartan party was expelled (Xen. *Hellenica* 1.1.32) or later in 390, when Thrasybulus was again operating in the area (Xen. *Hellenica* 4.8.26).

[86] Archebius of Byzantium is also mentioned as a friend of Athens at Dem. 23.189. Heraclides has been identified with the man of the same name in *IG* ii² 8. For recent discussion, see Culasso Gastaldi 2004: 35–55, who shows the decree should be dated to the early fourth century BCE.

trol,[87] with the result that you farmed out the ten-percent toll[88] and forced the Spartans despite their wealth to make the kind of peace that was in your interests?[89] When these men later fled into exile, you, men of Athens, voted them the very rewards that benefactors should receive from you: the rights of a *proxenos,* the title of benefactor, and exemption from all duties.[90] Are we to allow the men who were driven into exile because of you and who have received what they deserved from you to lose these rewards although we have no complaint against them? But that would be disgraceful.

[**61**] You might fully grasp this point if you were to consider it in the following manner. Imagine that some of the leaders of Pydna, Potidaea, or any of the other places that are now controlled by Philip and opposed to you[91] (in the same way that Thasos and Byzantium were when they belonged to the Spartans and not to you) were to approach you with a promise to bring these cities over to you, if you in return would give them the same rewards that you gave to Ecphantus and Archebius. [**62**] If some of these men here were to object to their request, alleging that it would be terrible if some group set apart from the rest of the metics were not to perform liturgies, how would you react to their arguments? Is it not obvious that you would not put

---

[87] This occurred around 390 (Xen. *Hellenica* 4.8.27).

[88] Byzantium levied a transit duty of 10 percent on all goods coming in and out of the Black Sea. On the nature of this duty, see E. M. Harris 1999. The Athenians took over this duty and farmed it out to the highest bidder. For the procedure, see And. 1.133–134 and *Ath. Pol.* 47.2.

[89] An allusion to the Peace of Antalcidas (cf. 54). In reality, the Athenians were forced to accept the treaty after the Spartans regained control of the Hellespont (Xen. *Hellenica* 5.1.25–9), and the treaty favored Sparta rather than Athens.

[90] On honors in Athenian decrees, see Henry 1983. A *proxenos* was a person who looked after the interests of citizens of a foreign city and gave them assistance when they came to his city. On this institution, see Herman 1987.

[91] Philip conquered Pydna around 357 (Diodorus 16.8.3) and Potidaea in 356 (Plut. *Alexander* 3.4–5). Both cities were in Northern Greece near Macedonia. Potidaea had been an Athenian cleruchy (Diodorus 15.81.6). The other places are probably Amphipolis and Crenides, taken in 357 (Diodorus 16.8.2–7). This is the earliest reference to Philip in the Attic orators and reveals that the Athenians did not yet view Philip as a serious threat. This changed after Philip's capture of Methone and his threat to the Chersonnese; see E. M. Harris 1995: 44–46.

up with their talk but would treat them like troublemakers?[92] In the case where you are about to receive help, you would treat the man who makes this argument like a troublemaker, but our opponents are talking about taking away rewards from men who helped you in the past: it would certainly be disgraceful for you even to listen to them. [63] Come, let us consider this question: what encouraged the men who betrayed Pydna and the rest of these places to wrong us? Is it not obvious to everyone that they were counting on the rewards that they expected to receive from Philip? You, Leptines, what then should you have done? Should you have persuaded our enemies, if you could, to withhold honors from their benefactors for the injustices that they did to us? Or should you have passed a law that removes some of the rewards that our benefactors already possess? The former, I think. But so that I do not wander too far from the present topic,[93] take the decrees that were proposed for the men of Thasos and Byzantium. Read.

[DECREES]

[64] Judges, you have heard the decrees. Some of these men may no longer be alive, but the deeds that they did remain once they are done. It is right to let these *stelai* remain valid forever so that these men may not be treated unjustly by you during their lifetimes, and so that after their deaths, they will remain as a memorial to the city's strength of character as well as provide examples that will show those who wish to help us how many people the city has rewarded for their services.[94] [65] Do not let this point escape you, men of Athens: nothing could be more shameful than for everyone in the world to see and hear that

---

[92] Demosthenes uses the word *sykophantes,* which normally referred to those who abused the legal system by bringing false charges and practicing extortion. Here the term has been extended to anyone who makes deceitful or dishonest arguments. On this term, see Harvey 1990.

[93] Because speakers swore to keep to the point, they could not stray from the main topic for long. See Rhodes 2004.

[94] Decrees passed by the Assembly were often inscribed on stone *stelai* and set up in public places. For the idea that the *stele* serves to remind others that the Athenians rewarded benefactors, see *IG* ii² 233, lines 18–24.

while nothing in all of time can revoke the misfortunes that these men endured for your sake, the rewards that they received from you as compensation have already been revoked. [**66**] It would be much more fitting to allow them to keep what they were given and take away their misfortunes than to take away their rewards and let their misfortunes remain. By Zeus, tell me who will be willing to help you if he is going to be punished on the spot by his enemies if he fails, and, if he succeeds, will receive rewards that he cannot trust?

[**67**] Well, now, I would be quite upset, judges, if I were to give you the impression that the only valid charge to be made against the law is that it takes the exemption away from foreign benefactors and that I believed that I could not name any of our citizens who deserved this honor. There are many other blessings that I would pray for us to receive, but above all I wish that the best and largest number of benefactors should be our own citizens. [**68**] Now consider first the case of Conon: does he deserve to have any of the awards granted to him canceled because some people have criticized either his character or his actions? As some of you from his generation can testify, this man was serving as general for the King after the return of the democrats from the Piraeus when the city was weak and did not have even one ship.[95] Without receiving any funds from you, he won a naval battle against the Spartans and taught them to respect you when before they had given orders to others.[96] He drove the harmosts out of the islands, and after that he returned home and rebuilt the walls.[97] He was the first person to put the city in a position where it could compete again with the Spartans for leadership. [**69**] In fact, he was the only citizen whose *stele* has this phrase written on it, saying, "Whereas Conon liberated

---

[95] Demosthenes exaggerates: in 404 the Spartans allowed the Athenians to keep ten (Diodorus 13.107.4) or twelve triremes (Xen. *Hellenica* 2.2.20).

[96] Conon commanded the Persian fleet and defeated the Spartans in a naval battle at Cnidus in 394 (Xen. *Hellenica* 4.3.11–12; Diodorus 14.83.4–7).

[97] After the victory at Cnidus, Conon liberated several Greek cities in Asia Minor (Diodorus 14.84.3–4). Harmosts were the Spartan officials placed in Greek cities. For the honors granted him at Erythrae, see Rhodes and Osborne 2003: no. 8. For his honors at Samos and Ephesos, see Pausanias 6.3.16. For his role in rebuilding the walls of Athens, see 73–74.

the allies of Athens."⁹⁸ This phrase is an indication of his ambition to earn your respect and yours to win the admiration of the Greeks, because whenever one of your citizens is responsible for conferring a benefit on another community, the city's reputation reaps the benefit of glory. [**70**] This is the reason why his contemporaries not only gave him an exemption but also made him the first person for whom they erected a bronze statue, just as they did for Harmodius and Aristogeiton.⁹⁹ They thought that by destroying the power of the Spartans he had put an end to a great tyranny. The clerk will therefore read you the actual decrees voted for Conon at the time so that you can better appreciate what I am talking about. Read.

[*DECREES*]

[**71**] Now, you, men of Athens, were not the only ones to honor Conon for the achievements that I have described. Many other communities rightly thought that they should show gratitude for the services that they received. It will certainly be disgraceful, men of Athens, if the rewards that he received from others remain secure while only the one that you gave him is taken away. [**72**] Nor is it honorable to reward him during his lifetime to the point where you considered him worthy of the kind of rewards that you just heard about, but now after his death, to take away one of the awards that you gave him. Many of this man's achievements, men of Athens, deserve praise—and all of them make it your duty not to revoke his awards—but the most distinguished of all is the rebuilding of the walls.¹⁰⁰ [**73**] Anyone could understand this if he were to com-

---

⁹⁸ Athenian honorary decrees normally began with a clause like this, giving the reasons for the award. See Henry 1983: 7–11.

⁹⁹ For the statue of Conon, see Isoc. 9.57; Pausanias 1.3.1–2, 24.3; Aes. 3.243; *IG* ii² 3774. Demosthenes' statement that Conon was the first person whom the Athenians honored with a statue during his lifetime appears to be accurate.

¹⁰⁰ In 404 the Spartans forced the Athenians to tear down the long walls and the walls around the Piraeus (Xen. *Hellenica* 2.2.21–23). After his victory at Cnidus, Conon returned to Athens with money from the satrap Pharnabazus to help rebuild the walls of Athens (Xen. *Hellenica* 4.8.9–10; Diodorus 14.85.2–3),

pare the way that Themistocles, the most famous person among his contemporaries, accomplished the same deed.[101] Now people say that this man told his fellow citizens to build the walls and if anyone came from Sparta, he instructed them to detain him. He then went away on an embassy to Sparta. During the debate some men reported there that the Athenians were rebuilding their walls, but he denied it and invited them to send ambassadors to see for themselves. When this group did not return, he advised them to send another group. I suppose all of you have heard the story about how he tricked them. [74] In my opinion—by Zeus, may none of you, men of Athens, feel envy when he hears what I am about to say, but just see whether it is true. Just as it is better to act openly than in secret and more honorable to achieve one's goal by winning rather than by cheating, so was Conon's way of building the wall better than that of Themistocles. One man acted in secret, the other by defeating the people who stood in our way.[102] You should certainly not treat such a man unjustly nor treat him less well than politicians who are going to demonstrate that one of his awards must be taken away.

[75] Enough about that. But, by Zeus, there is also Chabrias' son:[103] should we allow him to lose the exemption that his father justly received from you and passed on to him? I think that no person in his right mind would say this is fair. Perhaps you realize even without me telling you that Chabrias was an excellent man,[104] but certainly nothing prevents me from briefly recalling some of his achievements.

---

but the project appears to have begun before that; see Rhodes and Osborne 2003: no. 9.

[101] Demosthenes' account of Themistocles' role in building the walls of Athens agrees with the sources (Thuc. 1.89–93; Diodorus 11.39.1–40.4; Plut. *Themistocles* 19), but his knowledge of the event may have been based on oral tradition.

[102] Demosthenes overlooks "the fact that in 479–478 the Spartans, although opposed to the prospect of Athens' refortification, were still formally allied to Athens, while in 394 they were at war" with them (Chremmydas 2005: 183).

[103] Ctesippus, who is also mentioned at the beginning of the speech (1).

[104] Chabrias had a long and distinguished career that lasted from 390 to his death in 357/6. His most famous achievement was his victory over the Spartan fleet at Naxos in 376 (Xen. *Hellenica* 5.4.61; Diodorus 15.34–35).

[76] The way that he positioned you for battle against the Spartans at Thebes,[105] how he killed Gorgopas on Aegina,[106] the number of trophies that he erected on Cyprus and later in Egypt,[107] and how he traveled over almost the entire world without ever bringing disgrace on the city's name or on himself,[108] these are topics to which it would not be at all easy to do justice. It would also be very shameful for my words to make his actions appear inferior to what everyone thinks of them today.[109] But those deeds that I think my words could not diminish, I will try to recall. [77] Well, now, he defeated the Spartans in a naval battle, captured 49 triremes,[110] conquered most of the nearby islands and brought them over to your side, making former enemies into your friends. He brought 3,000 prisoners here and paid in a sum of more than 110 talents taken from the enemy. The older men among you are my witnesses for these events. In addition, he captured more than twenty other triremes, taking one or two at a time, all of which he brought back into your harbors. [78] In a nutshell, I am certain that he has been the only one out of all our generals who did not lose a city, a fortress, a ship, or a soldier when he was your leader. There is no trophy erected by your enemies from spoils taken

---

[105] Demosthenes probably alludes to an incident that took place in 377/6, when Chabrias ordered mercenaries under his command to face the Spartans with their shields against their knees as a gesture of contempt (Diodorus 15.32.4–6; Polyaenus 2.1.2), but he shades the truth by implying the soldiers were Athenians.

[106] Chabrias killed Gorgopas, the Spartan harmost on Aegina, in 388 (Xen. *Hellenica* 5.1.10–12).

[107] Conon fought with king Evagoras against the Persians on Cyprus in 388 (Xen. *Hellenica* 5.1.10) and in Egypt in 386 (Diodorus 15.29.1–4).

[108] Demosthenes exaggerates: Chabrias campaigned as far north as Thrace (Diodorus 15.36.4–5) and as far south as Egypt, but he went only as far east as Cyprus and never appears to have fought in Sicily.

[109] For a similar concern about a speech not doing justice to popular belief about courageous actions, see Thuc. 2.35.2.

[110] Demosthenes exaggerates again: Diodorus (15.35.2) reports only eight Spartan triremes captured and twenty-four destroyed. For these ships, see *IG* ii² 1606, lines 78–79, 82–83; 1607, lines 20–21, 114–115, 145–146.

from you under his command, but there are many that you erected over numerous foes when he was general. So that I do not omit any of his achievements from my account, the clerk will read you a list of the number of ships that he captured and the place where each was taken, as well as the number of cities, the amount of money, and the location of each of his trophies. Read.

[ACHIEVEMENTS OF CHABRIAS]

[79] This is how many cities this man captured and how many enemy ships this man defeated at sea. This is how much glory he has brought our city without ever causing it any disgrace. Do any of you think, men of Athens, that he deserves to lose the exemption that he received from you and passed down to his son? I do not think so. Indeed, it would not make sense. If he had lost one city or only ten ships, these men would indict him for treason.[111] If he had been convicted, he would have been destroyed forever.[112] [80] On the contrary, he took seventeen cities, captured seventy ships, and 3,000 prisoners, paid in 110 talents, and set up this many trophies. Are the rewards given to him for these achievements now going to be revoked? Men of Athens, everyone saw that during his lifetime Chabrias always acted in your interest and ended his life fighting for no one else.[113] As a result, it would be right to show your appreciation to his son not only for his achievements during his lifetime but also for the way he died. [81] Now, men of Athens, here is something else worth thinking about: we should avoid looking worse than the Chians in the way we treat our benefactors. Although he attacked these men as an enemy in arms, they have not now taken away any of the rewards that they previously gave him,[114] but they have placed more weight on his

---

[111] Generals who lost battles were frequently tried for treason. See Hansen 1975: 60–62.

[112] The penalty for conviction in an *eisangelia* was death, see Hansen 1975: 34–36.

[113] Chabrias was killed in 356 during the siege of Chios (Diodorus 16.7; Plut. *Phocion* 6).

[114] It is not known when the Chians gave Chabrias these honors. It may have been after the victory at Naxos.

past services than on their recent complaints. You, the men whom he died to protect while fighting them, are about to be seen taking away one of the rewards you gave him for his past services instead of granting him still more honors because of them. Shame on you! [82] Moreover, his son would not receive the treatment he deserves if he should have some of this reward taken away, because Chabrias led you in battle many times, he never caused anyone's child to become an orphan, yet his son has been raised as an orphan because of his father's ambition to win your respect. His devotion to the city was in my opinion truly unshakable. He had a reputation for being the most cautious of all your generals. When in command, he used this quality to protect you, but as for himself, when he was assigned to a dangerous position, he showed no concern for it and chose to lose his life rather than pour shame on the honors that he had received from you.[115] [83] Are we going to deprive his son of the honors for which he considered it his duty to die or win victory? And what are we going to say, men of Athens, when the entire world sees standing the trophies that he set up when serving as general for you, yet the rewards that he received for them are being taken away? Do you not realize, men of Athens, and understand that the law is not being judged whether it is expedient or not,[116] but you are being examined to see whether you deserve to be treated well in the future or not? [84] In fact, get the decree that was voted for Chabrias. Go and look for it. It must be here somewhere.

I want to say this too for Chabrias. When you honored Iphicrates, men of Athens, you honored not only him but also Strabax and Polystratus for his sake.[117] And again when you gave an award to Timotheus,[118]

---

[115] It is uncertain whether Chabrias fought as a general or only as a trierarch at the siege of Chios. See Chremmydas 2005: 197.

[116] Demosthenes' language here echoes the formal charge, i.e., that the law is inexpedient and thereby connects the argument with the substantive legal issue at stake.

[117] Strabax was a mercenary who fought for Athens (Arist. *Rhetoric* 1399b). Polystratus commanded mercenaries along with Chabrias and Timotheus during the Corinthian War (Dem. 4.24).

[118] Timotheus was the son of Conon and elected general in 378 (Diodorus 15.29.7). He won several victories but was removed from office in 373. Later he

you granted citizenship to Clearchus[119] and several others for his sake. But Chabrias received honors from you only for himself. [85] Imagine that when he received his award, he asked you to do what you had done for Iphicrates and Timotheus, that is, to reward some of the men who have received the exemption, all of whom these men are now criticizing and demanding that it be taken away. Would you not have done this as a favor to him? I think so. [86] Then are you going to take away this man's exemption because of those to whom you would have given this reward for his sake? But that would not make sense. It is not appropriate for you to have a reputation for being so enthusiastic after receiving some benefit that you not only reward your benefactors but also their friends, yet after a short period of time elapses, you take away all the honors that you have given them.

[DECREES OF CHABRIAS' HONORS]

[87] These are the men whom you will treat unjustly, men of Athens, if you do not annul this law, and that does not include many others whom you have heard about. Just think and imagine in your own minds how angry some of those who have died would probably be were they somehow to become aware of what is now going on.[120] The actions that these men performed for your benefit are judged from what we say, and their noble accomplishments have been done in vain, if our speeches do not do them justice. Would this not be a terrible way to treat them?

[88] So that you may know that all the arguments that we are presenting are truly based on all the principles of justice and that there is nothing in them designed to mislead or deceive you, the clerk will

---

captured Samos in 365 (Isoc. 15.111–112) and gained territory in Northern Greece, where he served continuously from 365 to 360/59 (see E. M. Harris 2006a: 355–363). After the defeat at Embata in 355, he was tried, convicted, and fined 100 talents. At this time he was living in exile. There is a lengthy account of his career in Isoc. 15.101–139.

[119] Clearchus has been identified with the tyrant of Heracleia in the Bosporus, who was educated by Plato and Isocrates (Isoc. *Epistle* 7.12–13).

[120] The Attic orators often appear to assume that their audience is uncertain whether the dead can perceive the actions of the living. See Currie 2005: 38.

read out to you the law that we propose to substitute in place of this one that we argue is inexpedient. You will realize from this that we have taken care to achieve three aims: that you avoid the appearance of doing anything shameful; that if someone finds fault with anyone who has received an award, he can take it away if you so decide; and finally that those whose awards meet with no objections can keep what they have been given. [**89**] Nothing in all of this is our innovation or even new. On the contrary, there is an old law, which this man has violated, that allows legislation to be enacted in the following way: if someone thinks that any of the existing laws is not good, he can bring a public action against it and substitute in its place another law, whatever he may propose, should the former law be abolished, and you then have the power to hear them and chose the better one.[121] [**90**] Solon was the man who created this method of enacting laws.[122] He did not think it right for the Thesmothetae, who are chosen by lot to administer the laws, to take office after having been examined twice, once in the Council and once before you in court,[123] but for the laws themselves, which these men and all citizens are obliged to follow in their public actions, to be passed haphazardly and go into effect without having been examined. [**91**] This is the reason why they kept to the traditional laws in the past as long as they used this method of legislation and did not enact new ones. But when some influential politicians, as I hear, arranged for themselves to make it possible to pass laws whenever they wanted in any possible way, the number of laws that contradicted each other grew so large that you have been electing men for a long time to straighten out the contradictions.[124] [**92**] In fact, there is no end in

---

[121] This law is also mentioned in *Against Timocrates* (Dem. 24.34) and required that anyone who wished to propose new legislation had first to repeal any opposing laws. Demosthenes here combines two procedures: first, the public action against the old law; second, the process of enacting the new law.

[122] It was customary to attribute all the laws of Athens to Solon, who enacted his laws in 594/3. In reality, the laws about legislation were passed around 403.

[123] The Thesmothetae, like all the Archons, had to undergo two examinations of their qualifications (*dokimasia*). See *Ath. Pol.* 55.2–5 with Rhodes 1981: 614–621. Other officials had to pass only one examination.

[124] In 330 there was a law instructing the Thesmothetai to examine the law code every year for conflicting statutes (Aes. 3.38). According to Hansen 1985:

sight for the matter. The laws do not differ one iota from decrees, and the laws to be followed when passing decrees are more recent than the actual decrees themselves.[125] But let me avoid relying on mere assertion; take the actual law that I am discussing in accordance with which Nomothetae used to be appointed. Read it.

[*LAW*]

[**93**] You see the excellent method that Solon provides for enacting laws. First, it comes before you, men who have sworn an oath and exercise supervision over this and other matters.[126] Next, opposing laws are repealed so that there is one law for each subject. This avoids confusion for private individuals, who would be at a disadvantage in comparison to people who are familiar with all the laws. The aim is to make points of law the same for all to read as well as simple and clear to understand.[127] [**94**] Even before this stage, Solon ordered that

---

355–356, Demosthenes is referring to this procedure, but according to MacDowell 1975: 66, 72, and Rhodes 1985: 60, this law was passed later, and Demosthenes is referring to ad hoc committees created by the Assembly to address the problem of contradictory laws.

[125] In the fourth century the Athenians drew a strict distinction between laws (*nomoi*), which were general provisions, and decrees (*psephismata*), which applied to individual cases and were subordinate to laws. Laws were also meant to remain fixed for long periods, while decrees were passed to handle temporary situations. Demosthenes claims that the Athenians now pass too many laws, which results in confusion. On the distinction between *nomos* and *psephisma*, see Hansen 1978. Demosthenes is probably exaggerating the degree of confusion for rhetorical effect; as Hansen has shown, the Athenians for the most part carefully maintained the distinction between laws and decrees.

[126] The Legislators (Nomothetae), who gave final approval to all laws, were selected from the judges serving in the courts, who had sworn the judicial oath (Dem. 24.21).

[127] This statement represents an ideal that was never attained in practice. In reality, ambiguities remained in the laws, which gave rise to problems of legal interpretation. See E. M. Harris 2000, 2004a. Although Demosthenes gives the impression that all Athenians (or residents of Attica) could read, scholars differ about the extent of literacy in Classical Athens. For an optimistic view, see Harvey 1966; for a pessimistic one, see W. V. Harris 1989: 65–115.

the laws be placed in front of the Eponymous Heroes[128] and handed over to the secretary for him to read at meetings of the Assembly.[129] The aim was for each of you to hear the laws many times and have a chance to study them at leisure and then enact those that were just and in the public interest. Now out of all these fair rules, this man here has not followed a single one. If he had, in my opinion you would not have been persuaded to pass such a piece of legislation. We, by contrast, men of Athens, have followed all of them and are substituting a law that is much better and more just than this one, as you will see when you hear it. [95] Take and read first the parts of the law that we are indicting, then the provisions that we say should be substituted in their place.[130]

[LAW]

These are the parts of the law that we are indicting as inexpedient. Next in order, read out the provisions that we say are better. Pay close attention, you men who are judging this case, as they are read out.

[LAW]

[96] Stop. Among the laws now in effect, men of Athens, this one is good and straightforward: "All awards granted by the people shall be valid."[131] By Earth[132] and the gods, this is fair. Leptines should not

---

[128] Each of the ten Attic tribes had an eponymous hero. Statues of these ten heroes were placed in the Agora. Public notices such as legal indictments (Dem. 21.103), lists of men summoned for military duty (Aristoph. *Peace* 1183–1184), and proposed laws (Aes. 3.38–39; Dem. 24.18, 23) were displayed here. For the location, see Rhodes 1981: 259.

[129] After the proposed law was posted, it was read out at three meetings of the Assembly (Dem. 24.21, 25).

[130] Some editors have proposed emending "Law (*nomos*)" to "Indictment (*graphe*)," but see Chremmydas 2005: 223.

[131] Sandys 1890: 79 suggests that this law was passed after the restoration of the democracy in 403 and was intended to abolish all privileges conferred by the Thirty and to confirm those granted by the people before the tyranny.

[132] For the connection between the goddess Earth and justice, see E. M. Harris 2006a: 73–74.

have proposed his law before indicting and repealing this law. As it is, although providing evidence against himself that proves he violates the law, he still tried to pass his law despite the existence of another law making his own subject to prosecution for contradicting previously enacted legislation. Take the actual law.

[*LAW*]

[**97**] Is not the provision "no one is to be exempt" of those who have received this privilege from the people contrary, men of Athens, to the rule "all awards granted by the people are valid"? Clearly so. But this is not the case with the law that this man[133] is proposing in its place. Instead, it keeps your awards valid and provides a legitimate means to prevent those who have used fraud, committed a subsequent offense, or are completely unworthy from keeping their award if you so decide. Read the law.

[*LAW*]

[**98**] Listen, men of Athens, and learn that in this way it is possible both for those who are worthy to keep the awards that they have received and for those who are judged to be not like this to have their awards taken away if they obtained them without just cause. And in the future, the power to grant or not to grant awards will remain, as is right, in your hands. This law is certainly just and fair; Leptines, I think, will not deny that, or if he does, he will not be able to prove it. Perhaps he will try to distract you by repeating what he said before the Thesmothetae.[134] He claimed that our substitute proposal was a ruse and that if his own law were repealed, this one would not be enacted. [**99**] As for the point that once this law has been rescinded by your vote,[135] the old law, which the Thesmothetae have followed

---

[133] Apsephion.

[134] All cases received a preliminary hearing (*anakrisis*) conducted by a magistrate before going to trial. See Harrison 1971: 94–105. In this case, the Thesmothetai conducted the hearing.

[135] MacDowell 1975: 70 believes that Demosthenes refers to the vote of the Nomothetae, who will invalidate Leptines' law and enact Apsephion's proposal, but see Rhodes 1985: 58–59.

when they wrote down this one beside it for you to read, permits the law substituted in its place to be ratified,[136] I will say nothing so as to avoid provoking a debate on this point but will move on to the following point. When he makes this argument, he surely admits that the other law is better and more fair than the one that he enacted, but he shifts the discussion to the manner in which it will be enacted. [100] First, there are many ways for him, if he wishes, to force the person making a counter-proposal, if he wishes to enact the law in question. Furthermore, I, Phormio, and anyone else he wishes to add, have pledged to enact the law. Certainly, you have a law that imposes the harshest penalties on anyone who makes a promise to the Assembly, the Council, or a court and does not fulfill it.[137] We are making a pledge and a promise. Let the Thesmothetae record it; let the matter rest in their hands. [101] Do not do anything that is beneath your dignity nor let an undeserving person retain his exemption, but let him be judged separately in accordance with this law.[138] If he[139] says that this is just words and idle talk, that by itself is not an argument. Let this man propose a law himself and not use the argument that we ourselves will not. It is no doubt better to introduce a law that has won your approval than the one he now proposes on his own.

[102] This is what I think, men of Athens. Leptines, do not, by Zeus, be angry with me; I am not about to disparage you. This man either has not read the laws of Solon or does not understand them.[140] Solon established a law granting the right to give one's property to

---

[136] Sandys 1890: 81 believes that the "law in question appears to have enacted that on the repeal of the law proposed for amendment, the amendment should *ipso facto* become law." Cf. Vince 1930: ad loc. Sandys implicitly translates the verb *keleuei* as "orders," but see MacDowell 1989b: 259–261, who shows that it often means "permit." At a session of the Nomothetae, either the old law would be upheld or the new law would be enacted in its place, but in this public action the defeat of Leptines' law would result in a return to the status quo ante, not the enactment of the alternative proposal.

[137] On this law, see *Ath. Pol.* 43.5 with Rhodes 1981: 527.

[138] This is addressed to the court.

[139] Leptines.

[140] All Athenians were expected to know the city's laws. See Aes. 1.39 with E. M. Harris 1994: 135–136.

whomever one wishes, provided that one has no legitimate children.[141] His aim was not to deprive the closest relative of the right to inherit but to encourage people to compete in doing good for each other by making this benefit open to all.[142] [**103**] Your proposal is the very opposite, to take away the people's right to give away its own property to anyone. How is anyone going to say that you have either read or understood the laws of Solon? You are depriving the people of the help given by men who will seek its honors because you are warning them and showing that they will not gain anything by doing good. [**104**] Indeed, there is among the excellent laws of Solon one that prohibits slandering the dead, even if it is done by one of his children.[143] But are you not doing this? Are you not slandering our dead benefactors by criticizing this one or saying that one was unworthy, when none of this has anything to do with them?[144] Is not this far removed from the spirit of Solon?

[**105**] Someone has quite seriously reported to me that to support their proposal that nothing be given to anyone, whatever they have done, they are prepared to make such an argument as this: the Spartans, who have a good government, and also the Thebans do not give any such honor to anyone in their communities, yet even in their communities there perhaps exist some good men. In my opinion, men of Athens, all such arguments are designed to stir you up with the aim of persuading you to take away the exemption, but they are in no way justified. I am not unaware that the Thebans and the Spartans do not have the same laws and customs as we do, nor even the same constitution. [**106**] First, the very thing that these men are about to do if they make this argument is not allowed in Sparta, namely, to praise the

---

[141] For this law, see Is. 6.9; Dem. 46.14; [Dem.] 44.68; Plut. *Solon* 21; Hyp. 3.17. Demosthenes uses an analogy and compares the Athenian people to a man making a will: just as the testator has the freedom to grant his property to anyone whom he chooses, so should the Athenian people have the right to grant honors to whomever they wish.

[142] Lit. "in the middle." Demosthenes compares the right to inherit to a prize in an athletic contest.

[143] For this law, see [Dem.] 40.49; Plut. *Solon* 21.

[144] Or, "who have nothing in common with them" or "who are not related to them."

laws of Athens or any other city; far from it. Instead it is necessary to praise what suits the interests of the community. Next, even though the Spartans refrain from this kind of award, they have other honors that our people would unanimously wish never to be introduced here. What are these? [**107**] I will not mention each one but will discuss one that sums up the others. When someone conducts himself in the correct way and is selected for what they call the Gerousia,[145] he becomes the absolute master over the masses. There the prize for excellence is to win control over the state along with one's equals. In our city, the people have control, and there are curses, laws, and safeguards to prevent anyone else from seizing power.[146] There are also crowns, exemptions, dining rights,[147] and similar honors that any good man might win. [**108**] These two practices are correct, both theirs and ours. Why? Because in an oligarchy the fact that all the leaders of the community have an equal share creates unanimity among them, and for democracies the competition among good men to win prizes awarded by the people protects liberty. [**109**] But as for the absence of honors at Thebes, I think that I can tell the truth. The Thebans, men of Athens, are prouder of their harshness and dishonesty than you are of your generosity and desire for justice.[148] Indeed, I wish (if I may utter a prayer) that the Thebans may never stop withholding honors and admiration from their benefactors and treating their fellow Boeotians in the way they do (you know how they treated Orchomenus).[149] Nor

---

[145] The Gerousia, or "Council of Elders," was the main deliberative body in Sparta. It consisted of thirty members: the two kings and twenty-eight others elected by the Assembly. See Michell 1964: 135–140.

[146] For the curse pronounced at meetings of the Assembly, see Dem. 19.70; Din. 2.16; Lyc. *Against Leocrates* 31; Aristoph. *Women at the Thesmophoria* 331–351. For the laws against tyranny, see 111n and 159n.

[147] The permanent right to dine in the Prytaneum was one of Athens' greatest honors. See Henry 1983: 75–78. A decree dated to 440–432 appears to give the categories of those eligible for the award (*IG* i³ 131). For a proposal about the location of the Prytaneum, see Schmalz 2006.

[148] For Athenian hostility to Thebes in this period, see Dem. 1.26, 14.33–34.

[149] In 364 some exiles from Thebes convinced 300 cavalrymen from Orchomenus to help them overthrow the government. After the conspirators betrayed the plot, the Thebans attacked Orchomenus, killed all the adult males,

may you ever stop doing the opposite, honoring your benefactors and using persuasion and the law to get citizens to perform their duties. [110] I think that it is right to praise the character and habits of others and to find fault with your own when it is possible to show that they are more successful than you are. But when you are prosperous and doing better than they are in terms of public affairs, achieving unity, and other matters,[150] what is the point of belittling our own way of life and adopting theirs? Even if their institutions appear better than ours in theory, it is still worth keeping our own because of the good fortune that they have brought you. [111] Aside from all these considerations, if I must say what I think is right, I would say this: it is not right, men of Athens, to discuss the laws of Sparta or of Thebes for the purpose of harming the laws here. Nor is it right for you to want to kill the person who wishes to impose on us the institutions that have made those cities powerful, yet on the other hand to be willing to listen to men who propose to destroy those practices that have made our people prosperous.[151]

[112] There is of course the ready-made argument that in fact even in the time of our own ancestors, some men who performed good deeds never asked for such a reward but were content to receive commemoration in the district of the Herms.[152] Perhaps he will read this inscription to you. I think that this argument, men of Athens, is not in the city's interest for many reasons, and besides it is wrong. [113] If

---

and sold the women and children into slavery (Diodorus 15.79.3–6; Pausanias 9.15.3).

[150] Although Athens was arguably in a better position than Sparta at this time, the city was certainly not stronger than Thebes after the Athenian defeat in the Social War.

[151] In Athens all attempts to subvert the democracy and establish a tyranny or an oligarchy were harshly punished. For prosecution against those subverting the democracy, see Hyp. 3.7–8 with Whitehead 2000: 186–189. For laws against tyranny, see Ostwald 1955.

[152] The district of the Herms was in the Agora between the Painted Stoa and the Royal Stoa; there also appears to have been a Stoa of the Herms in this area. Demosthenes probably refers to the epigrams honoring Cimon that are quoted by Aeschines (3.183–185), who makes a similar point.

he is going to say that even these men did not deserve to be honored, let him say who does deserve to be if there is no one either then or later. If he says there is no one, I for one would feel sorry for a city in which no one in its entire history ever deserved good treatment. And yet if he admits that these were excellent men who received nothing, he certainly is accusing the city of ingratitude. This charge is not true, not even close. Whenever someone deceitfully twists words to misrepresent reality, I think he inevitably appears offensive. [**114**] I will show you that this is the truth and that it is right to declare it. In the past there have been many excellent men, and our city granted honors to good men even then. Yet the honors and everything else in that period were appropriate for the customs of the time, and those granted now are suited to the present time. What then is my reason for saying this? I would say that the men of that time did not fail to obtain anything that they desired from the city. [**115**] On the basis of what evidence? The fact that Lysimachus, one of those who performed public service at that time, received as a gift twenty-two acres of woodland, the same amount of arable land, and in addition one hundred minas of silver coin, and four drachmas a day. In fact, there is a decree of Alcibiades that records these items.[153] At that time our city was well supplied with land and money, and soon it will be again (this is the way to speak and to avoid words of ill omen). Who in your opinion would right now not prefer one-third of these things instead of an exemption? To show that I am speaking the truth, get me the decree.

[*DECREE*]

[**116**] Certainly, men of Athens, your ancestors were accustomed to granting honors to good men; this decree here makes that clear. But if they did not do so in the same way that we do now, that is a somewhat different matter. Well, now, let us grant that neither Lysimachus nor anyone else ever received any reward from our ancestors: would

[153] Davies 1971: 51–52 shows that this decree must be a forgery. For other forged decrees from this period, see Habicht 1961.

that make it any more just to take honors away from those who have just now received them from us? [**117**] It is not those who do not give what they have decided not to give who have done anything disgraceful, but those who give something, but later go back on their word and take it away without any grounds for complaint. So if someone could show that those men took away one of the awards that they granted, I agree that you might too, but it would be disgraceful just the same. On the other hand, if no one could show that this ever happened, what reason would there be for starting such a practice in our time?

[**118**] You must certainly, men of Athens, keep in mind and observe the following point: you have come here having sworn to judge in accordance with the laws, not those of the Spartans or the Thebans, nor even those that your earliest ancestors followed, but those under which they received the exemptions that this man here is taking away through his law. As for matters where there are no laws, you have sworn to follow your most honest judgment.[154] Apply this kind of judgment to the entire law. [**119**] Is it not then right to give honors to your benefactors? It is right. What next? Is it not right to allow people to keep what someone once has given them? It is right. Then do this in order to abide by your oath, and show your anger if anyone claims that your ancestors acted differently. If anyone should cite examples of cases in which those men did not grant an honor to someone after receiving an important benefit, you should consider them dishonest and uncouth, dishonest because they tell lies about your ancestors and misrepresent them as ungrateful, uncouth because they are unaware that even if that was the way things were, it is their duty to deny it rather than to repeat it.

[**120**] I think that Leptines will also use this argument: he will say

---

[154]The judicial oath contained a clause whereby the judges swore to cast their votes "according to their most just judgment." Both here and at Dem. 39.40–41, it is stated that this clause applies only in cases in which there are no laws. At Dem. 23.96–97, however, the phrase is interpreted to mean that judges should cast an honest vote not influenced by hatred, partiality, or any other dishonest motive. Cf. Dem. 57.63. The clause did not grant judges the right to ignore the law and vote according to their consciences. On this part of the oath and its implications, see E. M. Harris 2007b.

that his law does not take away statues and the right to dine at public expense from those who have received them, nor does it abolish the city's right to grant honors to men who deserve them. It will still be possible both to erect bronze statues and to grant dining rights and anything else that you wish—except this. As for these rights that he will claim he is leaving the city, I have only this much to say: whenever you take away an award that you previously granted someone, you will destroy confidence in all awards that are made in the future. How will anyone have any more confidence in the award of a statue or of dining rights than in a grant of immunity that you will clearly have taken away after giving it to people? [121] Even if this problem were not about to arise, I do not think that it is a good idea to place the city in a position that forces it to choose between treating all men equally worthy of the same rewards as those given to its greatest benefactors or, if they do not do this, refusing to show gratitude to some men. When it comes to major acts of public service, it is not in your interest that the occasions to receive them occur frequently, nor is it any easier perhaps to be the party responsible for doing them. [122] On the other hand, the virtues of the average citizen and those qualities that anyone might display in peacetime and under constitutional government—loyalty, honesty, and diligence—such are the qualities that in my opinion it is both advantageous and necessary to reward with honors. There is thus a need to create different types of honors so that each person will receive from the people the kind of honor that he clearly deserves.

[123] As for the claim that he will make about leaving intact honors for those who have already obtained them, some might give the very simple and honest reply: "All the rewards you granted were in compensation for the same services; we deserve to keep all of them."[155] Another group might reply that the person who claims that their awards are being left intact is pulling the wool over their eyes. If someone is judged to have performed services that merit an exemp-

---

[155] The argument is very compressed, but the point of the first group is that the statues and dining privileges were given for the same services for which they also received an exemption, so that if they deserve to keep the former, they also should keep the latter.

tion, and has received only this reward, whether it be a foreigner or a citizen, when he loses this, Leptines, what reward does he have left? Obviously none at all. Do not take a reward from this group because you accuse another group of being worthless. Nor, on the other hand, should you take away the only reward that these men have because you are going to claim that you will leave another group some privileges. [124] To put it simply, it is not terrible for us to do an injustice to a single individual, no matter whether he be powerful or less important, but it is terrible if we are about to undermine the confidence in the honors that we grant to some people as rewards. The major issue in my view, at least, is not about the exemption but about the concern that this law introduces a pernicious habit, the kind that will destroy confidence in all the rewards that the people grant.

[125] Next comes the most insidious argument that they think they have come up with to persuade you to abolish the exemptions. It is better to warn you about it in advance so that you will not be taken in by it unawares. They are going to say that all the expenditures[156] are for religious rituals.[157] It would thus be terrible for someone who has an exemption to be barred from religious ceremonies. I think that it is right for men who have received this privilege from the people to be exempt from these duties, but what I think is terrible is what these men are about to do if they actually make this argument. [126] Suppose they have no other way of showing that it is right for you to abolish these privileges; how could they do anything more sacrilegious and terrible than attempting to accomplish this by invoking the name of the gods? Everything that one does when invoking the name of the gods should in my opinion clearly be the kind of acts that are clearly not wrong in the eyes of men.[158] Having an exemption from

---

[156] Some manuscripts add here "those for festival liturgies and the gymnasiarchy," but Dilts deletes as an intrusive gloss.

[157] Since the *choregos* regularly performed his duties at sacred festivals like the Dionysia, they had a religious aspect. See Dem. 21.51–55.

[158] The laws of the gods and those of men are not two different standards that might clash with one another but are based on the same moral principles. See E. M. Harris 2006a: 51–56 and Naiden 2004.

sacred duties is not the same thing as having one from festival liturgies. But these men will try to deceive you by substituting the term
"sacred rites" for the term "festival liturgies." I will present Leptines
himself as a witness for these facts. [127] At the beginning of his law,
he states in writing that "Leptines proposed that in order that the
wealthiest men perform festival liturgies, no person be exempt, except
the descendants of Harmodius and Aristogeiton." And yet if having an
exemption from religious duties is the same as having one from festival
liturgies, what was his motive for adding this last phrase? Not even this
family has received an exemption from religious duties. So that you
may see that this is the way things are, take for me first the copy of the
stele,[159] next the beginning of Leptines' law.

[*COPY OF THE STELE*]

[128] You have heard the copy of the *stele,* men of Athens. It orders
that they are to be exempt except in regard to religious duties. Now
read the beginning of Leptines' law.

[*LAW*]

Good. Put it away. After writing "So that the wealthiest men perform festival liturgies," he added the clause "no one is exempt except
the descendants of Harmodius and Aristogeiton." What is the reason
for this, because spending money for religious rites is the same as
performing festival liturgies? If this is what he says, it will be obvious
that what he has written stands in contradiction to the stele. [129] I
would like to ask Leptines this question: because you say that festival liturgies form a part of religious duties, what is the nature of the
exemption that you will claim to leave intact or that our ancestors
granted? By our old laws, they are not exempt from property taxes in
time of war or from trierarchies. They do not even hold an exemption
from festival liturgies because they are included as religious duties.
Yet it is in fact written that they are exempt. [130] From what? From

---

[159] This *stele* recorded the honors granted to the descendants of Harmodius
and Aristogeiton.

the tax for metics?¹⁶⁰ That is what is left. No, from the regular liturgies, as the *stele* makes clear and as you have specified in your law. Beyond that, there is the testimony of all the time that has passed before this, quite a long period, during which no tribe ever dared to appoint any of their descendants as chorus leader, nor did anyone who was appointed dare to challenge one of them to an exchange of property.¹⁶¹ If he has the audacity to claim the opposite, you must not listen to him.

[**131**] Well, perhaps they will carelessly assert that some Megarians and Messenians claimed they were exempt and later became so, this being a large group when taken altogether, and that some others are slaves and fit for whipping, and will pick out the men like Lycidas, men like Dionysius, and people of their ilk.¹⁶² When they make this argument, do as follows: if what they tell you is true, tell them to show you the decrees that granted them an exemption. No one receives an exemption from you without having it granted to him by a decree or a law. [**132**] Indeed many men like this have received the title of *proxenos* from you because of their services to the city. One of these is Lycidas. But it is one thing to become a *proxenos,* another to obtain an exemption. Do not let them distract you. Granted that Lycidas and Dionysius and perhaps someone else were slaves and became *proxenoi* thanks to men who willingly proposed this sort of decree for a fee, but do not for this reason let them try to steal away from other men who are free born and responsible for much good the rewards that they have justly received from you. [**133**] Would it not clearly be the worst possible way to treat Chabrias if the men who advocate this policy will not stop at granting the title of *proxenos* to Lycidas, who was that man's slave, but also take away on false grounds some of the rewards given

---

¹⁶⁰This is meant as a joke, because the descendants of the tyrannicides were Athenian citizens.

¹⁶¹On the procedure of the exchange of property (*antidosis*), see Dem. 20.40n. Because the descendants of Harmodius were never nominated or challenged to an exchange, this demonstrates that everyone recognized that they were exempt from the regular festival liturgies.

¹⁶²Lycidas was a former slave of Chabrias who was freed and made a *proxenos;* see 133. Nothing is known about Dionysius.

to the former because of the latter? No one receives an exemption as a result of becoming a *proxenos* unless the people explicitly grant an exemption. They did not give it to these people, nor will these men be able to show that they did. Should they be so shameless as to make such a claim, their conduct will be disgraceful.

[**134**] The most serious danger of all that you have to guard against still remains for me to describe to you. Let us assume that everything that Leptines is going to tell you about his law to demonstrate its good features is true. The ratification of his law will still bring about one shameful result for the city, which cannot be removed should it go into effect. What then is this? A reputation for deceiving those who have helped us. [**135**] That this is certainly shameful, I think everyone in the world would agree. But consider how much more shameful it would be for you than for other people. There is an old law, one of those that have an excellent reputation, that provides for trial if someone deceives the people after making a promise and, if he is convicted, imposes the death penalty.[163] Will you not be ashamed, men of Athens, if it becomes obvious that you are committing an act for which you punish others with death? Indeed, one should refrain from all actions that either seem to be or are morally wrong, but especially those for which one is seen to treat others harshly. There is no room for discussion about this issue: one should not do anything that one has oneself previously condemned as wrong.

[**136**] There is still another thing that you should be careful about: avoid doing something openly in public life that you would refrain from doing in private life.[164] Certainly none of you in private life would give something to a person and then would go back and take it away, nor would he even try. [**137**] Well, then, do not do this in public affairs either. On the contrary, if any of these men intending to defend the law claims that any recipient of this award does not deserve it or did not do the thing for which he was rewarded, or if they have any other charge to make, order them to bring an indictment under the law that we are now proposing to substitute in its place, whether

---

163 See 100n.
164 See 9n.

we introduce it (as we have pledged and promised to do) or they do it themselves during the next meeting of the Nomothetae. Every one of these men[165] probably has some personal enemy: for one it is Diophantus;[166] for another it is Eubulus;[167] for a third person, perhaps someone else. [138] If these men are reluctant and do not wish to do this, that is because each of them hesitates to be seen taking these honors away from their enemies.[168] Think then, would it be honorable for you openly to snatch these same honors from your benefactors, and to cause an entire group of men who have helped you in some way, people whom no one could criticize, to lose privileges legally granted, when one could use a public action to have them tried individually and given the same punishment? I do not think this course of action is dignified or worthy of you.

[139] Now, here is another point that you should not ignore. It was right to conduct an examination of qualifications for awards when we granted them. At that time no one objected. But after that, it is right to leave them in place unless the recipients later do you some wrong. If they are going to claim that this has happened (in fact, they

---

[165] Sandys 1890: 100 argues that these are Leptines and his supporters, not those with exemptions. Gagarin (*per litteras*), however, observes: "Demosthenes has just said that Leptines and company should indict those with undeserved exemptions. The next point is that if the exemptions are undeserved, they would be indicted by their enemies (unless they are reluctant, etc.). To say that Leptines and his associates have enemies only works if we assume everyone with undeserved exemptions is an enemy of Leptines and his associates, which is nowhere stated or implied. Also, do we know that Diophantus or Eubulus had exemptions? And that they were undeserved? Surely Demosthenes would say so if that is his point."

[166] Diophantus was active in politics (Dem. 19.84–86, 297; *IG* ii² 106, line 7; 107, line 8 [restored]), but little is known of his policies.

[167] Eubulus was one of the most prominent politicians of the time. On his career, see Cawkwell 1963. It has been thought that he advocated a more peaceful foreign policy and was opposed by Demosthenes, but see E. M. Harris 2006a: 133–134.

[168] It was considered wrong to initiate public actions merely out of a desire to harm a personal enemy. See Dem. 18.123, 278; Lyc. *Against Leocrates* 6 with E. M. Harris 2005 and Kurihara 2003.

have no proof of it), they need to show that they were punished at the time of their actual crimes.[169] Since such is not the case, if you put this law into effect, you will give the impression that you have taken away the awards out of spite, not because you caught them in the wrong. [140] Generally speaking, one should avoid all shameful actions, men of Athens, and most of all, this one. Why? Because spite is undoubtedly an indication of an evil nature, and there is no excuse that would entitle someone who feels it to any sympathy. Beyond that, there is no criticism that our city, which shuns all forms of shameful conduct, deserves less than the charge of being spiteful.[170] [141] Consider how much evidence proves this point. First, you are the only people in the world who hold public funeral orations for the dead, in which you celebrate the deeds of brave men.[171] Indeed, this is the way men act if they admire outstanding achievement, but not if they are jealous of men who are honored for this. Next, you have throughout history given the most generous awards to those who win crowns in athletic contests. Just because these crowns are naturally granted to few men, you are not jealous of those who win them, nor do you reduce their honors for that reason. Besides virtues like these, no other place has ever gained a reputation for outdoing our city in granting awards. This is how far our city outdoes others in granting prizes as rewards for the benefits we receive.[172] [142] All these things, men of Athens, provide examples of our justice, outstanding character, and magnanimity. Do not now destroy the reasons that long ago granted our city a good reputation for all time. Just so that Leptines can insult some of his personal enemies, do not

---

[169] I.e., not long afterwards.

[170] In his Funeral Oration, Pericles asserts that envy or spite is not part of the Athenian character. See Thuc. 2.37, 40. Demosthenes' speech is the only Attic oration that claims the practice of public burial is unique to Athens.

[171] Other Greek states granted honors to those who died in battle similar to those conferred in Athens (see Arist. *Politics* 1268a; Diodorus 20.84 [Rhodes]; Pouilloux 1971: 103–109 [Thasos]), but there is not evidence for other states instituting funeral orations.

[172] Or: "This is how far the rewards that we give outstrip the benefits that we are repaying."

destroy the glorious reputation that the city and you yourselves have acquired over the course of centuries. Do not think that this trial is about anything other than the city's reputation: will it remain secure and equal to what it was before or will it change and be damaged?

[143] I have found many astonishing things in Leptines' law, but there is one that astonishes me most of all: he is unaware that just as a person who assigns heavy penalties for offenses does not seem ready to commit a crime himself, in exactly the same way one creates the appearance of being unprepared to do anything useful if one abolishes the honors given for public service. If this fact has escaped him (this is certainly possible), he will soon make it obvious, and he will agree with you and rectify his mistake. But if he is clearly eager and putting all his effort into making the law valid, although I have no way of approving his actions, I do not wish to censure him. [144] Do not be so bent on victory, Leptines; do not try to force through the kind of measure that will not make you and those persuaded by you look any better, especially since this trial carries no risk for you. As a result of the death of Bathippus (he was the father of Apsephion, who is here now), the man who indicted him when he was still subject to prosecution, the deadline has expired so the case involves only the law itself, and this man is in no danger.[173]

[145] You will say, I am told, that in fact three previous accusers did not bring their cases against you to trial.[174] If you are actually criticizing them by saying that they did not put you at risk, there is no one else in the world who loves danger more than you do. But if you are taking this as proof that your proposal is right, you are quite naïve. How would it improve your law if one of the people who indicted it died before bringing his case to court, or another withdrew his charge after reaching an agreement with you, or another was completely corrupted by you? These are not good arguments to use.

[146] Advocates have been elected to support the law, men who are very impressive speakers: Leodamas of Acharnai, Aristophon of

---

[173] The person who proposed the law was subject to prosecution for only one year.

[174] It was not illegal to drop a public case once it was initiated, provided that one did it in the correct way. See E. M. Harris 2006a: 405–422.

Azenia, Cephisodotus from the Ceramicus, and Deinon of Erchia. Listen to the right way to answer these men and see if it seems just to you. First in response to Leodamas.[175] This man brought a public action against an award made to Chabrias, which contained a grant of exemption among the privileges given to him.[176] When he came before you, he lost his case. [**147**] The laws do not allow one to bring the same charge twice, whether it be a private action, a rendering of accounts, an inheritance case, or anything similar.[177] Apart from that, it would be quite bizarre if at that time the actions of Chabrias carried more weight than the words of Leodamas, but later, now that his achievements remain and those of other benefactors have been added to them, all of them taken together should prove to be weaker than this man's words.[178]

[**148**] Well, now, in response to Aristophon,[179] I think I would have many reasonable points to make. This man received from you an award that contained this privilege. That is not what I am criticizing; you should have the right to give away what belongs to you to whomever you wish. This, however, is what I say is not right: when he was about to receive this privilege, he saw nothing terrible about it,

---

[175] Aeschines (3.139) says that Leodamas was sent on an embassy to Thebes and praises his oratory. He prosecuted Callistratus and Chabrias after the loss of Oropos in 366 (Arist. *Rhetoric* 1364a).

[176] This award was probably made after the victory at Naxos. Aristotle (*Rhetoric* 1411b) quotes from a speech delivered by Lycoleon at the trial.

[177] The laws of Athens recognized the principle of *res iudicata* and did not allow the same charge to be brought twice (Dem. 38.16). By supporting the law, Leodamas is not bringing the same charge again against Chabrias but defending Leptines' law. The effect, however, would be to remove Chabrias' exemption. Demosthenes therefore construes this as in effect the same case. But in fact, the issues at the two trials were quite different, and the court could have sided with Leodamas in this case without being inconsistent.

[178] Another specious argument. Demosthenes argues that because the court earlier rejected Leodamas' charges against Chabrias, they should also do so now. But the issues at the two trials were quite different, and the court could have sided with Leodamas in this case without being inconsistent.

[179] Aristophon had a long career in Athenian politics and was one of the most powerful Athenian politicians at the time. He had recently convicted Timotheus of treason. See Hansen 1975: 101.

but after it has been given to others, then he gets angry and persuades you to take it away. **[149]** Here is another point: this man proposed to return five talents to Gelarchus[180] for providing this money to supporters of the people in the Piraeus, and he did the right thing. These loans were made without witnesses, and you made sure that they were repaid in the name of the people; do not then recommend the cancellation of those privileges that the people themselves have witnessed and recorded on inscriptions placed in sanctuaries and that everyone knows. Do not openly propose that we must pay back debts but then recommend that we take back privileges that someone has already received from the people. **[150]** In response to Cephisodotus[181] I would have this much to say. This man is inferior to no one when it comes to eloquence. Yet it is much better for him to use that eloquence to punish those who wrong you rather than to wrong those responsible for doing good. If you must be angry with any people, I think it should be those who wrong the people, not those who do them some good. **[151]** Now for my reply to Deinias.[182] Perhaps this man will talk about his trierarchies and festival liturgies. If Deinias proves himself to be someone who deserves much from the city (by the gods, I believe that he does), I would advise him to ask you to give him an honor rather than demand that honors already granted be taken away from others. The better sort of person typically asks to be honored for the good that he has done rather than to act jealous of the honors granted to others for their services. **[152]** But this is cer-

---

[180] Gelarchus is otherwise unknown.

[181] Cephisodotus was one of the ambassadors who negotiated peace with Sparta in 371 (Xen. *Hellenica* 6.3.2) but later worried about the consequences of the Athenian alliance with Sparta (Xen. *Hellenica* 7.1.12–14). Earlier he passed a decree in honor of Straton, the king of Sidon (Rhodes and Osborne 2003: no. 21, who date it to around 378–376), and in 367/6 he was the author of a decree protesting the arrest of the men sent to announce the Eleusinian Mysteries (Rhodes and Osborne 2003: no. 35).

[182] Deinias served as joint trierarch possibly in 366/5 (*IG* ii² 1609, lines 54, 93). He may also be the Deinias who gave some land to the city at the request of Lycurgus ([Plut.] *Moralia* 841d). He passed on his wealth to his son Deinon, who also served as a trierarch (*IG* ii² 1631, lines 144–146, 158–159, and 210).

tainly the most serious objection of all and applies to all the advocates in common. Each one of these men has served as public advocate many times before. There is a law that is very good in many respects—one that was not passed with them in mind but to prevent this activity from becoming a profession and a method of abusing the legal system—that forbids anyone to be elected and serve as public advocate more than once.[183] **[153]** The men who are about to defend this law and prove to you that it is expedient should make clear they too obey the laws now in force. If not, it is ridiculous for them to defend one law while breaking another. Read the law that I am discussing.

[LAW]

This law, men of Athens, is both old and good. If these men are sensible, they will take care not to violate it.

[154] After saying a few more words, I will step down. You should take seriously, men of Athens, the task of making all your laws (this is my opinion) as good as possible, above all those that are responsible for making the city weak or powerful. Which ones are these? Those that grant honors to men who do some good and inflict penalties on those who do the opposite. If all men should truly fear the penalties found in the laws and refrain from doing harm, and if all men should choose to do their duty in their desire to win rewards for public service, what prevents the city from becoming extremely powerful, all its men good, and none evil?

[155] Well, now, men of Athens, this law of Leptines not only commits the injustice of rendering pointless the generosity of citizens who are ambitious to serve you by abolishing rewards for public service, but it leaves the city with a shameful reputation for breaking the law. You certainly know that for each of the most serious offenders, the laws impose just one punishment. It expressly states, "For

---

[183] This law is mentioned only here, and there is no way of telling whether Demosthenes' summary of its contents is misleading or not. It appears to apply only to supporting speakers elected by the Assembly and may have been limited to those appointed to defend an indicted law. See Rubinstein 2000: 52–54.

a judicial decision there is to be no more than one penalty, either corporal or monetary, at the discretion of the court. It is illegal to impose both." [**156**] This man, however, did not follow this rule. On the contrary, if anyone asks you for a reward, he states, "Let him lose his rights, and let his property be confiscated."[184] These are two penalties. "And there are procedures for denunciation and arrest. If he is convicted, let him be subject to the same law that is in effect for public debtors who hold office." This means death; this is the punishment for that offense. That then makes three penalties.[185] This is shocking and terrible, men of Athens: people will think that it is more dangerous to ask for a reward for doing good than to be caught perpetrating the very worst crimes! [**157**] The law is shameful and wrong, men of Athens! It has a spiteful and divisive air about it and—I spare you the rest. Such are the motives that seem to guide its author. And such are not the kind of qualities that you should emulate! Nor should you appear to harbor thoughts that are beneath your dignity. Think now, by Zeus, what would all men pray most to avoid? What is the most serious aim in all our laws? To prevent men from killing each other. The Council of the Areopagus has been assigned to act as the special guardian of this task. [**158**] In the laws on this subject, Draco makes the act of taking another person's life the object of fear and terror. He writes that the murderer is banned from lustral water, libations, bowls of wine, holy places, and the marketplace, and goes through all the other measures that he thinks will deter people from committing this crime.[186] Just the same, he does not eliminate all consider-

---

[184]The argument is fallacious. As Sandys 1890: 109 notes, "the law against double penalties, as above quoted, only affects penalties *assessed by a court*, not those fixed by a law." In fact, loss of rights and confiscation of property were often joined. See Dem. 21.43.

[185]This argument is also fallacious. The penalty here is not aimed at the person asking for an exemption but at the person who has lost his rights and illegally tries to exercise them. See Sandys 1890: 109.

[186]After receiving an accusation of murder, the Basileus made a proclamation banning the defendant from sacred rites and places to avoid pollution. For the proclamation, see Ant. 6.35–36; *Ath. Pol.* 57.2. Cf. Sophocles *Oedipus the King* 236–242. On pollution for homicide, see Parker 1983: 104–143.

ations of justice but specifies in what circumstances it is permitted to kill,[187] and if one does so in the correct way, he sets him apart as free from pollution.[188] Will your laws then grant the right to kill with just cause but take away the right to ask for a reward, whether it be justified or not, thanks to this man's law? [**159**] Not at all, men of Athens. Do not be willing to give the impression that you are more serious about taking away the right to receive a reward from those who help you than preventing murder in the city. Remember instead the circumstances in which you received the help and rewarded the men who received these privileges. Remember too the *stele* of Demophantus, which Phormio mentioned,[189] where this oath has been inscribed: "If anything happens to someone defending the democracy, the same rewards are to be given to him as were given to Harmodius and Aristogeiton" and vote against the law.[190] You cannot avoid breaking your oath if you fail to do this.

[**160**] In addition to these arguments, listen to this further one: a law that uses the same language about the past and the future cannot be good. It states, "No one is exempt except the descendants of Harmodius and Aristogeiton." So far, so good. "Nor is it permitted to grant one in the future." Not even if there are men similar to them, Leptines? If you were disparaging the past, what of it? But did you know the future too? [**161**] You may say, "By Zeus, we are now far from expecting anything like that!"[191] I wish that it were so, men of Athens. But since we are human beings, we ought to propose and en-

---

[187] On the circumstances in which one had a right to use deadly force, see MacDowell 1963: 70–81.

[188] Normally a person who killed incurred pollution, but a person who committed "just homicide" or "homicide according to the laws" was considered ritually pure. See Parker 1983: 366–369.

[189] Phormio gave one of the previous speeches for the prosecution.

[190] The decree of Demophantus was passed after the fall of the Four Hundred in 411; a document preserved at And. 1.96 purports to be a copy of the law. Lycurgus (*Against Leocrates* 124–127) dates it to after the fall of the Thirty in 403. For discussion, see Ostwald 1955.

[191] I.e., the tyranny of the Peisistratids, which ended several years after the tyrannicide of Harmodius and Aristogeiton.

act laws that would not stir the gods' wrath, then hope for prosperity, and pray to the gods to grant it, but we must realize our limits as mortals. The Spartans did not expect to end up in such a position.[192] Nor perhaps did the Syracusans, who for a long time had a democracy, collected tribute from the Carthaginians, ruled over all their neighbors, and defeated us in battle at sea,[193] ever expect to live under the tyranny of a single clerk.[194] [**162**] And the Dionysius alive now did not expect that Dion would ever come in a merchant ship with a handful of soldiers and drive him into exile, and he a man who controlled many triremes, mercenaries, and cities.[195] No, in my opinion, men cannot know the future; minor events are responsible for major upheavals. For that reason one should practice moderation in times of prosperity and show that one is looking ahead to the future.

[**163**] Someone else might have more points to make and might go through other reasons why this law is neither good nor beneficial to you in any respect. But in order to grasp the main point and allow me to finish my speech, do the following: compare the two alternatives and consider in your mind what will happen if you vote against the law and what if you do not. Then keep in mind and remember what you think will result from each so that you may choose the better alternative. [**164**] If you vote against it, as we are asking, you will maintain the rights of those men who deserve them, but if someone is undeserving, which might happen, in addition to having his award

---

[192] In 403 the Spartans were the most powerful state in Greece, but their defeat at Leuctra in 371 and the liberation of Messenia in 369 ended their leading position.

[193] Demosthenes alludes to the defeat of the Athenians by the Syracusans in the Great Harbor in 413 BCE. See Thuc. 7.51–54.

[194] Dionysius I started as a clerk and became tyrant of Syracuse in 406 (Diodorus 13.96; Polyaenus 5.2.2). The Athenians considered the job of public clerk as undignified. Demosthenes (18.127, 19.237) ridicules Aeschines for having held this position. The manuscripts add the phrase "who was an underling" after the word "clerk." The phrase is deleted by Reiske as an intrusive gloss, but retained by Dilts.

[195] Dionysius II was expelled by Dion in 356 (Diodorus 16.6; Plut. *Dion* 25; Nepos *Dion* 5). On Dion, see Westlake 1969.

taken away, he will pay the penalty that you determine under the terms of the law that has been proposed in its place.[196] The city will appear trustworthy, just, and free from deceit in the eyes of everyone. If you vote for it, which I wish you would not do, good men will be wronged because of evil ones, and those who deserve no reward will cause others to suffer and will pay no penalty at all themselves. The city's reputation will be the opposite of the one I just now described: it will appear unreliable, spiteful, and dishonest to everyone. [165] This alternative is not worth choosing, men of Athens, namely, to acquire such a poor reputation instead of one for the good qualities that belong to you. Indeed, each of you will personally have his own share of the renown gained through your common verdict. None of those attending the trial[197] nor anyone else is unaware that although Leptines is our opponent in court, in the mind of each of you seated here, generosity is set against envy, justice against evil, and noble sentiments against the worst. [166] If you are influenced by the better of these, if you follow our advice when voting, you will appear to have come to the right decision and to have voted what is best for the city. And if any occasion should ever arise, you will not be short of men willing to court danger to protect you. All these matters, I think, demand your keen interest and attention so that you will not be compelled to make a mistake. Many, many times, men of Athens, you have not been instructed as to what is the right decision[198] but have been misled by shouting, intimidation, and lack of scruples on the part of orators. Do not let this happen to you today: it is beneath your dignity. [167] Instead, make the right decision, then fix your mind on it and remember it until you vote. This way you will cast a vote in keeping with your oath that rejects those who give bad advice. I am amazed that

---

[196] Demosthenes gives the impression that the law proposed by Apsephion will go into effect if the court votes against Leptines' law, but this is misleading because the former still had to be passed by the Assembly and ratified by the Nomothetae. See Rhodes 1985: 58.

[197] Important trials in Athens were often attended by numerous bystanders. See Lanni 1997.

[198] Sandys, followed by Dilts, accepts Weil's insertion of *ouk* before *dikaia*, but this seems unnecessary.

although death is the punishment you impose on men who debase our currency,[199] you will grant the right to speak to men who make the entire city counterfeit and unreliable. By Zeus and the gods, certainly not!

I do not know what more I should say; I think that you understand everything I have said.

---

[199] This law is attested only here, but see *IG* ii ^{2} 1013, lines 56–60 (second century BCE), where those who violate the laws about standard weights and measures are subject to the law about *kakourgoi* ("wrongdoers"). This law provided for the death penalty to those who were caught "red-handed" and confessed. See *Ath. Pol.* 52.1 with E. M. Harris 2006a: 373–390.

21. AGAINST MEIDIAS

〜〜〜〜〜〜〜〜〜〜〜〜〜〜〜〜〜〜〜〜〜〜〜〜〜〜〜〜〜〜〜〜〜〜〜

INTRODUCTION

Meidias, the defendant in this case, was born around 395 or later[1] and came from a wealthy family; his father Cephisodorus served as trierarch.[2] Meidias made enough money from mining in Attica (see 167) to perform liturgies (151, 156), to qualify for inclusion among the Three Hundred in the naval symmories (157), and to donate a trireme to the state (160). He served as trierarch several times[3] and was elected to the prestigious posts of cavalry leader, treasurer of the sacred ship *Paralus*, overseer of the Eleusinian Mysteries (see 171– 174 and notes there), and Pylagoros to the Amphictyony at Delphi (Aes. 3.115).[4] By 346 he was associated with the influential leader Eubulus (205–207) and counted many politicians and affluent men among his friends (189–190, 208–215).

The origin and reasons for Demosthenes' quarrel with Meidias are obscure.[5] Demosthenes claims that his quarrel with Meidias began

---

[1] Demosthenes says that Meidias was "fifty or a little less" at the time of the trial (154) but may be adding a few years to his age. See E. M. Harris 1989: 124 n. 18.

[2] Cephisodorus: *IG* ii² 1609, line 29. His son Thrasylochus was also eligible for the trierarchy; see 77–80.

[3] For Meidias as trierarch, see *IG* ii² 1612, line 291; 1629, line 770; 1631, line 132.

[4] On Meidias' career, see Davies 1971: 385–387.

[5] *Pace* Cohen 1995: 90–101, it would be incorrect to call this quarrel a feud in the sense that the term is used by legal anthropologists. Strictly speaking, this kind of feud occurs only between kinship groups and lasts for many years, if not several generations. But there is no evidence that the quarrel between Meidias and

in 364/3, when he was involved in a dispute with his guardians, and Meidias' brother Thrasylochus challenged him to an *antidosis* (77–80). But the version of this event that he gives in his speech against Meidias is very different from the one that he gave shortly after the incident, and the two versions cannot be reconciled.[6] In the earlier version, which was told to judges who were in a better position to know what happened, Demosthenes does not mention Meidias. It is also suspicious that Demosthenes can mention no further acts of hostility by Meidias from 364/3 down to 349/8. Demosthenes may well have invented Meidias' participation in this incident in 346 to make it appear that his hostility toward him was longstanding, when in reality it was a recent development.

Some scholars have thought that the quarrel was caused by differences between the two men over Athenian foreign policy in 348.[7] In that year the Athenians were sending troops to help defend Olynthus against the attacks of Philip II of Macedon. Early in that year Plutarch, the leader of Eretria on the island of Euboea, asked for Athenian support against his rival Callias of Chalcis. The Athenians sent an army under the general Phocion, which marched inland to Tamynae, where it was besieged by local troops (Plut. *Phocion* 12). Phocion called for reinforcements but was able to win a decisive victory over the Euboeans before they could arrive (see 160–167). Sometime later, Molossus took over command of Athenian troops on the island but was defeated and forced to withdraw, leaving Euboea under the control of Callias.

Demosthenes claims that Meidias was a supporter of Plutarch (110, 200), but this is probably no more than slander, an attempt to pin the blame for the debacle in Euboea on his enemy. The statement is

---

Demosthenes involved two large kinship groups, and it may have lasted only two years. See E. M. Harris 2005. Wilson 1991 attempts to analyze the speech in terms of an alleged conflict between democratic values and the aristocratic values of competition. See, however, Fisher (2003), who rightly points out that competition was not contrary to democratic values and questions much of Wilson's analysis.

[6] For the method of evaluating the historical reliability of statements found in the orators, see E. M. Harris 1995: 7–16. On this incident, see E. M. Harris 2005: 137–138.

[7] See MacDowell 1990: 4–7.

not reliable evidence. No more reliable is Demosthenes' statement in his *On the Peace* (5) that he opposed the expedition to Euboea.[8] He certainly says nothing about his protest in this speech against Meidias. In the same passage in *On the Peace* Demosthenes also claims that he argued against Neoptolemus when he conveyed Philip's invitation to begin negotiations about peace, but other evidence shows that he was in fact a fervent supporter of peace talks as early as 348.[9] The view that Meidias and Demosthenes quarreled because of differences about Athenian foreign policy therefore rests on no solid foundation.

Despite Demosthenes' assertions, the quarrel may not have started until 348. Early in that year Demosthenes volunteered to act as chorus producer for his tribe Pandionis at the Dionysia, which took place in Elaphebolion (March/April) (13–14). Meidias then did everything that he could to prevent Demosthenes' chorus from winning the prize: Meidias bribed Demosthenes' trainer, attempted to ruin the costumes of the chorus, and blocked up the entrances to prevent the chorus from performing. Finally, he punched Demosthenes in the face before thousands of spectators from Athens and abroad (15–18; cf. Aes. 3.52). This caused Demosthenes to use the procedure of *probole* (see below) to secure a vote of the Assembly condemning Meidias' disruption of the festival (1–2, 226).

Demosthenes at first appears to have been satisfied with the Assembly's vote of censure, but he alleges that Meidias' campaign of harassment continued long after the Dionysia. Shortly afterward, Demosthenes was accused of desertion by a certain Euctemon (103). The charge was a serious one: if convicted, Demosthenes would have lost his rights as a citizen. But Euctemon did not pursue the case and lost his right to make public charges. Demosthenes claims that Meidias hired Euctemon to bring the charge, but he calls no witnesses to prove his allegation. At about the same time, Demosthenes may have also been prosecuted on the same charge by Nicodemus

[8] MacDowell 1990: 5 accepts this statement as reliable but does not study it in context.

[9] For Demosthenes' support for sending an embassy to Philip, see Aes. 2.12–20 (with the evidence of documents), 3.62–63 and the discussion of E. M. Harris 1995: 50–53.

(Aes. 2.148). After Nicodemus was murdered, Aristarchus, a friend of Demosthenes, was charged with the crime by the victim's relatives (116–122). Aristarchus either went into exile before the trial and was convicted *in absentia* or left Athens during the trial. Demosthenes claims that Meidias attempted to convince the victim's relatives to bring the charge against him, but apparently Meidias did not succeed.[10] This allegation may have led Demosthenes to bring a private charge of slander (*dikē kakegorias*) against Meidias.[11] According to Demosthenes (83–92), Meidias attempted to delay the proceeding before the arbitrator, an inexperienced man named Strato, but on the day when the verdict was to be rendered, he did not show up and therefore lost his case by default. Meidias then brought a charge of misconduct against Strato before the other arbitrators and won a conviction. Demosthenes claims that Meidias still owed him money from the judgment against him, but it is more likely that the conviction of Strato annulled his decision. When Strato appealed his conviction to a court, the judgment of the arbitrators was upheld, resulting in the complete loss of his rights as a citizen. Demosthenes portrays Meidias' case against Strato as a vindictive attack on a defenseless citizen, but the court's decision casts doubt on Demosthenes' account.[12] Meidias may have dredged this charge up again in the summer of 347, when

---

[10] Demosthenes calls witnesses to support his charges (121), and there may therefore be some truth to his statements about Aristarchus. Moreover, the charge that he persuaded Aristarchus to kill Nicodemus was repeated by Aeschines (1.170–73) in late 346. But it is not clear what the witnesses testified about. Demosthenes' summary of their testimony indicates that all they may have stated was that Meidias denounced Aristarchus as a murderer at the same time as he was asking Aristarchus to bring about a settlement between himself and Demosthenes.

[11] Demosthenes gives the impression that this charge was brought because of Meidias' violent entry into his house as a result of the *antidosis* in 366 and his insults to his mother and sister (79), but this impression is probably false. His earlier version of the *antidosis* omits Meidias and clashes with the account given in 346. Furthermore, the insults to his mother and sister do not fall under the kinds of slander covered by the *dike kakegorias*. See 81n.

[12] Demosthenes calls witnesses at 93 but does not indicate what their testimony stated.

Demosthenes says that Meidias attacked him during his *dokimasia* for the Council in the summer of 347 (111).[13]

Demosthenes initiated his case against Meidias soon after the Dionysia in the spring of 348 by the procedure of *probole*, then two years later in 346 brought a public charge, probably of outrage (*graphē hybreos*) against Meidias.[14] In most cases the accuser started legal proceedings by summoning the defendant to appear before a magistrate on a certain day.[15] In a *probole* the accuser made his charge at a meeting of the Assembly (9). A *probole* could be brought against sykophants (those who abused the legal system) and those who deceived the people by making promises and not keeping them. This kind of *probole* could be brought only at the first (or *kyria*) meeting of the sixth prytany. Three charges could be brought against three citizens and three metics (*Ath. Pol.* 43.5). At a special meeting in the theater, convened shortly after the festival, a person could bring a *probole* against someone who committed an offense against the Greater Dionysia (9). The procedure was later extended to cover offenses against the Eleusinian Mysteries (175).[16] At the meeting of the Assembly the accuser and the defendant spoke, and a vote was taken whether or not to censure the defendant (2; Aes. 3.52). The vote had no legal effect, and a vote against the defendant did not require the accuser to pursue his case in court: Demosthenes says several times that he could have reached a private settlement with Meidias without taking him to court (2, 151, 216).

Some scholars believe that the *probole* procedure included both the vote in the Assembly and the trial in court, but the evidence clearly shows that the two were separate, and the *probole* was only a means of initiating legal proceedings.[17] First, Demosthenes in several passages

---

[13] For the suggestion that the charge was repeated at Demosthenes' *dokimasia*, see MacDowell 1990: 10.

[14] For the date of the speech, see E. M. Harris 1989: 121–123 and MacDowell 1990: 10–11.

[15] See Harrison 1971: 86–87.

[16] The only evidence that the procedure could be used for other festivals is the document at 10, but this is a forgery (see the notes ad loc.).

[17] See the scholion to 214 and Pollux 8.46, which call the procedure a "summons" (*proklesis, klesis*). Cf. Harrison 1971: 59: "the preliminary stage . . . to certain actions rather than an integral part of an action."

---

refers to the *probole* as an event that took place in the past and never calls the trial in court part of the *probole* (193, 214, 226). Second, the vote in the Assembly and the proceedings in court examined separate issues. This is best seen in the case of Ctesicles: the Assembly considered whether he had committed an offense about the festival, while the court decided whether he was guilty of *hybris* against the defendant (180–181).[18] Aeschines (3.52) also distinguishes between the vote in the Assembly against Meidias (*katacheirotonia*) and the charge of *hybris* brought by Demosthenes and does not conflate the two. This is similar to the distinction that Demosthenes makes between the charge of impiety at the vote in the Assembly (199, 227) and the charge at the trial, which was *hybris* (7, 21, 34, 38, 41–42). Third, the *probole* was not a public procedure like a *graphe* or *eisangelia,* in which the accuser could ask only for the death penalty, permanent exile, or a fine paid to the state, but only a preliminary procedure that left the accuser with the choice of whether to pursue a public or a private suit. This is clear in the case that Evandrus brought against Menippus (175–177). After gaining a vote against Menippus in the Assembly, Evandrus must have brought a private suit against him because he was awarded a payment of damages, which would not have been possible in a public suit.[19] Demosthenes, however, decided to bring a public charge of *hybris* against Meidias.[20] His speech was delivered at the first of the two parts

---

[18] Rowe 1995 does not discuss this case.

[19] See 176–177. This case is misunderstood by Harrison 1971: 64, by Rowe 1995: 57–58 n. 12, and by Rubinstein 2000: 209 n. 42. Rowe claims that there was a special feature of the *probole* as an *agon timetos*, which "allowed the prosecutor and the dicasts to come to an agreement about the penalty, whether for damages or confiscation of property or death." But an *agon timetos* allowed only for payment of penalty to the state, not to a private individual. See 28 with Harrison 1971: 78 for the general rule. There were a few exceptions to the rule, but they do not cover this case. Rubinstein's view is vulnerable to the same objections. Scafuro 2004 unconvincingly attempts to explain the case with information found in the law at 10, but this document is a forgery, and the evidence contained in it unreliable. See note 50.

[20] Rowe 1995 attempts to deny this and claims that the charge was impiety (*asebeia*), but this flies in the face of Demosthenes' repeated statements that the

of the trial, at which the court determined whether the defendant was guilty; Demosthenes states in several passages that the assessment of the penalty (*timesis*) lay in the future (21, 151) and for this reason indicates that he has not yet decided what penalty he will propose.[21] That the charge brought by Demosthenes was *hybris* is often made clear in the speech: the word occurs dozens of times in the speech, and Demosthenes constantly says that his arguments are designed to show that Meidias committed *hybris*.

The crime *hybris* was a complex offense, which covered a broad range of actions. Despite the variety of actions that fell under this label, all shared certain characteristics. As with all legal offenses, there were two sides to *hybris*, a subjective aspect and an objective aspect. As a state of mind, *hybris* was the opposite of the Greek virtue of *sophrosyne*. The person who has *sophrosyne* is able to control his or her desires and appetites, exhibits self-restraint, and shows respect for others; *sophrosyne* for a woman is chastity. The person who has *hybris* lacks self-control, acts without restraint, and treats others with contempt. As MacDowell puts it, "*Hybris* is therefore having energy or power and misusing it self-indulgently."[22] The main causes of *hybris* are youth, overindulgence in food and drink, and excessive wealth. On the objective side, *hybris* is an action that causes dishonor and a sense of humiliation in the victim.[23] As Demosthenes says (180), *hybris* is the crime of "treating free men like slaves." The victim of *hybris* feels

---

burden of the case is to prove that Meidias committed *hybris* and the explicit statement of Aeschines (3.52) that the charge was *hybris*.

[21] See 70, 112, 118 (death penalty possible); 152, 211 (fine possible). See E. M. Harris 1989: 125.

[22] MacDowell 1976: 21 (a tendency "to indulge his own desires and wishes without respecting the wishes, rights, and commands of others").

[23] Cf. Arist. *Rhetoric* 1378b: "Dishonor is the result of *hybris*, and one who dishonors demeans someone since what has no value has no honor either for good or for bad." Fisher (1976, 1992) tends to stress the objective side of *hybris* and pays less attention to the subjective side of the offense. His approach is well criticized as too narrow by MacDowell 1990: 19–20 and Cairns 1996. The analysis of *hybris* as a legal offense in Fisher 1992: 36–85 is undermined by his reliance on the law of *hybris* at 47. For the evidence proving that this document is a forgery, see 47nn.

a deep sense of rage and loses status in the eyes of society if he does not avenge his insult. On the one hand, there is the offender's state of mind, which is revealed by his expression and behavior;[24] on the other, there is the reaction of the victim, who feels insulted and is beside himself with rage.[25] To prove that Meidias has committed *hybris*, therefore, Demosthenes must show not only that Meidias struck him but that he did so with the intent to humiliate him.[26]

Demosthenes begins his speech by establishing the most important fact for his case, namely, that Meidias hit him at the Dionysia: he reminds the court of the vote in the Assembly condemning Meidias' conduct at the Dionysia of 348 and how everyone witnessed his abusive behavior. In contrast to Meidias, Demosthenes followed the law and the wishes of the people when using the *probole* (1–12). Next he recounts the incidents leading up to the vote in the Assembly: he describes his voluntary service as chorus producer and Meidias' efforts to deny his chorus victory, culminating in his assault on Demosthenes during the Dionysia (13–18). For the events that occurred in public, he relies on the knowledge of the court but provides the testimony of the goldsmith to prove that Meidias tried to destroy the sacred clothing made for Demosthenes' chorus. At the same time, he outlines the basic structure of the speech (19–24), which first discusses Meidias' other attacks on him (77–127), then his offenses against others (128–142).

Before discussing these topics, however, Demosthenes anticipates three arguments that he expects to be used by Meidias: first, he has used the wrong procedure to initiate his case (25–28); second, his dispute is private, not public (29–35); third, there are several precedents for his actions (36–41). In response, Demosthenes argues that Meidias'

---

[24]Cf. Dem. 54.9 for a description of the behavior of the man who commits *hybris*.

[25]Cf. Isocrates 20.5–6: "If there was no *hybris* present in his actions, I would never have come before you. But as it is, I am here in front of you to obtain justice from him not for the other damage incurred from his blows, but for the mistreatment and the dishonor. These are the things that are most likely to cause men to grow angry and seek the greatest revenge."

[26]Cf. Arist. *Rhetoric* 1374a13–15: "If one hits, one does not in all cases commit *hybris*, but only if it is for a purpose such as dishonoring the man or enjoying oneself."

offense is very serious because it was done with deliberate intent to humiliate him and shows that the laws provide more severe penalties for offenses committed willingly and with violence (42–50). Meidias' offense is aggravated by being committed at a festival in honor of a god (51–61). Rivalry and ambition are no excuse for Meidias' actions; other men who were competing against personal enemies did not act as he did (62–69). Demosthenes' failure to retaliate by hitting back should not be taken as a sign that he did not feel a deep sense of rage and humiliation at Meidias' blows. He refrained from striking Meidias out of fear that his response would not be proportionate to the harm that he suffered (70–76).

Demosthenes then turns to Meidias' other attacks on him: Meidias' breaking into his house and insulting his mother and sister during the *antidosis* (77–82), his attempt to evade the charge of slander and his effort to disenfranchise Strato (83–101), his charges of desertion and murder (102–122). Although all these actions were directed at Demosthenes, they represent a threat to the peace and safety of all Athenians (123–127). Demosthenes next charges that Meidias has also committed numerous crimes against others (128–131), but he adduces only his criticism of those serving in the cavalry with him (132–135). He tries to explain away the absence of witnesses to testify about these offenses by alleging that they have all been threatened, intimidated, or paid off, but this is a transparent effort to cover up a significant weakness in his case (136–142).

In the following section, Demosthenes anticipates the arguments Meidias may use at the second phase of the trial, the assessment of the penalty (*timesis*), namely, that he should not be punished harshly because of his public service (143–174). To undercut this argument, Demosthenes compares Meidias to Alcibiades, whose public services were greater but who was still sent into exile for less serious crimes (143–150). He then argues that Meidias' public service is not all that impressive, that he donated a trireme only to avoid military duty (151–170), and that his performance in office was abysmal (171–174). Others who received an adverse vote in a *probole* have received harsh sentences, and so Meidias should too (175–181). The court should not allow social status or the pleas of family members to influence their vote (182–183).

The final part (*epilogos*) of the speech (184–227) covers various topics. Demosthenes replies to Meidias' charges that his speech is not sincere because it is written down and that he should not be trusted because he is a politician (189–192). Meidias' contempt for the people merits the court's indignation (193–204). He predicts that Meidias' supporters will ask the court to violate its oath and to ignore the law as a personal favor to them, but he urges that their request should be denied (205–218). He ends his speech with a ringing endorsement of the rule of law, which is the best protection against the violence and arrogance of powerful men (219–225), and he reminds the court once more about the Assembly's vote of censure against Meidias (226–227).

Some scholars believe that Demosthenes reached a settlement with Meidias and never delivered the speech, which was left in an unrevised state. The main evidence for this view is a statement made by Aeschines (3.52) in 330:

> Why do I need to mention these events now and the events concerning Meidias and the punches that he received in the *orchestra* while serving as chorus-producer and how he sold for thirty minas at the same time both the *hybris* against him and the motion of censure against Meidias, which the people voted in the precinct of Dionysus?[27]

This statement has been interpreted to mean that Demosthenes came to a settlement with Meidias by which he agreed to drop his charge of *hybris* in return for a payment of thirty minas. Because Demosthenes did not bring his case to trial, it is further assumed that he did not finish his speech *Against Meidias* and that the version found in the *corpus demosthenicum* is an unrevised draft.[28] There are several objections to be made against this view. First, it is unclear what Aeschines means by "sold the charge of *hybris* and the motion of censure." It may refer to an out-of-court settlement, but other interpretations are possi-

---

[27] According to Plutarch (*Demosthenes* 12), Demosthenes agreed to drop the suit in return for a payment. This story is probably nothing more than an inference from Aeschines' statement, because there is no indication that Plutarch had any other source for this event than the speeches of the Attic orators.

[28] E.g., Dover 1968: 172–174.

ble.[29] Second, Aeschines presents no evidence to prove his charge that Demosthenes accepted payment from Meidias; the charge may be no more than slander. Third, this charge is one of six made by Aeschines in 330 about Demosthenes' activities in 346 that are missing from the speech that he delivered against Demosthenes in 343, just three years after 346. Two of these charges must be false, which casts doubt on the other four unsubstantiated charges.[30] Fourth, the passages cited as evidence that the speech was not delivered rest on misunderstandings of the rhetorical strategy and tactics of the speech.[31] Fifth, stylistic evidence indicates that the speech is just as polished as other speeches known to have been delivered by Demosthenes.[32] In short, there is no good reason to believe that Demosthenes reached a settlement with Meidias, dropped the suit in return for a payment of money, and left the speech in an unfinished state.[33]

On the other hand, there are strong grounds for thinking that Demosthenes brought his case against Meidias to court and delivered the speech that he composed for the trial. An accuser would not normally compose the final version of his speech for a case before attending the *anakrisis*, at which he would learn how the defendant intended to reply to his charges. This is clear from several references in speeches given by accusers to statements made at the *anakrisis* (Dem. 20.98–99; Is. 5.16, 10.2). But if Demosthenes made his charge against Meidias, did not formally withdraw it at the *anakrisis*, and then did not bring the case to court as the result of a settlement with Meidias, he would have lost his right to bring any public suits in the future. Yet he brought a public charge against Aeschines at his *euthynai* later in 346. Finally, it is difficult to understand why Demosthenes would

---

[29] See Rubinstein 2000: 208–209, who believes that Aeschines may have accused Demosthenes of agreeing to propose a small penalty at the assessment of the penalty in return for a payment. For a similar interpretation, see Erbse 1956: 150–151.

[30] E. M. Harris 2006a: 94–95.

[31] See Erbse 1956 and E. M. Harris 1989.

[32] See McCabe 1981: 119–168, 170–172.

[33] MacDowell 1990: 28 concludes, "There is no proof, then, that the speech was not delivered."

have reached a settlement with Meidias and dropped his suit, then published a speech in which he boasts several times that he would not accept payment from Meidias because many Athenians urged him not to do so. Publication of the speech in those circumstances would have damaged his reputation and made him appear to be a liar and hypocrite. The most probable scenario is that the court convicted Meidias, then imposed a small penalty on him. He was not executed, sent into exile, or deprived of his rights as citizen because he served as Pylagoras to Delphi in 340 or 339 (Aes. 3.115).

The documents found in the manuscripts of Demosthenes' *Against Meidias* were not included in the earliest copies of the speech but were inserted later, either in the Hellenistic or Roman period.[34] All these documents are forgeries. The laws lack the standard prescript for this type of document[35] and contain errors about Athenian political and legal procedures.[36] Many of the laws and witness statements have post-Classical words and forms, which reveal that they were composed several centuries after the fourth century BCE.[37] They may contain

---

[34] For the evidence of stichometry, which demonstrates that the documents were inserted later than the earliest stages of the text's transmission, see MacDowell 1990: 43–46. MacDowell believes that later editors might have found genuine copies of laws and inserted them then, but see E. M. Harris 1992.

[35] The laws of this period begin with a formula indicating that they have received the approval of the Nomothetae: see Rhodes and Osborne 2003: no. 25, line 1; no. 79, line 6; no. 81, line 7; *IG* ii² 140, lines 7–8; 244, line 6; and the text of the law given by Themelis 2002: 112, lines 8–9. All these contain the formula *dedochthai tois nomothetais*, except for Rhodes and Osborne no. 25, which has a similar formula, and Rhodes and Osborne no. 26, lines 2–4, which lacks the formula but still indicates that the measure is a *nomos*. The prescript of *IG* ii² 333 has not been preserved, but the Nomothetae are mentioned in line 13. These officials also appear to have been named in an unpublished law; see *SEG* 35.83. The prescripts of the laws inserted into the text of Dem. 21 do not mention the Nomothetae in their prescripts or in the rest of their contents and are thus without parallel in the laws preserved in contemporary inscriptions. On prescripts of *nomoi*, see Rhodes 1972: 276.

[36] See the notes to the documents at 8, 10, and 47.

[37] See the notes to the documents at 22, 47, 52, 82, 93, 94, and 121. MacDowell 1990 takes an inconsistent approach to the documents. He considers the witness statements forgeries, but he accepts the authenticity of some of the laws. He does not, however, take into account the errors about legal procedure found in these

reliable information about Athenian law but should not be used as sources unless their contents can be corroborated by contemporary evidence.

21. AGAINST MEIDIAS

[**1**] The bullying, judges, and the insolence with which Meidias always treats everyone, I think is well known to all of you and to the other citizens. I myself have done the very thing that each of you would have chosen to do had you been the victim of outrage: I brought a *probole*[38] against him for committing an offense in regard to the festival, not just because of the blows I received from him at the Dionysia but also for suffering many other acts of violence throughout all my service as chorus producer. [**2**] The entire Assembly acted honorably and did what was right: they were so angry and furious and so seriously concerned about the injustices that they knew I had suffered that, despite all his efforts and those of several others acting on his behalf, they were not persuaded to relent and paid no attention to their wealth and their promises, but unanimously voted against him.[39] Right after this, judges, many of you now in court and many other citizens approached me, asking and encouraging me to pursue my case and to bring him before you. By the gods, I think they had two reasons, men of Athens: they thought that I had suffered terrible abuse, and they wished at the same time to punish him for his arrogant, offensive, and unbridled behavior, which they had observed on other occasions. [**3**] Given this situation, I have rightly looked after all your interests that I should protect. As you see, I am here to accuse him because the case is proceeding to trial.[40] Although I could have received a large amount of money in return for dropping my prosecution, I did not accept anything and stood firm in the face of

---

documents and linguistic features like the late form of the imperative and the use of the adjective *idios*.

[38] For this legal procedure, see the Introduction.

[39] At 193 we learn that Meidias claimed that most citizens were abroad at the time and that only a handful voted against him.

[40] After the vote in the *probole*, the case was introduced to the court by one of the Thesmothetae. See *Ath. Pol.* 59.2.

repeated appeals, offers to do favors, and, by Zeus, even threats.⁴¹ [4]
As for what remains after this, which lies in your hands, I think that
the more people that this man has pestered and asked for help (I was
observing the sort of things that he was just now doing in front of the
courts),⁴² the greater is my hope for obtaining justice. Indeed, I would
not assume that any of you are about to abandon the support that you
have personally shown for my case, nor that you will permit Meidias
in the future to carry on his abusive behavior without fear by casting
any vote except one you consider just while you are under oath.⁴³

[5] Now if I were going to accuse him of proposing an illegal decree,
committing treason on an embassy, or any other such charge, I would
not consider it right to make a personal appeal to you;⁴⁴ I think that
the accuser in such cases should confine himself to proving these kinds
of charges, while the defendant is allowed to make appeals. But after
this man corrupted the judges and thereby caused my tribe unjustly to
lose the tripod,⁴⁵ [6] and after I myself was beaten and insulted (I do
not know if any other chorus producer has ever endured such insults)
and am now pursuing the case in which the Assembly passed a vote of
censure in its rage and fury over these incidents, I will not hesitate to
add a personal appeal.⁴⁶ If one may say so, I am now in the position

---

⁴¹On the story that Demosthenes accepted money in return for dropping the
case, see the Introduction.

⁴²All the judges met in one place, possibly the Agora, to be assigned to different courts (see *Ath. Pol.* 63). Litigants might then appeal to them as they made
their way to court. See Boegehold 1995: 33–34. For a humorous account of the
practice, see Aristoph. *Wasps* 552–558.

⁴³An allusion to the Judicial Oath.

⁴⁴In cases in which the charge was passing an illegal decree or committing
treason as an ambassador, the offense was not committed against an individual but
the entire community, and so a personal appeal would be out of place.

⁴⁵The tripod was the prize awarded for victory in the men's chorus (Lys. 21.2).
On the tripods awarded at the Dionysia, see Amandry 1976.

⁴⁶Demosthenes expresses his request for a sympathetic hearing in solemn
terms, using the language of supplication. Normally, it was the defendant who
supplicated the court (e.g., Aes. 2.179–180) and asked the judges to acquit him.
But Demosthenes claims that an acquittal will harm him as much as a conviction
would hurt a defendant. For the relationship between supplication and the law,
see Naiden 2004.

of the defendant because it is a disaster for the victim of abuse not to obtain justice. [7] I am therefore appealing to all of you, men of the court, and solemnly implore you to give me a favorable hearing as I present my case, and then, if I prove that Meidias here committed outrage not only against me but also against you, the laws, and everyone else, to help me as well as yourselves. This is roughly how matters stand, men of Athens: in the past I have been the victim of outrage, and my person has been subjected to physical abuse. Now the issue that is about to be debated and decided is whether or not someone should be allowed to do this sort of thing and to commit outrage with impunity against anyone whom he encounters.[47] [8] Therefore, if any of you previously thought that this trial was about some private quarrel, let him now bear in mind that it is in the public interest for no one to be allowed to commit this sort of crime. Let him listen carefully because the matter affects the community and let him cast his vote for the side that appears most just to him.

First, the clerk will read to you the law in accordance with which *probolai* take place. After that, I will try to explain the other issues. Read the law.[48]

---

[47] This passage shows that the case before the court was a *graphe hybreos*. Because Demosthenes has brought a public case, not a private one, he must show that Meidias' crime affects not only him but everyone in the community.

[48] This document is a forgery. First, when the speech was delivered, the duty of presiding over meetings of the Assembly belonged to the Proedroi (as Demosthenes correctly states in 9), not to the Prytaneis, who had ceased to exercise this role in the 380s. See Rhodes 1972: 25–27 and Rhodes 1981: 533–534. Second, the document contains a late form of the imperative (*paradidotosan*) that is not found in the epigraphic laws and decrees before 352/1 and is extremely rare between 351 and 300 BCE. See Threatte 1996: 462–466. MacDowell 1990: 228 cites a few examples of this form before 350, but they are all from literary sources and thus irrelevant because this is documentary prose. Third, the document states that the meeting about business arising from the Dionysia took place at a fixed time, the next day following the Pandia, whereas Demosthenes (9) says that it merely takes place "after the Pandia." Inscriptions indicate that Demosthenes' statement is more accurate. Fourth, the document implies that *probolai* were fines collected by the Prytaneis, not the name of the procedure in the Assembly. Fifth, the syntax of the document is inconsistent, switching from infinitives to an imperative. For detailed analysis of the document, see E. M. Harris 1992: 76–77.

[*LAW*]

The Prytaneis are to hold a meeting of the Assembly in the precinct of Dionysus on the day after the Pandia. During this meeting they are to conduct business first about sacred matters, then let them hand over all *probolai* arising as a result of the procession or the contests at the Dionysia that have not been paid off.

[**9**] This is the law, men of Athens, according to which preliminary actions are brought. As you heard, it requires that a meeting of the Assembly be held in the precinct of Dionysus after the Pandia,[49] and that when the Proedroi hold a discussion about the Archon's administration, a discussion also be held about any offenses or violations of the law concerning the festival. This law is good, men of Athens, and serves the public interest, as this case itself attests. When some men are clearly no less prone to commit abuse when this fear hangs over them, how should one expect that men like this would act if they are not facing any trial or danger?

[**10**] Now I want to read to you the next law in order after this one. This law will make clear to all of you how scrupulous all the rest of you are and how arrogant this man is.[50]

---

[49]The Pandia was a festival in honor of Zeus (see *IG* ii² 1140, line 5), which probably occurred on 16 Elaphebolion (MacDowell 1990: 227–228) or 17 Elaphebolion; see Mikalson 1975: 137.

[50]Like the previous document, this law is a forgery. First, the records of victories at the City Dionysia (*IG* ii² 2318) record performances of children's choruses, men's choruses, tragedies and comedies, but they do not mention a revelry (*kōmos*). Second, the document confuses the Attic month of Thargelion with the festival of the Thargelia. Third, the document contains a late form of the imperative (*estōsan*) that is not found in the epigraphic laws from this period (see note 48). Fourth, the document does not mention those who commit violence, a category of offenders included in Demosthenes' summary of the law's content. Fifth, the document implies that after the Dionysia in the Piraeus, the Lenaea, and the Thargelia, there was a meeting of the Assembly in the theatre of Dionysus, but there is no evidence for such a meeting. For discussion, see MacDowell 1990: 230–235. Sixth, Demosthenes states at 9 and 175 that this law concerned only the Dionysia, but the text says that it pertained to the Dionysia and Lenaea.

[*LAW*]

Euegorus proposed: When the procession for Dionysus in the Piraeus, the comedies and the tragedies take place, and the procession at the Lenaea, the tragedies and the comedies, and the procession at the City Dionysia, the children's choruses, the revelry (*kōmos*), the tragedies, and the comedies, and during the procession and contest in Thargelion, it is not permitted to seize a security or to take anything from anyone, not even from a defaulting debtor during these days. If anyone violates any of these measures, let him be subject to an action brought by the victim, and let there be *probolai* at the meeting of the Assembly in the precinct of Dionysus against him as an offender just as has been written concerning other offenders.

[**11**] Notice, men of the court, that whereas in the previous law the *probole* is directed against those who commit an offense in regard to the festival, in this law you have provided for *probolai* also against those who collect from debtors in default, those taking anything else from someone, or those using force. Not only did you think it necessary to prevent abuse against a person's body in this period or against the equipment that he might provide from his own funds for his liturgy, but you also allowed property belonging to those who had won it through a verdict in a lawsuit to remain, at least for the duration of the festival, in the hands of the losing parties who originally owned it. [**12**] Indeed, men of Athens, you are all so filled with generosity and piety that you suspend the execution of judgment for prior offenses during these days. But Meidias will be shown to have committed acts during these same days that deserve the harshest penalty. After recounting each thing that happened to me from the beginning, I wish to speak also about the blows that he finally rained down on me.[51] Every single act of his will make it clear that he deserves to die.

---

[51] Demosthenes indicates that he has ended the preliminary section of his speech and is moving on to the narration.

[**13**] This was the situation two years ago:[52] the tribe Pandionis had not appointed a chorus producer;[53] the meeting of the Assembly during which the Archon was legally required to conduct the lot for the selection of *aulos* players for the chorus leaders was in session;[54] there were arguments and insults flying back and forth, with the Archon blaming the tribal supervisors, the tribal supervisors, the Archon.[55] At this point I came forward and promised to volunteer my services as chorus producer. When the lots were cast, I won the first pick of the *aulos* players. [**14**] All of you, men of Athens, welcomed both these events, my promise and my piece of good luck, in the warmest possible way: you gave the sort of shouts and applause that you do when you praise someone and share his joy. But this man here, Meidias, alone out of all, was apparently irritated; throughout my entire liturgy he kept following me around, harassing me both in minor and in more serious ways. [**15**] As for all the times he annoyed me by opposing my efforts to gain an exemption from the army for the members of my chorus[56] or by getting himself nominated and asking to be elected supervisor for the Dionysia,[57] and all the other things like this, I will

---

[52] This was in 349/8.

[53] Demosthenes was a member of the deme Paeania, which belonged to the tribe Pandionis.

[54] The Archon determined by lot the order in which chorus producers chose *aulos* players. The individual chorus producer was then free to select any *aulos* player he wished. See *Ath. Pol.* 56.3. The *aulos* was a pair of pipes attached to a single mouthpiece. On this instrument, see Wilson 1999. For those who played the instrument, see Wilson 2002.

[55] Each of the ten tribes appointed three supervisors (*epimeletai*). Their duties were to nominate chorus producers, conduct sacrifices, and look after the tribe's funds. They were different from those elected to assist the Archon with the Dionysia, who are mentioned below. See MacDowell 1990: 237.

[56] The members of a chorus were granted exemption from military service during the festival. See Dem. 3.11–12 with scholia ad loc.; 39.16 with MacDowell 1989a: 70–72.

[57] In this period the Assembly elected ten supervisors (*epimeletai*) to assist the Archon in organizing the Dionysia. Later they were chosen by lot (*Ath. Pol.* 56.4 with Rhodes 1981: 627–628). Wilson (2000: 159–162) believes that Meidias was actually elected and was thus acting legally when he assaulted Demosthenes.

not mention them. I am not unaware that although each one of these actions aroused in me the same feeling of anger at being insulted and humiliated that one might feel for the very worst crimes, in your eyes these same actions by themselves might not appear worth the trouble of a trial in court because you were not involved in the situation. But the actions that will make all of you equally angry, these I will discuss. [16] His subsequent actions, which I am about to describe, went far beyond this. I would not have even attempted to bring this charge against him now unless I had immediately proven my case earlier in the Assembly. The sacred clothing (I consider all clothing that one has prepared for the festival sacred while it is worn) and the gold crowns, which I had made as an adornment for the chorus, he plotted to destroy, men of Athens, by breaking into the goldsmith's house at night. He actually did ruin them, but to be sure not completely; he was not able to. Certainly no one claims to have ever heard of anyone in the city daring or succeeding in doing such a thing. [17] This was not enough for him, but he also, men of Athens, corrupted the trainer for my chorus.[58] In fact, if Telephanes, the *aulos* player in the men's chorus, had not been extremely good to me, seen what was going on, then chased the man away, and thought it his duty to weld together and train the chorus, we would not have competed, men of Athens, but the chorus would have gone on stage without any training, and we would have been completely humiliated. His outrages did not stop there: there was so much arrogance still left in him that he corrupted an Archon wearing a crown[59] and brought together the chorus producers against me, shouting, threatening, standing next to the judges as they swore their oaths,[60] blocking and nailing up

---

But Demosthenes states twice (17 and 61) that Meidias was a private citizen when he struck him, and this was public knowledge.

[58] The trainer (*didaskalos*) was "the poet who composed the words and music as well as directing the chorus" (MacDowell 1990: 240).

[59] Officials wore crowns when performing their duties to distinguish them from private individuals. See MacDowell 1990: 239–240. Demosthenes adds this detail to make Meidias' crime appear worse.

[60] The Archon selected ten men by lot, one from each tribe, to judge the contests at the Dionysia (Isoc. 17.33–34; Plut. *Cimon* 8.7). They all swore an oath

the side rooms[61]—a private citizen doing this to public property! He was constantly causing me harm and trouble that beggars description. [18] For all these events that took place in the Assembly or in front of the judges in the theater, I have all you, men of the court, as witnesses. And one must certainly regard as most reliable any statements that those who are seated here testify to be true. After corrupting in advance the judges in the contest for the men's chorus, he added two actions like crowning achievements to all these youthful pranks: he committed outrage against my person and was primarily responsible for preventing the winning tribe from gaining the prize!

[19] These are the acts of insolence that he committed against me and the members of my tribe and the offenses in regard to the festival for which I brought the *probole* against him, men of Athens. There are many other actions of which I will soon describe as many as I can. I have many other thoroughly wicked crimes of his to discuss, this foul man's insults toward many of you and his many terrible and shameless actions. [20] Some of his victims, men of the court, were afraid of him, his reckless behavior, his cronies, their wealth, and all the other advantages this man possesses, and kept silent. Others tried to obtain justice but were unable to, while still others reached settlements with him, perhaps thinking this would be better. Those who came to an agreement at least received compensation for themselves. You, on the other hand, have inherited the task of defending the laws that this man broke when he wronged the first two groups and now me and all the others.[62] [21] Take all his crimes together and assess whatever

---

to give the award to the best performers. The author of one of the hypotheses to this speech suggests that Meidias urged them to add "except Demosthenes" when they swore to vote for the one who danced the best.

[61] According to Theophrastus, these were rooms where the chorus made ready for its performance; according to Didymus, they were the entrances on each side of the stage (*orchestra*). Meidias was probably trying to prevent Demosthenes' chorus from reaching the stage. See MacDowell 1990: 242–243.

[62] MacDowell 1990: 245 claims that "the sense of the metaphor is that Meidias has incurred many debts, which now fall due to be paid by the jury." Yet the judges have not inherited Meidias' debts but the duty to uphold the law, which has been passed on to them by those who did not prosecute Meidias in court for his previous crimes.

single penalty you consider just.[63] I will prove, first, how many times I
was the victim of his insults, and then how many times you were. After
that, men of Athens, I will examine the rest of his life and will show
that he deserves to die not just once, but many times. Take and read
for me the first witness statement, that of the goldsmith.[64]

[**22**] *[TESTIMONY]*

I, Pammenes, the son of Pammenes,[65] from the deme of Erchia,
have a goldsmith shop in the Agora, where I reside and practice the
trade of goldsmith. Demosthenes, for whom I am testifying, gave
me a gold crown to prepare and clothing to embroider with gold so
he could march in them in the procession for Dionysus. When I
had completed the work and had them ready in my shop, Meidias,
the man being prosecuted by Demosthenes, burst in on me at
night, bringing others along with him and tried to destroy the
crown and the clothing and damaged some of these but just the
same was not able to destroy them all because I showed up and
stopped him.

[**23**] Now I also have much to say, men of Athens, about the crimes
he committed against others (just as I said at the beginning of my
speech), and I have collected a list of his outrages and insults, all of
which you will hear in a moment.[66] The job of collecting them was

---

[63] Demosthenes refers to the second part of the trial, when the court
determined what penalty the defendant would receive after being found guilty.

[64] This witness statement contains two words that are not Attic Greek (*kata-
gignomai* and *diachryson*) and is thus a later forgery. See MacDowell 1990:
245–246.

[65] MacDowell 1990: 245 believes that this was "a name used in the Roman
period, not known before the second century BC," but see *SEG* 14.155 for an example from around 300 BCE. The manuscripts add the otherwise unattested word
eperchos after Pammenes' patronymic, and Buttman emended this to the demotic
for the deme of Erchia. Other editors have made other suggestions.

[66] Dover 1968: 173 finds the connection between this section and what precedes
very weak. But Demosthenes here refers to the beginning of his speech (1, 7),
where he referred to Meidias' crimes against everyone. He later discusses these at
128–142. See E. M. Harris 1989: 128–129.

easy: the victims themselves approached me. [**24**] But before this, I want to talk about the ways in which I have heard he will try to deceive you. In my opinion, it is absolutely necessary for me to discuss these matters first, and it is extremely useful for you to hear them. Why? Because by preventing you from being deceived, this discussion will cause you to cast a vote that is just and in keeping with your oath. By far your most important duty is to pay attention to these points, to remember them, and to counter every objection when this man speaks. [**25**] It is no secret (it was reported to me that he was rehearsing these arguments in private before a small group)[67] that he will say first that if I had actually been the victim of the crimes I am alleging, it was more appropriate for me to initiate a private action for damages for ruining the cloaks and the gold crowns and for all the harm done to the chorus and an action for outrage for physical insults I claim to have suffered—but not, by Zeus, to bring a public charge and introduce an assessment of the penalty to be imposed or paid![68] [**26**] One thing I know well, and you should know it too, is that if I had not brought a *probole* against him, I would have immediately been confronted with the opposite argument, namely, that if there were any truth in the charges, I should have brought a *probole* and imposed punishment at the actual time of his offenses. The chorus belonged to the city, all the clothing was made in preparation for the festival, and I was the victim of these crimes when I was a chorus producer. Who would then have chosen any other penalty than the one provided by law for those who commit offenses in regard to the festival? [**27**] In that case, I am certain that he would have made all these arguments. Indeed, I think that it is typical for an offender who is on trial to try to evade punishment by arguing that the present procedure is inappropriate,[69] but it is the duty of prudent judges to ignore these arguments and to punish whomever they catch acting insolently.

---

[67] Accusers, who spoke first at a trial, sometimes say that they have learned about the defendant's arguments from friends or gossip. See Dorjahn 1935.

[68] Demosthenes anticipates Meidias' argument that he should have brought a private action (*dikas idias*) for the wrongs he suffered, not a public action (*dēmosia krinein*), as he in fact did by bringing a *graphe hybreos*.

[69] For other passages where a defendant objects to the procedure used by the accuser, see Ant. 5.8 and Dem. 22.21–24.

[**28**] Do not let him say now that the law provides me with private actions.[70] It does in fact provide them. But let him show either that he did not commit the actions I have charged him with or that he has done them but is not guilty of an offense against the festival.[71] This is the reason I brought the *probole*, and this is the issue about which you will cast your vote.[72] If I am giving up my chance to gain from private actions, thereby yielding to the city my right to punish him, and have therefore chosen this kind of trial from which I receive no profit, it would certainly be reasonable for my decision to earn your gratitude and not to damage my case.

[**29**] Now I am aware that he will also make much use of the following argument: "Don't hand me over to Demosthenes nor destroy me because of Demosthenes. Just because I am at war with him, will you destroy me for this reason?" I know that he will repeatedly shout this sort of thing with the aim of using these words to rouse up hostility against me. [**30**] This is not the way matters stand, not even close. You do not turn over anyone who is guilty to any of his accusers; not even when someone is the victim of a crime do you impose punishment in whatever way the victim persuades you to. Quite the opposite: you pass laws before crimes are committed without knowing who will commit them and who their victims will be. What do these laws do? They promise to all people in the city that if someone suffers an injustice, they will enable him to obtain justice. Thus, whenever you punish anyone who violates the laws, you do not hand this man to his accusers but keep the laws strong for your own benefit.

---

[70] The manuscripts add the words "and with the public action for outrage," which are retained by MacDowell and Dilts, but they are omitted by Syrianus Sopater Marcellinus in his quotation of the passage. They should be deleted because in the last sentence in this section, Demosthenes says that he is giving up only private actions and thus renouncing the possibility of receiving personal compensation. This would not have applied to the *graphe hybreos*.

[71] Demosthenes here clearly distinguishes arguments based on the facts and those based on the law.

[72] This statement is misleading. The issue of whether Meidias had committed an offense concerning the festival was decided at the *probole*. The issue before the court at this trial was whether Meidias committed an outrage against Demosthenes. See 7.

[**31**] Next, in response to the following sort of argument, when he says that "it was Demosthenes who is the victim of outrage,"[73] there is a reply that is just, serves the public interest, and protects the rights of all. He did not bully me alone, Demosthenes, on that day, but also your chorus producer. You could best understand what this means from the following considerations. [**32**] You know of course that the word Thesmothete[74] is not the name of any single one of the men who are Thesmothetae, but each has his own name, whatever it may be. Now, if anyone outrages or slanders someone who is a private individual, he will stand trial on a public charge for outrage or a private charge of slander, but if he does this to a Thesmothete, he will lose his citizen rights once and for all.[75] Why? Because the man who commits this crime also insults the laws, your public crown, and the name of your city. The title of Thesmothete belongs to no individual but to the city. [**33**] Again, the situation is the same in regard to the Archon. If someone hits him after he has put on a crown or slanders him, he loses his rights as a citizen, but when he strikes him as a private citizen, he is subject to a private action. And this is the case not only for these officials but also for all those who receive the right to wear a crown or some other honor from the city.[76] Certainly such is the case with me also: if Meidias had committed one of these offenses against me on

---

[73] Demosthenes anticipates that Meidias will argue that he should bring a private suit since the offense was committed against a single individual and did not harm the community.

[74] The Thesmothetae were six of the Archons who were selected by lot annually and were responsible for supervising the courts. See *Ath. Pol.* 59.1–6 with Rhodes 1981: 657–667.

[75] The person who was convicted of striking an official had no possibility of regaining his rights, unlike the public debtor, who could recover them by paying his debt. This passage is the only evidence for this law. For the principle that it is far worse to insult an official than a private citizen, see [Arist.] *Problems* 952b28–32.

[76] The manuscripts also include "some immunity" (*adeian*) in this list, but MacDowell 1990: 251 notes that this privilege seems out of place in this context and deletes it, while Dilts retains it. Some officials wore crowns, but they might also be given to victors in athletic contests or those honored for their services to Athens.

some other days, it was appropriate for him to pay a private penalty. [34] But if he clearly has committed all his crimes of outrage against your chorus producer during a sacred season, he deserves to receive the people's anger and their punishment. For together with Demosthenes, the chorus producer was also the victim of outrage; he is a public official, and this occurred on those days when the laws prohibit it. It is necessary whenever you pass laws to examine their merits, but after passing them, to protect and follow them. That is what your oath requires,[77] and it is also just in other respects. [35] A law about damage has been in effect for a long time,[78] as has one about assault, and another about outrage. If it were sufficient for those who commit one of these offenses during the Dionysia to pay the penalty according to these laws, there would be no additional need for this law. But it is not sufficient. Here is the proof: you have established a sacred law for the god himself about the sacred season.[79] If anyone then is subject to the previous laws already in existence and to the latter one, which was passed after them, and to all the rest of the laws, does such a man not deserve to pay any penalty on those grounds or a greater one? A greater one, I think.

[36] Someone has been reporting to me that Meidias was going around making a list and finding out who had ever happened to be the victims of outrage and that they are going to speak and tell you their stories.[80] For instance, men of Athens, the Proedros[81] who they say was once struck by Polyzelus, the Thesmothete who was recently struck while rescuing a woman who played the *aulos*, and some people like them. He is doing this on the assumption that if he shows that many others have been the victims of many terrible crimes, you will be less angry about what has happened to me. [37] On the contrary, I

---

[77] Another allusion to the Judicial Oath.

[78] For this law, see 43.

[79] This is the law read out at 8. On sacred laws in general, see Parker 2004.

[80] Demosthenes predicts that Meidias will list cases of men who were struck and did not prosecute and use these as precedents to show that he should not be convicted of *hybris*. For the use of precedents in Athenian law, see E. M. Harris 2006b.

[81] On the office of Proedros, see 8n.

think that you would be right to do the very opposite, men of Athens, given that it is your duty to show concern for what is in the community's best interest. Who among you does not realize that the reason why many crimes of this sort occur is the failure to punish offenders and that what is alone responsible for preventing someone from being the victim of outrage in the future is to have the person who is caught each time receive the appropriate punishment?[82] Well, if it is to our advantage to discourage other criminals, this man must also be punished for these crimes, and indeed all the more so to the extent that they are greater in number and more serious. Yet if it is to our advantage to encourage both him and all men, he should be let off. [38] Furthermore we will indeed discover that the former and the latter do not deserve the same amount of compassion. In fact, in the first case, the man who struck the Thesmothete had three excuses: drunkenness, passion, and ignorance because the event took place in darkness and at night.[83] Next, Polyzelus struck in anger and because of his aggressive nature and made a mistake before he had time to think; his victim was certainly not an enemy, and he did not act with the intent of insulting him.[84] But Meidias cannot make any of these arguments. In fact, he was my enemy and knowingly committed outrage against me in broad daylight. Besides, he clearly made up his mind to commit outrage not just at this time but at every opportunity. [39] And I certainly see no similarity between what I did and what these men did. First, it will be obvious that the Thesmothete showed no concern for you and the laws and felt no anger but agreed to a private settlement for some amount of money or other and let the case drop. Next, as for the man who was struck by Polyzelus, this same thing happened: he reached a private settlement and said goodbye to the laws and to you and did not even bring Polyzelus into court.[85] [40] Now if someone wishes at the pres-

---

[82] One of the main rationales for punishment was to act as a deterrent to future crime.

[83] For ignorance providing a reason for lenience and fairness (*epieikeia*), see E. M. Harris 2004b: 9–11.

[84] To commit an act of *hybris* one had to have the intention (*mens rea*) to insult. See Arist. *Rhetoric* 1374a.

[85] Demosthenes says only that the Thesmothete and the man struck by Polyzelus did not take advantage of the law, but he does not imply that they did

ent time to bring charges against those men, these are the points that he must discuss. But if someone wants to defend himself against my charges, he must present any arguments but these. I myself did completely the opposite of these men: it will be clear that I did not accept or attempt to get any money. Instead, I have maintained the right to punish him for the sake of the laws, for the sake of the god, and for your sake, and have now handed this decision over to you. Do not let him make this argument; if he forces you to listen, don't be convinced as if his point were justified. [41] If you remain firmly decided about these issues, he will not be in a position to make any argument. What kind of pretext, what human or reasonable excuse will emerge clearly from his actions? Anger, by Zeus: yes, perhaps this is what he will say. When someone is carried away and acts on the spur of the moment before having a chance to think, one would say that his actions, even if performed in an insulting manner, have been done because of anger. On the other hand, if someone is detected doing something for a long time, repeatedly over many days, and in violation of the laws, his actions are certainly far removed from those done in anger, but it is clear that such a person is deliberately committing outrage.

[42] Yet as soon as it is obvious that he has committed the offenses that I am charging him with and has done them with intent to outrage, we must examine the laws, men of the court, because you have sworn to follow them when you judge this case. Consider how much more anger and punishment they prescribe for those who commit offenses willingly and through insolence than for those who do wrong in some other way. [43] Now first, all these laws about damage, to begin with these, provide for payment for twice the amount if one does damage willingly, but if unwillingly, simple payment for the value of the damage.[86] Rightly so: the victim has a right to receive help in all respects, but the law has not prescribed the same amount of anger for the offender if he acts willingly or unwillingly.[87] Next, the laws about

---

anything illegal. It was possible to drop a public case provided one did it in the correct way. See E. M. Harris 2006a: 405–422; cf. MacDowell 1990: 256.

[86] This was a general law dealing with cases of damage, but there were other laws that covered specific types of damage. See MacDowell 1990: 253–254.

[87] For a law about the Eleusinian Mysteries making a similar distinction, see *IG* i³ 6b, lines 4–8.

homicide punish those who kill deliberately with death or permanent exile and confiscation of property,[88] but consider that those who kill unwillingly deserve the chance to obtain pardon and a large amount of sympathy.[89] [44] One can see that the laws are harsh to those who commit outrage with deliberate intent not only in these cases but also in all cases. Why in the world, if someone owes a judgment and does not pay it, has the law not yet made ejectment a private matter but imposes an additional fine to be paid to the public treasury?[90] And again why in the world, if someone, after receiving one or two or ten talents from another when both parties are willing, then defrauds him of this amount, does the state pay no attention, while if a person takes something of very slight value but grabs it away by force, the laws order the payment of an additional fine to the public treasury precisely equivalent to that paid to the private individual?[91] [45] The reason is that the legislator thought all offenses that a person commits when using violence are public wrongs that threaten even those who are not directly involved. Although few possess physical strength, the laws belong to all people; the man who has given his consent needs protection suitable for an individual, but the victim of violence requires the protection of the community. For this reason, the lawgiver has granted

---

[88] Those who killed deliberately were tried at the Areopagus (*Ath. Pol.* 57.3). Those who were found guilty on this charge were put to death, but the defendant who feared conviction could go into permanent exile before the verdict. See Dem. 23.69, with MacDowell 1963: 110, 115. For confiscation of property as an additional penalty, see Dem. 23.45, 24.7; Lys. 1.50. For the meaning and potential ambiguity of the term *phonos ek pronoias*, see E. M. Harris 2004a: 248–251.

[89] If one was convicted of killing someone unwillingly (*akon*), he went into exile until he came to an agreement with the kin of the victim. See Dem. 23.72, 77, 37.59. The adjective *akon* should not be translated "unintentionally" (MacDowell); see Rickert 1989.

[90] A private action for ejectment (*dike exoulēs*) could be brought against someone who refused to turn over property awarded to the plaintiff by a court judgment. See Harrison 1968: 217–220.

[91] If someone stole property without using violence, he was merely liable to the private action for theft (*dike klopes*). This action covered cases of embezzlement and larceny and provided a payment of twice the value of the object stolen. See E. M. Harris 2006a: 373–389. For the *dike biaion*, see Harpocration s.v. *biaion*.

to anyone who wishes the right to bring a public action for outrage and has made the entire penalty payable to the state: he thought that the man who attempts to outrage harms not only the victim but the city and that punishment of the offender was a sufficient amount of justice for the victim, but that he should not receive money for his own benefit as a result of such crimes. [**46**] In fact, the lawgiver went so much further that even if someone commits outrage against a slave, he granted a public action in the same way on behalf of the slave.[92] In his opinion, it was necessary to consider not the identity of the victim but the nature of whatever action took place.[93] When he found a type of behavior inappropriate, he did not permit it either toward a slave or in any way at all. There is nothing, men of Athens, nothing at all that is more intolerable than outrage nor anything that more deserves your anger. Read for me the actual law about outrage (*hybris*). There is nothing like hearing the law itself.[94]

[**47**] [*LAW*]

If anyone commits an outrage against anyone, either a child or a woman or a man, whether slave or free, or does anything illegal to any of these people,[95] let any Athenian to whom it is permitted

---

[92] This law covered only abusive treatment of slaves belonging to other people; it did not protect slaves from beatings by their own masters, who could kill them with impunity (see Ant. 6.4). One could also administer physical punishment to a slave owned by someone else who was caught while committing an offense against one's own property. See Dem. 53.16 with E. M. Harris 2006a: 275.

[93] For a similar view of the law about *hybris,* see Aes. 1.17.

[94] This document is an obvious forgery. See the following notes. For detailed discussion, see E. M. Harris 1992: 77–78.

[95] Athenian laws were aimed at specific offenses or limited the jurisdiction of officials to certain classes of individuals. Outrage in particular was a distinctive type of offense (see 38, 41; Arist. *Rhetoric* 1374a13–15 with MacDowell 1990: 264) and was not a general category covering all types of crimes. This statute, by contrast, has an unlimited range of application. The document at Dem. 43.75 is not a true parallel, because it limits the jurisdiction of a particular magistrate (*pace*

bring a public action before the Thesmothetae and let them bring the case to the Heliaea within thirty days[96] from the time of the accusation unless some public business prevents it, but if not, at the earliest possible time. Whatever the Heliaea decides, let it immediately assess whatever penalty it thinks he deserves to suffer or pay. As for everyone who brings his own public actions[97] according to the law, if someone does not bring the case to court or does bring the case to court and does not gain one-fifth of the votes, let him pay one thousand drachmas to the public treasury.[98] If he is assessed a sum of money for his outrage, let him be put in prison until he pays, if he has outraged a free man.[99]

[48] Listen, men of Athens, to how humane this law is: it states that not even slaves deserve to be the victims of outrage. Why is this, by the gods? Imagine if someone were to bring this law to the barbarians, who provide the Greeks with their supply of slaves,[100] and were to praise you and talk about your city, telling them, [49] "There are

---

Fisher 2001: 139), who does not address the other grounds against authenticity discussed in notes 97, 98, and 99. The person who composed this document was probably misled by the tendentious paraphrase of the law given by Aes. 1.15.

[96] Hansen 1981: 167–170 argues that a thirty-day time limit was normal, but see MacDowell 1990: 266–267.

[97] If one assumes that the law is a genuine document composed in the early fourth century, the phrase *graphas idias* (public actions that are private) makes no sense. But the document is clearly a forgery written during the Hellenistic period when the adjective *idios* meant "one's own" and was equivalent to the Latin *suus* (see *LSJ* s.v. I.6). MacDowell, followed by Dilts, assumes the document is genuine and deletes the word, but his explanation of how the word entered into the text is unsatisfactory. See E. M. Harris 1992: 77–78.

[98] The author of this forged document did not realize that the person who did not gain one-fifth of the votes or did not follow through his case also lost the right to bring any public cases. See E. M. Harris 2006a: 405–422.

[99] This sentence, in which the subject is the defendant, clashes with the previous sentence, in which the subject is the accuser, another indication that the document is a forgery.

[100] Though most slaves in Athens were non-Greek (see, for example, *IG* i³ 421, lines 34–47, 49; 422, lines 70, 77, 80, 195–197, 199, 206; 426, line 11; 427, lines 4–13), the Greeks often enslaved fellow Greeks. See Pritchett 1991: 223–245.

some Greeks who are so kind and generous in their character that despite the many injustices you have done them and the ancestral hostility that exists by nature between you and them, they still do not think it right to commit abuse against those men for whom they pay a price and buy as slaves. On the contrary, they have made this very law to prevent this abuse and have already punished with death many men who have violated this law."[101] [**50**] If the barbarians should hear and understand this law,[102] don't you think that they would collectively choose you to protect their interests?[103] Since this law is not only famous among the Greeks, but would also enjoy a good reputation among the barbarians,[104] think about what kind of punishment the person who violates it deserves to suffer.

[**51**] Now, if I had not been the victim of these crimes when acting as chorus producer, someone would have condemned only the abusive nature of his actions. But as it is, if this person should also condemn his impiety, I think he would be acting in an appropriate way. For you are certainly aware that you perform all these choruses and hymns for the god not only in obedience to these laws about the Dionysia but also to the oracles where you will find it has been proclaimed, both by Delphi and similarly by Dodona,[105] that the city should institute choruses in accordance with the ancestral rules and fill the alleyways with the smoke of sacrifices and wear crowns. [**52**] Take the actual oracles and read them for me.[106]

---

[101] For death as the penalty for conviction on a charge of *hybris,* see Din. 1.23 with E. M. Harris 2006a: 288. Demosthenes may exaggerate here; we know of no free person convicted for committing *hybris* against a slave.

[102] Demosthenes suggests that the barbarians might not be intelligent enough to understand the law. For the racial stereotype of the dim-witted barbarian, see Hall 1989: 122–123.

[103] Demosthenes uses the term *proxenos,* a person appointed by a foreign community to protect the interests of their citizens when they were in the former's community. The Athenians granted special privileges to those whom they appointed to be their *proxenoi.* On the *proxenos,* see Dem. 20.60 with n. 90.

[104] I.e., if the barbarians knew about it.

[105] There was an oracle of Zeus located at Dodona.

[106] The texts of these oracles are forgeries composed in the late Hellenistic or Roman period. The two oracles appear to be from Delphi, but the first contains a

[ORACLES]

I proclaim to all the sons of Erechtheus, who in the city of Pandion
dwell and conduct their festivals by ancestral rules,
be mindful of Bacchus and along the wide avenues
establish a thank offering of ripe crops to Bromius, all mingled together,
and make the altars fragrant with sacrifice, covering your heads with
   crowns.
Sacrifice for health and pray to Zeus the highest, to Heracles, to Apollo
   the protector; for good fortune to Apollo of the avenues, to Leto, to
   Artemis; and
set up mixing bowls in the avenues and choruses, and put on crowns
following the ancestral rules for all the Olympian gods and goddesses,
raising high their right and left hands, and show gratitude.

[53] [ORACLES FROM DODONA]

To the people of Athens, the oracle of Zeus commands that since you
have neglected the times of sacrifice and of sacred missions, nine
chosen sacred envoys be sent and that these men promptly sacrifice with
   good
omens to Zeus three oxen and for each ox three pigs, and an ox to Dione
   and
set up a bronze table for the dedications that the Athenian people have
   dedicated.
The oracle of Zeus commands the performance of sacrifices at Dodona

---

chaotic mixture of Attic (*Erechtheidais*) and Ionic/Epic forms (*ithyneth', Bacchoio,*
karē), the second an equally strange combination of Doric (*tychās agathās, Lātoi,*
histamen, mnasidorein) and Attic forms (*stephanēphorein, kata ta patria*). Demosthenes states that these oracles contained provisions similar to those in the Athenian laws about the Dionysia and instructed the Athenians "to establish choruses
in accordance with ancestral practices, to fill the alleyways with the smoke of
sacrifices, and to wear crowns." The first oracle does not appear to order the performance of choruses, and the second does not mention Dionysus, the patron god
of the festival in whose honor all the choral and dramatic contests were performed. The second oracle from Delphi also contains the adjective *idias* with the
meaning "one's own" found only in the Hellenistic period (see note 97). Attempts
to emend these oracles are thus unjustified.

to sovereign Dionysus,[107] *and to fill mixing bowls, and to establish dances, and to wear crowns, both free and slaves, and to take rest for one day; to sacrifice an ox to Apollo the averter of evil and a white ox to Zeus, Protector of Wealth.*

[54] Men of Athens, the city possesses these and many other fine oracles. What then should you conclude from them? That while they command other sacrifices to the gods indicated in each oracle, they also ordain in all the oracles you receive that you institute choral dances and wear crowns in accordance with ancestral rules. [55] Now, all of us who dance in a chorus or serve as chorus producers on those days when we meet for the contest have obviously put on crowns for your sake in accordance to these oracles, both the man about to win and the person who will place last. But during his victory celebration, the winner puts on a crown for himself.[108] What then about the man who outrages one of these dancers or a chorus producer out of hatred and does this during the actual contest and inside the god's shrine? Are we going to say that he does anything other than commit sacrilege?

[56] Now, you are certainly aware of this fact: although you do not want any foreigner to compete,[109] you simply do not permit any of the chorus leaders to issue summons to dancers and to question them. On the contrary, if he issues a summons, you have imposed a fine of fifty drachmas, and if he orders him to sit down, one thousand drachmas.[110] For what reason? So that on that day no one summons

---

[107] The oldest manuscripts read "to sovereign (*dēmotelei*) Dionysus." Buttman, followed by MacDowell and Dilts, adopted the reading of a later manuscript and read "sacrifices at public expense (*dēmotelē*) to Dionysus." But there is no reason to reject the reading of the earlier manuscripts; see Parker 1996: 5 n. 17 with *IG* xii 9.20.

[108] The other crowns are worn as part of the religious ceremony. The winner is given a crown as an award.

[109] According to a scholion on Aristophanes (*Wealth* 953), it was illegal for foreigners to dance in a chorus only at the Dionysia; it was not illegal for them to dance at the Lenaea.

[110] The terms of this law are slightly obscure. If one suspected a foreigner of joining a chorus, it was permissible to issue him a summons to appear before the Archon (cf. 60). But it was illegal to question him or to remove him during

nor insults nor intentionally commits outrage against someone who has put on a crown and is serving the god. [**57**] Will then the man who issues a summons to a dancer for a legitimate reason not be exempt for a fine, while the man who has beaten up a chorus leader in defiance of all the laws clearly escapes punishment?[111] No, there is not any advantage in making laws to protect the majority in a noble and generous spirit if you who hold the power to decide at any given time will feel no anger against those who disobey and break them.

[**58**] Now, by the gods, consider also the following point. I am going to ask you not to be angry with me if I mention by name some people who have fallen on hard times. I will do this, by the gods, not out of a desire to rebuke any of them but rather to show that all the rest of you refrain from using violence, humiliating people, and doing things like this. There is, you know, a certain Sannion[112] who trains tragic choruses. This man was convicted for desertion and found himself in trouble.[113] [**59**] After his misfortune an ambitious chorus leader in the tragic competition hired this man; I think it was Theozotides.[114] At first, the rival chorus leaders were angry and said they were going to stop him, but when the theater filled up and they saw the crowd gathered for the contest, they grew reluctant and left him alone; no one touched him. On the contrary, anyone of you might see that each man possesses so much respect for the god that during the entire period since this, he has been training choruses and not one of his personal enemies stands

---

a performance. The penalty for the former was fifty drachmas, for the latter 1,000. On these laws, see MacDowell 1989a: 72–77.

[111] As MacDowell 1990: 276 notes, Demosthenes' argument "is strictly invalid. The special law about choristers concerned challenges to their citizen status, and its purpose was to minimize disruption and delay to the choral performances when an individual chorister was suspected of not being entitled to participate. There was no reason why this law should apply to *khoregoi*, not only because the identity of a *khoregos* was known and his status could be challenged long before the festival, but also because a *khoregos* did not himself perform and an attack on him would therefore not delay the performance."

[112] Sannion is identified as a trainer of choruses in a fragment of Demochares (*FGrHist* 75 F6) preserved in a life of Aeschines.

[113] The penalty for desertion was the loss of citizen rights. See [Dem.] 59.27; And. 1.74; Aes. 3.175–176.

[114] On Theozotides, see Davies 1971: 222–223.

in his way. This is how far removed the chorus-leaders are from this behavior. [**60**] There is another man, Aristides of Oeneis;[115] this man also had this sort of bad luck. He is now an old man and perhaps not as good a dancer, but at one time he was the leader of his tribe's chorus. You are of course aware that should someone take away the leader, the rest of the chorus is ruined. Yet despite the intense competition among the chorus leaders, none of them ever saw this as a way of gaining an advantage or dared to drag him away or stop him. Because it would have been necessary to do this by laying a hand on him, and it was not permitted to summon him before the Archon as one could if he wanted to remove a foreigner, everyone was reluctant to be seen physically shoving him around. [**61**] Men of the court, isn't this a terrible and awful state of affairs? On the one hand, not one of the chorus producers, men who think they might win for this reason, who have often spent all their money on liturgies, has ever dared to lay their hands on people whom the laws permit them to seize but conducted themselves with such caution, such respect for the god, and such restraint that despite spending money and competing, they still hold back and show concern for your wishes and enthusiasm about the festival. Yet, on the other hand, when Meidias, though only a private citizen who has spent nothing, runs into someone who happens to be an enemy, he humiliates him—a man who is spending money, serving as chorus leader, and possesses the rights of a citizen—and beats him in utter disregard for the festival, the laws, your reaction, or the god!

[**62**] Now, although there are many people, men of Athens, who hate each other not only for personal reasons but also because of politics, no one has ever reached the point where he is so lacking in shame that he has dared to do something like this. In fact, they say the famous Iphicrates[116] once got into a very bitter quarrel with Diocles of Pithos.[117] Furthermore it happened that Teisias, Iphicrates' brother,[118]

---

[115] On the possible identity of this Aristides, see MacDowell 1990: 280–281.

[116] Iphicrates was awarded the honors of dining in the Prytaneion (Dem. 23.130) and having his statue placed on the Acropolis (Pausanias 1.24.7).

[117] Diocles, son of Diochares of Pithos, was a wealthy man who is known to have performed two trierarchies (*IG* ii² 1604, line 91; 1609, line 118) and may have derived his wealth from mining. See Davies 1971: 158–159.

[118] There is no other evidence about Teisias aside from the names of his sons Timotheus (*Hesperia* 7, 1938, 92, no. 12) and Timarchus (Aes. 1.157).

was competing as chorus leader against Diocles. Yet although Iphicrates had many friends and a great deal of money and held the high
opinion of himself that you would expect in a man who has won the
kind of fame and honors that you have awarded him, [**63**] he did not
enter into the houses of goldsmiths at night, nor tear up clothing
prepared for the festival, nor bribe the trainer nor prevent the chorus
from learning its part, nor did he do any of the things that this man
was doing. On the contrary, he deferred to the laws and to the wishes
of others and endured the sight of his enemy gaining a victory and
winning a crown. He was right: he believed that such matters did
not take precedence over the constitution that he knew had made his
own success possible. [**64**] Next, we all know the story of Philostratus
of Colonus.[119] He was an accuser of Chabrias[120] when the latter was
on trial about Oropos[121] on a capital charge, and he was the harshest
of all the accusers. Later, when he was a chorus leader in the boys'
competition at the Dionysia and won,[122] Chabrias did not beat him
or snatch away his crown or go anywhere where he was not permitted. [**65**] Though I still have many people I could mention who hated
each other for many reasons, I have never heard or seen anyone who
has reached such a pitch of insolence as to do such a thing. None of
you, I know, remembers before this any of those men who hated each
other, whether it be for personal or political reasons, standing nearby
when the names of the judges were called out or dictating the oath to
them when they swore it or in general displaying outright hostility in
such circumstances. [**66**] Someone who is a chorus producer, men of
Athens, and does all these things and things like them while carried
away by ambition has some excuse. But for a person to do these things
out of malice while deliberately harassing someone at every opportu-

---

[119] Philostratus was a wealthy Athenian; see MacDowell 1990: 284. This is his
only known political activity, but he is later called a politician (Dem. 42.21).

[120] On Chabrias, see Dem. 20.75–86 and the notes there.

[121] Oropos was a town on the border between Attica and Boeotia. The Athenians lost it to the Thebans in 366 (Dem. 18.99; Aes. 3.85; Xen. *Hellenica* 7.4.1;
Diodorus 15.76.1). Chabrias and Callistratus were prosecuted for betraying the
town. See Plut. *Demosthenes* 5; Arist. *Rhetoric* 1364a, 1411b6–7.

[122] The tripods commemorating Philostratus' victory are mentioned at Dem.
42.22. For a possible fragment of these tripods, see *IG* ii² 3055 and *SEG* 19.194.

nity and showing that his personal influence is greater than the laws, by Heracles, this conduct is oppressive, and it is certainly neither just nor to your advantage. Suppose that each person who leads a chorus could clearly expect the following treatment: "If I have so-and-so as an enemy, whether Meidias or some other man equally arrogant and wealthy, first I will have my victory taken away even if I compete more successfully than someone else, and then I will be always put in a weak position and continually humiliated." Who is so lacking in common sense or so pathetic that he would willingly choose to spend a single drachma? Certainly no one.

[**67**] On the contrary, I think that what makes all men eager to win honor and willing to spend money is this: each man believes that in a democracy he has a share of equality and justice. I was deprived of these rights, men of Athens, because of this man. Apart from the outrages I suffered, I also had victory stolen from me as well. I will clearly show all of you that without committing any outrage or abuse or hitting me, Meidias could have annoyed me, displayed to you his ambition, and obeyed the laws—and I would not now be able even to open my mouth about him. [**68**] When I agreed in the Assembly to be chorus producer for Pandionis, men of Athens, he should have stood up and at that time agreed on his part to serve for Erechtheis, his own tribe, placing himself on the same level and spending money just as I did, and should have taken victory away from me in this way. He should not have committed such outrage and hit me, not even then. [**69**] But as it was, he did not do the thing that would have demonstrated his respect for the people, nor did he show his youthful exuberance in this way. Whatever my motive, men of Athens—if someone wants to consider it madness (perhaps it is madness to do something beyond one's means) or a desire for honor that I agreed to serve as chorus leader—I was the one whom this man followed around and insulted so openly and in such a foul manner that in the end, he did not keep his hands off the sacred garments, or the chorus, or even my own person.[123]

[**70**] Now if any of you, men of Athens, does not feel the kind

---

[123] Dionysius of Halicarnassus (*Demosthenes* 9) quotes this section as an example of Demosthenes' use of parentheses to create a style that is "overwrought" (*periergos*), "unusual" (*asynēthēs*), and "outlandish" (*exēllagmenē*).

of anger one does when a man deserves to die, he is mistaken.[124] It is neither just nor right for the caution shown by the victim to contribute toward saving a man who has made no attempt to rein in his insolence. Instead, it is right to punish the latter for being guilty of all sorts of intolerable behavior and to repay the former by helping him. [71] Nor again can you claim that since nothing terrible has ever happened as a result of actions like these, I am now using words to exaggerate what he did and make it sound terrifying. Far from it. On the contrary, all men know (if not all, then at least many) the story of the young Euthynus, the once famous wrestler, and Sophilus the pancratiast; he was a strong man with a dark complexion. I am sure that some of you know whom I mean. During some gathering, a private party, Euthynus hit him back, because he thought he was insulting him, and with such force that he actually killed him.[125] Many people know Euaeon, the brother of Leodamas,[126] who killed Boeotus at a banquet, a public gathering, because of a single blow. [72] It was not the blow that aroused his anger, but the humiliation. Being beaten is not what is terrible for free men (although it is terrible), but being beaten with the intent to insult. A man who strikes may do many things, men of Athens, but the victim may not be able to describe to someone else even one of these things: the way he stands, the way he looks, his tone of voice, when he strikes to insult, when he acts like an enemy, when he punches, when he strikes him in the face.[127] When men are not used to being insulted, this is what stirs them up, this is what drives them to distraction. No one, men of Athens, could by reporting these

[124] Accusers ask the judges to show anger toward the defendant only in public speeches and in private speeches in which there is a vital matter of public interest. See Rubinstein 2004.

[125] In the Greek there is some ambiguity as to who was the killer and who was the victim. See MacDowell 1990: 288. Euthynus and Sophilus are not mentioned in other sources.

[126] Euaeon is not otherwise known, but his brother Leodamas may be the politician mentioned at Dem. 20.146–147.

[127] Longinus (*On the Sublime* 20) admires this passage for its combination of asyndeton (absence of conjunctions), anaphora (repetition of words), and diatyposis (vivid description). "By these words the orator produces the same effect as the assailant—he strikes the mind of the judges by the swift succession of blow on blow" (trans. Roberts).

actions convey to his audience the terrible effect of outrage in the exact way that it really and truly appears to the victim and those who witness it. **[73]** Consider, by Zeus and the gods, men of Athens, think and calculate in your own mind how much more anger I was likely to have felt when Meidias did things like this than Euaion did then, the man who killed Boeotus. He was struck by an acquaintance, and that man was drunk, in front of six or seven men, and those men were acquaintances who were going to blame one man for what he did and praise the other for holding back and restraining himself. Besides, this happened when he went to a house for dinner, a place where he did not have to go. **[74]** I, on the other hand, was the victim of outrage at the hands of an enemy who was sober, in the morning, acting to humiliate me not under the influence of wine, in front of many people, both foreigners and citizens, and this happened in a shrine where as a chorus leader, I was under a strong obligation to go. Because of good sense or rather good fortune, I think, men of Athens, I decided to hold back and not get carried away to do any irreparable damage; but I have much sympathy for Euaeon and all men if someone has been the victim of outrage and has come to his own rescue. **[75]** I think that many of the men who judged the case at the time also shared my opinion. In fact, according to what I personally hear, he was convicted by a single vote, and this happened without him shedding any tears or begging any of the judges or doing anything at all, large or small, to make the judges sympathetic to him. So let us draw the following conclusion: on the one hand, the judges who decided against him voted to convict not because he struck back but because he struck back in such a way that he actually killed him; on the other, those who voted to acquit allowed an extreme amount of retaliation to a man who was the victim of physical indignity.[128] **[76]** What follows then? I have acted so cautiously to prevent any irreparable damage from being done that I did not even strike back; from whom should I receive revenge for the wrongs that I have suffered? From you and the laws, I think. This case

---

[128]The charge was deliberate homicide and would have been tried at the Areopagus (*Ath. Pol.* 57.3). *Pace* MacDowell 1990: 292–293, it was not a case of just (*dikaios*) homicide, which would have been tried at the Delphinion. Euaeon was not defending himself, because he could have left the house without striking back, but retaliating for an insult. See E. M. Harris 1992: 78. For an analysis of the split verdict, see E. M. Harris 2004b: 11–12.

indeed should serve as an example that one should not strike back in
the heat of anger at all men who commit outrage and are abusive, but
bring them before you because you are the men who maintain and
preserve the protections for victims provided by the laws.

[77] Now, I imagine that some of you are eager to hear about the
quarrel we have with each other,[129] for these men think that no one
in the world would treat a citizen with such abuse and such violence
unless there was some important matter that he owed him for in the
past. I certainly want to tell you also about this quarrel from the beginning so you will realize that he clearly deserves to be punished for these
incidents as well. My account of these events will be brief, even if I
decide to start from long ago. [78] When I brought my action against
my guardians to recover my father's property, I was just a mere boy;[130]
I was not even aware of this man's existence, nor did I know him—and
I wish that I still did not! On about the third or fourth day before the
trial was set to begin, this man and his brother burst into our house as
part of their challenge to me to undertake a trierarchy.[131] Thrasylochus
reported my name and lodged the challenge, but everything was done
and carried out by this man.[132] [79] First, they smashed in the doors to

[129] In a modern court the background to the case is usually not considered
pertinent to the legal issue. As Rhodes 2004: 155 notes, however, in Athenian law
"when the case currently before the court was one item in a long and compli-
cated dispute, it was accepted as within the bounds of relevance not to limit
oneself to the current case but to set that case in the context of the dispute as a
whole." Here the account of the quarrel shows that Meidias struck Demosthenes
with deliberate intent and not only on a sudden whim and that his assault thus
fitted into a pattern of abusive behavior. This was necessary to prove to obtain a
conviction for *hybris*.

[130] Demosthenes was eight years old when his father died (see E. M. Harris
1989: 124–125). His father's property was placed in the hands of his guardians
Aphobus, Demophon, and Therippides (Dem. 27.13–15, 29.45). When Demosthenes reached the age of majority in 367/6, he received only a fraction of his father's property. He therefore brought a suit against his guardians in 364/3 (Dem.
30.15–17). The cases that he brought against them are the subject of Dem. 27–31.

[131] For the challenge (*antidosis*) brought by Meidias' brother Thrasylochus, see
Dem. 28.17. For the *antidosis* procedure, see Dem. 20.40 with note 68.

[132] Demosthenes' version here of Thrasylochus' actions is markedly different
from that given at Dem. 28.17 in 364/3. In the earlier version, Demosthenes says

our rooms—as if they already belonged to them as a result of the property exchange! Next, in front of my sister, who was still living at home then and was a young girl, they repeatedly shouted disgraceful words of the sort that men like this shout (no one could induce me to repeat to you any of the things they said), and they were uttering insults, speakable and unspeakable, at my mother, at me, and at all of us. But what was most shocking was not what they said but what they finally did. They were trying to have the suit against my guardians dropped on the grounds that the property belonged to them.[133] [**80**] Although these events took place long ago, I think that many of you remember them all the same. The entire city knew about the challenge and their plot at the time and their abusive behavior. I was completely without resources and a very young man. To avoid losing the property held by my guardians, and hoping to recover not the amount I was able to get turned over but everything I knew had been taken from me, I gave them twenty minas—this was the price that they paid someone to perform the trierarchy. These are the acts of outrage these men committed against me at that time.

[**81**] Later, I brought an action for slander against this man and won a judgment by default because he did not appear.[134] Although he

that he barred Thrasylochus from his property after receiving the challenge, then decided to perform the trierarchy himself to avoid a trial and does not mention Meidias' involvement. Here he claims that Thrasylochus and Meidias invaded his house and that he paid Thrasylochus twenty minas to hire out the trierarchy. Demosthenes has obviously altered the story considerably in the later version and has invented details to slander Meidias. It is certainly suspicious that no witnesses are provided to corroborate this later account. *Pace* MacDowell 1990: 297, the two versions are markedly different and cannot be reconciled. See E. M. Harris 2005: 137–138.

[133] If Demosthenes had been forced to accept the exchange of property, his father's estate would have passed into the hands of Thrasylochus, and he would not have been able to recover what his guardians had embezzled from his inheritance.

[134] There was a private suit for slander, which could be brought against those who falsely accused someone of murder, beating their father or mother, or throwing away his shield in battle. See Lys. 10.6–9. On this charge, see Loomis 2003. Demosthenes probably brought the charge because Meidias claimed that he had killed Nicodemus; see 105. His actions during the *antidosis* were not suitable for this charge (*pace* MacDowell 1990: 300).

did not pay in time and still has not paid, I never touched any of his property, but despite bringing another suit for ejectment, I have not yet even today been able to bring the case to trial.[135] This man always evades me by finding so many tricks and excuses. And yet I consider it right to do everything carefully, justly, and according to the laws. But this man, as you hear, thought it necessary to outrage not only me and my family abusively but also the members of my tribe because of me. [82] To show then that I am speaking the truth, call for me the witnesses of these events so that you know that before obtaining justice under the laws for the wrongs he did me earlier, I have been the victim of the kind of outrages you have just heard about.[136]

[TESTIMONY]

We, Callisthenes of Sphettus, Diognetus of Thoricus, and Mnesitheus of Alopeke, know that Demosthenes, for whom we are testifying, brought a suit for ejectment against Meidias, who is being prosecuted in public by Demosthenes, that the case was decided eight years ago, and that Meidias has been responsible for the entire delay by always making excuses and seeking postponement.

[83] Well then, men of Athens, hear what he did about the lawsuit and observe his insolence and arrogance in each case.[137] For this lawsuit (I mean the one that I won against him) I had Strato of Phaleron as an arbitrator, a poor man, inexperienced, but otherwise not a scoundrel and actually quite honest. These are the very qualities that have destroyed the poor man in a way that was neither right nor just, but quite disgraceful. [84] This man Strato was our arbitrator when the appointed day arrived and all the legal means had been exhausted,

---

[135] On the suit for ejectment, see 44 and the note there.

[136] This document is regarded as spurious because it contains two non–Attic forms. See MacDowell 1990: 320. There is a Mnesitheus of Alopeke attested on a *horos* from this period (see *Hesperia* 35, 1966, 277, no. 4), but this does not indicate that the document is genuine.

[137] This is the most detailed account of official arbitration in Athens. All private cases were submitted to the four judges of the defendant's tribe, who assigned the case to an arbitrator (*diaitetes*) drawn from a panel of citizens in their sixtieth year. See *Ath. Pol.* 53.5 with Rhodes 1981: 587–596.

motions for delay and objections to the charge,[138] and there was nothing more left. At first he asked me to adjourn the arbitration, then to delay it to the next day. Finally, because I was not yielding, and this man did not show up, and the hour was late, Strato made his decision against him.[139] [85] When it was already evening and dark, this man Meidias went to the office of the magistrates[140] and caught the magistrates on their way out; Strato had already left after giving a decision by default, as I learned from one of the men who were present. Well, at first, Meidias had the nerve to try to persuade him to report the decision that he had decided against him at the arbitration as one in his favor and to have the officials change the record, and he tried to give them fifty drachmas. [86] Because those men were getting annoyed by what he was doing and he was not persuading either of them, he threatened and insulted them—and then what does he do after he leaves? Just look at how malicious he is: he brought a suit to reverse the judgment, then did not swear the oath, and allowed the judgment to stand, and he was reported as not having sworn the oath.[141] Wishing to escape the inevitable, he waits for the arbitrators' last day in office,[142] when one of the arbitrators shows up but another does not. [87] He

---

[138] "If a litigant was unable to attend a trial or arbitration, he could apply for a postponement, sending a relative or a friend to swear an oath that he was ill or absent from Attika" (MacDowell 1990: 305). Some scholars have argued that the "objections to the charge" (*paragraphai*) were motions to postpone the arbitration similar to the motion for postponement, but the word probably has its normal meaning and refers to an action brought by the defendant charging that the accuser was bringing his case in an illegal manner. See MacDowell 1990: 306–308.

[139] The arbitrator normally held a preliminary meeting with litigants (Dem. 54.29), then set a date on which to hear the case and render a verdict. This passage indicates that this date could be postponed only with the mutual consent of the litigants.

[140] These were the judges of the tribe.

[141] If an arbitrator gave a judgment against a defendant who was absent, the latter could swear an oath that he could not attend and ask for the judgment to be overturned. According to Demosthenes, Meidias asked to have the judgment canceled, but did not swear the oath, with the result that the arbitrator's decision remained binding. See MacDowell 1990: 309–310.

[142] The manuscripts add the phrase "which was in Thargelion or Skirophorion," the last months of the Attic year, but MacDowell 1990: 310, followed by Dilts, suggests that this is an intrusive gloss.

persuades the one who is presiding to take a vote without writing the name of a single witness on the written charge—which is in violation of all the laws—then he brings a charge against Strato in his absence without anyone present[143] and has him thrown out and makes him lose his rights.[144] And so, just because Meidias had to pay a judgment by default, an Athenian has lost his entire stake in the community and completely lost his rights. It is not at all safe, it seems, to bring an action if one is wronged or to act as an arbitrator for Meidias or even to walk on the same street!

[88] Here then is the way that you should look at this issue: consider what happened to Meidias that made him plot to exact such a savage retribution for actions done by a man who was a citizen. If it was something truly awful and unusual, you ought to feel some sympathy for him, but if it was nothing, look at the brutality and savagery with which he treats everyone he meets. What then happened to him? "By Zeus, he had to pay a large judgment, one so large that he would lose his property." But the judgment was only a thousand drachmas.[145] [89] "Yes, certainly," someone might say, "but the fact that it is unjust for him to pay irritates him, and because he felt wronged, he happened to forget that he missed his payment." On the contrary, he realized it that very same day—which is the greatest indication that Strato did nothing wrong—and he had not yet paid a single drachma. [90] But more about that later. Of course, he could have brought an action to reverse the judgment and kept the dispute just against me, his original adversary in the lawsuit. But he did not want to do this. No! Just so that Meidias could avoid contesting a lawsuit for the fixed sum of ten minas, which he failed to show up for

---

[143] When an accuser presented his summons to the defendant, he had to bring two witnesses (*kleteres*). If the defendant failed to answer the summons, these witnesses would testify that it had been served. See Harrison 1971: 85.

[144] A charge against an arbitrator was brought before all the other arbitrators. If the arbitrator was convicted, he had the right to appeal his case to a court. The penalty for conviction was loss of citizen rights. See *Ath. Pol.* 53.6 with Rhodes 1981: 595–596.

[145] Normally, the penalty for conviction in a suit for slander was five hundred drachmas (Lys. 10.12; Isoc. 20.3). For possible reasons why it may have been double in this case, see MacDowell 1990: 300.

when required, and, if guilty, could avoid paying a penalty, or, if innocent, could be acquitted, an Athenian had to lose his rights without obtaining pardon, or the chance to speak, or any fairness, all of which are granted even to men who are actually guilty.[146] [91] But even after he deprived the man whom he wanted of his rights, and you did Meidias this favor,[147] and he fulfilled the shameful plan that he chose for that task, and accomplished those goals, has he paid off the judgment that led him to destroy this man? Even today he has not yet paid a penny but is allowing himself to stand trial in an ejectment suit. One man has lost his rights and been completely ruined, yet the other has suffered nothing at all, and turns upside down the laws, the arbitrators, everything that he likes. [92] Moreover, he has made the decision against the arbitrator, which he deceitfully won without issuing a summons, binding to profit himself, but the judgment that he had to pay after receiving a summons,[148] in full knowledge, and without contesting it, he gets reversed![149] And yet if this man considers it right to punish so severely an arbitrator who issued a decision against him by default, what kind of penalty is it right for you to impose on this man who flagrantly breaks your laws and commits outrage? If loss of rights and being stripped of all recourse to the laws and legal procedures and everything else is an appropriate punishment for that man's offense, death is clearly a small punishment for his outrage. [93] Now

---

[146] Although the judges swore to decide according to the laws, they could take extenuating circumstances into consideration. This was "fairness" exercised in exceptional cases. It should not be equated with the modern concept of "jury nullification." On *epieikeia*, see E. M. Harris 2004b.

[147] Demosthenes alludes to Strato's appeal of his conviction by the arbitrators to the court and his failure to overturn the decision. As MacDowell 1990: 314 notes, "This fact, which D. has almost but not completely concealed, makes his whole complaint that Meidias treated Strato unfairly a good deal less convincing."

[148] Normally, the summons was issued by the accuser to the defendant, requiring him to appear before a magistrate, but here it seems to refer to the notice given by Strato to Meidias about the date of his decision in the arbitration. See MacDowell 1990: 315–316.

[149] Demosthenes appears to assume that Strato's conviction did not overturn his verdict against Meidias.

then, to show that I speak the truth, call for me the witnesses to these events and read the law about the arbitrators.[150]

[TESTIMONY]

We, Nicostratus of Myrrhine and Phanias of Aphidna, know that Demosthenes, for whom we are testifying, and Meidias, the man who is charged by Demosthenes, chose Strato as arbitrator when Demosthenes brought an action for slander against him; when the day appointed by law arrived, Meidias did not appear at the arbitration but forfeited it. When a judgment by default was entered against Meidias, we know that Meidias attempted to persuade Strato and us, who were in office at the time, to change the verdict of the arbitration for him and to give us fifty drachmas; when we did not yield, he threatened us and in this way departed. We also know that Strato was convicted by Meidias and lost his rights as a citizen in violation of all the principles of justice.

[94] Read also the law about arbitrators.[151]

[LAW]

If any persons have a dispute about private transactions and wish to select any arbitrator whatsoever, let it be permitted for them to select whomever they wish. After they jointly select one, let them abide by what this man decides and let them not transfer the same charges to another court, but let the decision of the arbitrator remain binding.

---

[150] This testimony is a forgery. It contains three non-Attic forms or expressions (*oidamen, kakēgoriou, katabrabeuthenta*) and mistakenly assumes that public arbitrators were selected by litigants, not by lot. See MacDowell 1990: 316–317.

[151] Public arbitration was introduced in 400/399 (see MacDowell 1971), but this law refers to private arbitration. The document contains the late forms of the imperative (*menetōsan, metapheretōsan*) and other errors. See MacDowell 1990: 317–318.

[95] Call also Strato himself, who was the victim of these crimes. He will surely be permitted to stand up.[152]

This man, men of Athens, is perhaps poor, but he is certainly not a bad person. Yet although he was a citizen, had served on all the campaigns when he was eligible,[153] and had never done anything terrible, this man stands now in silence, deprived not only of other common privileges but even of the right to speak or express his grief. He is not even allowed to tell you whether what happened to him was just or unjust. [96] This is what he suffered at the hands of Meidias and Meidias' wealth and arrogance because of his poverty and isolation, one man in a crowd. If he had broken the law and accepted the fifty drachmas from Meidias, then reported the judgment entered against him as one decided in his favor, he would have kept his rights and shared without any disadvantages equal privileges as the rest of you. But, because he paid more attention to justice than to Meidias and feared the laws more than this man's threats, he has fallen into such a deep and serious misfortune thanks to this man. [97] If this man is so brutal and insensitive and inflicts such an enormous punishment for injustices that he only claims to have suffered (in fact, he has suffered no wrong), will you acquit him after catching him committing abuse against a citizen? Will you not convict him when he shows no concern for the festival, the sacred rites, the law, or anything else? [98] Won't you make an example out of him? What will you say, men of the court? What honest or respectable reason, by the gods, will you be able to offer? By Zeus, that he is abusive and disgusting? That is certainly true. But, men of Athens, you surely ought to hate such men, not protect them. Or because he is wealthy? But I dare say you will find that this is the very reason for his insolence; it is more appropriate therefore to take away the assets that make him abusive rather than to save him because of them. If you allow this sort of bold

---

[152] A person who was disenfranchised was not allowed to address the court. See [Dem.] 59.26–27.

[153] All Athenians eligible for military service could be called for duty until the age of 59, after which they could serve as public arbitrators. See *Ath. Pol.* 53.4–5 with Rhodes 1981: 591–593.

and disgusting person to retain control of such a large sum of money, you are giving him assets to be used against you.

[**99**] What else then is left? Pitying him, by Zeus. He will place his children next to him and weep and in these ways beg for acquittal.[154] This is what is left. But surely you know that it is right to pity the victims of some injustice that they will not be able to endure, not those who are being punished for the terrible things that they have done.[155] Who would justly pity those children when he sees that this man showed no pity for that man's children,[156] who, apart from the rest of their misfortunes, see no support for their father in his misfortune? There is no debt that this man here must pay to regain his rights. On the contrary, he has completely lost his rights just like that through the sheer force of Meidias' rage and insolence. [**100**] Who then will stop committing outrage and lose the wealth that makes him do these things if you are going to take pity on this man as if he were the victim of terrible crimes, but when some indigent man who has done nothing wrong but has suffered the worst misfortune because of this man, you are not going to share his anger toward him?[157] Do not do this. No one who feels no pity for anyone has a right to be pitied; no one who feels no sympathy has a right to obtain sympathy. [**101**] In my opinion, all men consider it right in everything they do to make contributions to a charitable fund (*eranos*) to benefit their own lives.[158] For instance, suppose I am this kind of man, moderate

---

[154] For the practice of bringing one's family into court to ask for pity, see Lys. 20.34–35; And. 1.148; Aes. 2.179. The practice is parodied by Aristophanes in his *Wasps* 976–984.

[155] An appeal to pity was not a request to ignore the law because the Athenians believed that only those who were innocent deserved to be pitied. See Konstan 2000.

[156] The children of Strato.

[157] I.e., share Strato's anger.

[158] I have translated the Greek word *eranos* as "charitable fund." Originally, the term *eranos* referred to a common meal that was held either for conviviality or as part of a religious celebration. The distinctive feature of this kind of meal was that each of the participants recompensed the host for his generosity either by bringing a contribution to the meal (*eranos*) or by later taking his turn in offering a meal to the group. This practice gave rise to clubs called *eranoi*. As early as the fifth

in my dealings with everyone, capable of pity, who does many people favors. If some crisis or time of need comes upon a man like this, all men ought to make a similar contribution to him. Take another man: this one is violent and shows no pity to others, whom he does not even treat as human beings. It is right for this man to receive similar contributions from everyone else. Because you have indeed collected these sorts of contributions for yourself, you certainly deserve to receive its payments.[159]

[**102**] Well then, men of Athens, I think that even if I had no other charge to make against Meidias, and the charges I am about to make were no more astonishing than those I have already made, on the basis of what has already been said you would be justified in convicting him and assessing the ultimate penalty for him.[160] But the case certainly does not stop here, and I do not believe that I will be at a loss for charges to make, given such a generous supply of reasons he has given me to accuse him. [**103**] I will pass over the fact that he trumped up a public charge of desertion[161] against me and hired this disgusting and quite unscrupulous man, the filthy Euctemon, to do this.[162] For neither did that blackmailer show up at the prelimi-

---

century BCE, however, the term acquired another meaning and could also denote a loan of money collected from several individuals, usually relatives and friends (e.g., [Dem.] 59.31; Ant. 2.2.9) or from a group of people such as an *eranos* club. An *eranos* loan appears to have generally been given to friends and relatives in need. That is probably why we never find interest being charged for an *eranos* loan. For a brief summary with references to earlier literature, see E. M. Harris 2006a: 335–336.

[159] The *plerotes* was one who collected the contributions for the *eranos* and exacted repayment, not (*pace* MacDowell 1990: 323) a contributor. See E. M. Harris 2006a: 335, 352–353.

[160] This passage reveals that Demosthenes brought a *graphe* against Meidias where the court voted first about guilt, then about the penalty (*timema*).

[161] There was a *graphe* against cowardice (*deilia*) (Aes. 3.175–176; Lys. 14.5–7), which covered three main offenses: failure to report for military duty (*astrateia*), leaving one's position in battle (*lipotaxion*), and throwing away one's shield (And. 1.74). See E. M. Harris 2004a: 256–258. The penalty was complete loss of citizen rights (Dem. 15.32).

[162] The identity of Euctemon is uncertain; see MacDowell 1990: 325–326.

nary hearing, nor did this man hire him for any other reason than to have everyone see a notice displayed in front of the Eponymous Heroes[163] stating "Euctemon of Lousia indicted Demosthenes on a charge of desertion." If it were in any way possible, I think he would gladly have added that Meidias hired him to bring the charge. But I will let this go. Because that man did not bring his case to court and therefore made himself lose his rights,[164] I ask for no further penalty, but consider this punishment enough. **[104]** But I will tell you something he has done which I for one think is terrible and awful, men of Athens, not just a crime but an act of sacrilege affecting the entire community. After the wretched and miserable Aristarchus, the son of Moschus, found himself facing a pernicious and difficult charge, men of Athens, at first Meidias went around the marketplace and dared to tell blasphemous and terrible stories about me, that I was the one who committed this crime.[165] When he was getting nowhere with this tactic, he approached the men who were bringing the charge of murder against him, the relatives of the deceased,[166] and promised to give them money if they were to charge me with the crime. Not letting the gods or a sense of piety or anything else stand in his way, he showed no hesitation at all in making this allegation. **[105]** In front of the men that he spoke to he showed no shame about bringing a vicious charge like this, one so devastating, without any justification, but he set himself one goal, to destroy me by any means. He thought

---

[163] For the statues of the Eponymous Heroes, see Dem. 20.94n.

[164] The penalty for failure to follow through a public case was a fine of 1,000 drachmas and the loss of the right to bring public cases. See E. M. Harris 2006a: 407–408, correcting MacDowell 1990: 327–328.

[165] It is impossible to separate gossip from fact in Demosthenes' and Aeschines' stories about Aristarchus. In his speech *Against Timarchus*, Aeschines (1.170–173) alleges that Demosthenes became Aristarchus' lover and persuaded him to kill Nicodemus. After Aristarchus went into exile, Demosthenes embezzled three talents given to pay for his living expenses. In a later speech, Aeschines (2.148, 166) repeats these charges and adds that Nicodemus accused Demosthenes of desertion and this was the reason why he was killed, but says nothing about Meidias' role in the affair. For discussion, see MacDowell 1990: 328–330.

[166] A charge of homicide was a private suit, which could only be brought by the relatives of the victim. See Tulin 1996.

he must leave no stone unturned but had to drive out and destroy any victim of his abuse who saw fit to seek justice and did not keep silent, not leaving him alone, but convicting him on a charge of desertion or bringing him to court for murder and all but crucifying him.[167] Yet when he is proven to have committed these crimes in addition to his outrages against me while I was chorus producer, what sympathy or pity does he deserve to receive from you? [106] I think that he has actually murdered me by these tactics, both earlier at the Dionysia when he inflicted abuse on my equipment and on my person and everything I spent money for, and now by all his deeds and actions and everything else, he has abused my city, my family, my privileges, my hopes. If he had succeeded with just one of his plots against me, I would have been robbed of everything and would not be allowed to be buried at home.[168] For what reason, judges? If the victim of Meidias' illegal abuse who tries to defend himself faces the prospect of suffering this and other similar treatment, it will be best not to resist but to kowtow before those who abuse us just as the barbarians do.[169] [107] So then, to show that I speak the truth and that this disgusting and shameless man has committed these crimes too, call for me the witnesses of these events.[170]

[*WITNESSES*]

We, Dionysius of Aphidna and Antiphilus of Paiania, carried through a charge of murder against Aristarchus after our relative Nicodemus perished by a violent death at the hands of Aristarchus.

---

[167] One method of executing criminals was to nail them to a board. See MacDowell 1963: 111–113.

[168] Those who committed serious crimes were denied burial in Attica. See Xen. *Hellenica* 1.7.22; Lyc. *Against Leocrates* 113. This should not be confused with complete denial of burial, which was against the established laws of the Greeks. See E. M. Harris 2006a: 65–67.

[169] Among the Persians it was customary for inferiors to prostrate themselves before superiors (Herod. 1.134), but the Greeks found the practice abhorrent (Herod. 7.136.1; Arist. *Rhetoric* 1361a36). See Frye 1972. For Greek attitudes to the practice, see Bosworth 1988: 284–287.

[170] This document is another forgery. See MacDowell 1990: 333.

When Meidias, the man brought to trial by Demosthenes, for whom we are testifying, saw this, he tried to persuade us to let Aristarchus go free and to change the charge[171] and bring it against Demosthenes by offering some coppers.[172]

Come, get for me also the law about gifts.

[108] During the time it takes him to get the law, I wish to say a few words to you, men of Athens, and, by Zeus and the gods, to make a request of you, men of the court. Listen to everything you hear with this thought in mind: what would each of you do if he were the victim of these crimes? How angry would your sufferings make you feel toward your abuser? Although I found it hard to endure the abuse that I suffered during my liturgy, I have found it far more difficult, men of Athens, to put up with what happened after that, which made me even more angry. [109] What could someone say that truly goes beyond this level of malice, what exceeds the shamelessness, brutality, and insolence of someone who, after committing many terrible acts of injustice, by Zeus, instead of making amends and showing remorse, would later go on committing other more terrible crimes and to use his wealth not in ways that somehow improve his personal affairs without harming anyone, but the very opposite, in ways that make him congratulate himself for his superiority in driving someone unjustly into exile and vilifying him?

[110] Well now, men of Athens, this man has done all these things to me. For example, he brought a false charge against me that has nothing to do with me, as the facts themselves have made clear. He indicted me for desertion after having himself left the ranks three times.[173] And as for the debacle in Euboea that his host and friend Plutarch brought about (I almost forgot to mention this), he tried to make out that I was the one responsible, before it became obvious

---

[171] The word here is *graphe*, the term for a public charge, but homicide was a private charge.

[172] The term used here (*kermata*) is colloquial and out of place in a formal document.

[173] It was Euctemon who actually brought the charge; see 103. Demosthenes discusses Meidias' desertion at 162–164; it is obvious that no one ever prosecuted him for this offense.

to everyone that the situation came about because of Plutarch. [**111**] Finally, when I was selected by lot to serve in the Council[174] and was having my qualifications examined,[175] he made accusations against me, and my position became extremely dangerous. Instead of obtaining justice for what had happened to me, I was in danger of being punished for something that had nothing to do with me. During this ordeal, when I was being harassed in the way that I have just now been describing to you, I was not able to perform my duty, men of Athens, even though I am not completely without friends or lacking in resources. [**112**] Perhaps I need to say something about this too right now: in comparison to the wealthy, the rest of us do not share equal rights and access to the laws, men of Athens; we do not share them, no.[176] These men are given the dates to stand trial that they want, and their crimes come before you stale and cold, but if anything happens to the rest of us, each has his case served up fresh. These men have witnesses ready to testify and well-trained men all available to speak with them and against us.[177] Yet, as you can see in my case, a few men are not willing even to give truthful testimony.[178] [**113**] Well, someone could wear himself out shedding tears over this, but read for me next in order the law, just as I began. Read it.[179]

---

[174] Demosthenes served in the Council in 347/6. See Aes. 2.17, 3.62; Dem. 19.154.

[175] For the *dokimasia* of officials, see Dem. 20.90n.

[176] Demosthenes gives the impression that he was not among the wealthiest men in Athens, but in reality his fortune was one of the largest. For his property, see Davies 1971: 126–139.

[177] For supporting speakers, see Rubinstein 2000. It was illegal to accept payment for being a supporting speaker (Dem. 42.26), but Demosthenes suggests Meidias' supporters did so.

[178] One could bring an action for failure to testify (*lipomarturion*) against a witness who agreed to testify then did not (Dem. 49.19). One could also issue a summons to a witness who did attend. If he refused, he was subject to a fine of 1,000 drachmas. See Carey 1995.

[179] This law differs from other contemporary laws on bribery and may be spurious like the other laws inserted into this speech. See, however, MacDowell (1983), who argues that this is a sixth-century law because it contains the older form of *atimia*. Yet there is no reason to believe that such a law would have been

[*LAW*]

If any Athenian receives from someone, or he himself gives to another, or corrupts some people by making promises, to bring harm to the people or privately to some citizen, in any way or manner, let him and his children and property be deprived of his rights.

[**114**] This man is so impious, so foul, so ready to stoop to say or do anything—whether it be true or false, against an enemy or a friend, and so on, he makes no distinction at all—that even after accusing me of murder and bringing such a serious charge, he still allowed me to conduct the inaugural rites for the Council[180] and to conduct the sacrifice and to preside over the rituals for you and the entire city, [**115**] then allowed me to head the sacred delegation sent out on behalf of the city and lead it to Nemean Zeus,[181] and did not stop me from being elected out of all Athenians along with two others to serve as *hieropoios* for the August Goddesses[182] and to preside over their rites. If there were a shred or shadow of truth in any of the charges that he was trumping up against me, would he have allowed these things to happen?[183] I do not think so. These facts certainly prove that he is trying to have me exiled from our country with the clear aim of humiliating me.

---

preserved in the Metroon after the revision of the laws in 400. Besides, the law contains no Archaic forms or terms similar to other laws from this period. Cf. Lys. 10.15–20.

[180] These rites would have been held in the summer of 347 when the new Council came into office. See Rhodes 1972: 130. If Meidias had actually charged him with murder, Demosthenes would not have been permitted to sacrifice. See Dem. 20.158n. For the religious role of public officials, see E. M. Harris 2006a: 54–55 and Parker 2005: 96–97.

[181] The *architheoros* led a delegation of Athenians to one of the international festivals.

[182] The *hieropoios* was an official who carried out public sacrifices (*Ath. Pol.* 54.6–7). The August Goddesses were the Erinyes or Eumenides, who formed the chorus of Aeschylus' *Eumenides* and pursued Orestes for the murder of his mother. They had a shrine at the Areopagus (Thuc. 1.126.11; Pausanias 1.28.6).

[183] If Demosthenes had actually committed murder, he would have been polluted and thus ineligible to perform sacrifices. On pollution for homicide, see Parker 1983: 104–143.

[**116**] Now, when he was not able to make the charge stick against me—not one part of it despite all sorts of contortions—he now began to bring this malicious prosecution against Aristarchus, obviously because of me. I will not mention the other events except this one: when the Council was in session investigating this matter, he came forward and said, "You men in the Council, don't you realize what is going on? You have the murderer" (meaning Aristarchus) "yet you go on hesitating and investigating and acting like fools! Aren't you going to put him to death?[184] Won't you go into his house? Aren't you going to arrest him?"[185] [**117**] This is what this disgusting, shameless creature was saying. Yet he had just left Aristarchus' house the previous day and prior to that dealt with him the same way anyone else would have, and when things were going well for Aristarchus, he kept pestering me about reaching a settlement with this man. Yet even if he thought that Aristarchus had done any of the things responsible for his downfall, and he believed any of the allegations made by his accusers when he made these statements, he should not have acted this way. [**118**] When people think that a friend has committed some terrible crime, they impose a moderate penalty by no longer maintaining their friendship; punishment and legal proceedings, on the other hand, are left to victims and enemies. Still, let us forgive him for this. But if it becomes obvious that Meidias chatted with him under the same roof[186] as if he did nothing wrong but also slanders and accuses him with the aim of maliciously prosecuting me, does not justice demand that he die not ten, but ten thousand times? [**119**] So then to prove that I am speaking the truth and that he had entered his house and spoken with him the day before he said these things and then on the following day he went to his house again (nothing, men of Athens, nothing is filthier than this behavior)[187] and sat as close to him as this

---

[184]Citizens could not enter the houses of private citizens to carry out an arrest, but the Council could pass a decree instructing an official to do so. See E. M. Harris 1995: 172.

[185]The Council of 500 had the right to conduct investigations, but it did not have the power to execute men without trial. See Rhodes 1972: 179–180 ("Demosthenes is representing Meidias' conduct as outrageous . . .").

[186]A murderer could spread his pollution by sharing a roof with another person. See Parker 1983: 122, 336.

[187]"Unclean" because polluted through contact with a murderer.

and took his right hand in front of many people—after that speech in the Council in which he called Aristarchus a murderer and other most appalling things!—and he kept swearing oaths, calling down curses on his head that he had said nothing damaging about him and not caring about committing perjury even in the presence of people who knew the facts, and then asked him to bring about a settlement between me and himself, for all these events I am going to call for you witnesses who were present at these events. [**120**] Yet how is it not shocking, men of Athens, or rather impious, to call him a murderer, then turn around and deny on oath that he said this, to blame him for murder and share the same roof with him? Even if I let him go and betray the vote you cast against him, I am doing nothing wrong, it seems. But if I proceed with the case, I have deserted my post, I am an accomplice to murder, and I must be eliminated. Well, my opinion is quite the opposite: if I had let him go, I would have deserted the cause of justice, and I could plausibly have brought a charge of murder against myself. Had I done this, life would certainly not be worth living. [**121**] Now, to show that my account of these events is also true, call for me the witnesses to the events.[188]

[*TESTIMONY*]

We, Lysimachus of Alopeke, Demeas of Sounion, Chares of Thorikos, Philemon of Sphettos, and Moschus of Paiania, know that at the time when the report (*eisangelia*)[189] was made to the Council that Aristarchus, the son of Moschus, had killed Nicodemus, Meidias, the man charged by Demosthenes, for whom we are testifying, came into the Council and declared that no one other than Aristarchus was the one who murdered Nicodemus with his own hands, then advised the Council to go to Aristarchus' house and arrest him. He said these things to the Council after dining together with Aristarchus and us on the previous day. We also know

---

[188] This document contains a non-Attic form (*oidamen*) and is another forgery. See MacDowell 1990: 343–344.

[189] In this period, the procedure of *eisangelia* was used for offenses such as treason and bribery but not for homicide. See MacDowell 1978: 184–186.

that after making these statements, Meidias went out of the Council and returned to Aristarchus' house, and shook his right hand and swore destruction on himself that he had said nothing derogatory about him to the Council and asked Aristarchus to arrange a settlement between Demosthenes and himself.

[122] What could ever surpass this man's egregious behavior? What has or ever could equal it? This is a man who decided he should bring malicious charges against someone who was down on his luck but had done him no wrong (I pass over their friendship) at the same time that he was asking him to bring about a settlement with me! Yet while he was doing this, he was also spending money to have me as well as Aristarchus unjustly sent into exile!

[123] Yet practices and schemes like this, men of Athens, which involve heaping still more troubles on those who bring just cases to court to protect themselves, are not things that deserve my anger and indignation but should be ignored by the rest of you.[190] Far from it. All of you ought to feel as angry as I do when you take into account the following considerations, that those among you, men of Athens, who are the poorest and most vulnerable are also the most likely to be the victims of casual mistreatment, whereas these disgusting men who have money are the most likely to commit outrage and avoid punishment for their actions but retaliate by hiring men to cause trouble. [124] We must certainly not overlook behavior like this but realize that the person who uses fear and terror to stop any of us from punishing him for any wrongs that they suffered is doing nothing other than taking away the equality and freedom shared by all of us. To be sure, granted that I may have fended off his false allegations and malicious charges—or someone else might—and I have not been rubbed out. But what will the majority of you do if you do not publicly deter everyone from misusing his wealth for these purposes? [125] One should repel unjust attacks by giving an account of one's actions and by standing trial on any charges that might be brought before retaliating against his attackers, not by eliminating the accuser

---

[190] This section (123–127) forms a transition between the account of Meidias' wrongs against Demosthenes and the discussion of his offenses against other Athenians.

before the trial or trying to gain acquittal without a trial by bringing false charges. One should not chafe at paying the penalty but should refrain from any bullying from the beginning.

[126] You have heard, men of Athens, about all the acts of outrage that he committed against my liturgy and my person, and all the plots of every sort against me and the harm that I have managed to escape. Indeed, I am leaving many things out because it is perhaps not easy to recount everything. This is the situation: I am not the only one who has been wronged by what he did, but my tribe, a tenth part of you, was wronged along with me by the crimes committed against the chorus, and the laws, which keep each one of you safe, were also wronged by his acts of outrage and his plots against me. And the god for whom I had served as chorus leader was also wronged by all these crimes and the solemn and divine element of holiness whatever its precise nature.

[127] Those who wish to impose the correct penalty on this man in proportion to the crimes he committed should not be angry only because this matter concerns me but because it similarly affects the laws, the god, and the city, which have all been wronged together, and they should impose punishment in this way. They should also think about those who help him and are huddled at his side: they are not just speaking on his behalf, but they have stamped his crimes with their approval.[191]

[128] Now, if Meidias had otherwise behaved in a restrained and moderate way, had harmed no other citizen, and had been abusive and violent only toward me, first I would have counted this as just my own bad luck, and then I would be afraid that he might evade punishment for his acts of abuse against me by henceforth living a life conspicuously filled with moderation and kindness. [129] But as it is, he has committed so many other crimes like this against many of you that I have nothing to worry about on that score. On the contrary, I am afraid of the very opposite, namely, that after hearing about other victims of his many terrible crimes, some such thought as this might enter your minds: "What, then? Are you angry because you have suf-

---

[191]Demosthenes compares Meidias' henchmen with the public Tester (*doki-mastes*) of coinage, a public slave who examined coins to see if they were genuine or counterfeit. For the *dokimastes*, see Rhodes and Osborne 2003: no. 25.

fered more terribly than each of his other victims?" I would not be able to tell you all the things that this man has done—nor would you have the patience to hear about them. There would not be enough time even if our two portions of water still remained, both all of mine and his added to it.[192] So I will describe the most serious and best known incidents. [130] Or rather, I will do the following: I will have read out to you all the notes that I have written out for myself, and then I will discuss whatever you wish to hear first, then the next thing, and so on in the same way for as long as you are willing to listen. These are all sorts of crimes, many outrages, crimes against family and friends, and many acts of sacrilege against the gods—there is no area where you will find that he has not committed many crimes deserving death.

[NOTES ABOUT MEIDIAS' CRIMES]

[131] Now, these are all the things he has done, men of the court, to people he has run into at any given time. I have left out the other things. No one would be able to recount at one sitting all the acts of outrage that this man has repeatedly committed throughout his entire life. It is worth considering how arrogant he has become as a result of not being punished for any of these: he does not believe, it seems, that the kind of crime one individual commits against another is prestigious or dashing or impressive.[193] If he is not going to throw mud on an entire tribe, the Council, an entire class, and harass many of you altogether at the same time, he thought his life would not be worth living. [132] I will not mention the rest although I have thousands of things to speak about. But as for the cavalrymen who accompanied him on the expedition to Argoura,[194] all of you doubtless know what sort of public speeches he made about them before

---

[192] Speeches given in court were measured by a waterclock. In a public case, each litigant was allowed about 132 minutes. See Rhodes 1981: 719–728.

[193] The manuscripts read "worthy of death" (*axion thanatou*), but this makes no sense in the context and has been emended to "worthy of admiration" (*axion thaumatos*) by some editors, including MacDowell and Dilts. Others emend in different ways.

[194] Argoura was located in the territory of Chalcis near Eretria on the west coast of Euboea. Knoepfler 1981: 305, 308, locates it near the modern town of Lefkandi, in the eastern Lelantine plain, but see Tritle 1988: 188.

you after his return from the area near Chalcis, when he flung about accusations and charges that the departure of this expedition was a disgrace to the city. You remember the slurs about this that he made against Cratinus, who, as I discover, is going to support him.[195] A man who picks such a great quarrel for no reason with so many citizens *en bloc*—how much malice and arrogance must one think drives him to do it? [**133**] And yet, Meidias, who is the greater disgrace to the city? The men who crossed over [196] in an orderly fashion carrying the kind of equipment that is suitable for men who are going out to meet the enemy and fight alongside their allies? Or you, who prayed not to be selected among those sent out when you were in the lottery,[197] you, who never once put on a breastplate, but rode back from Euboea on a silver mule-chair,[198] carrying woolen cloaks, drinking cups, and wine jugs, items that the customs officers confiscated?[199] This story was reported to those of us serving in the infantry (we did not cross over to the same place these men did). [**134**] And so if Archetion [200] or someone else made a joke about this, would you give them all a hard time? If you did the things your companions in the cavalry said about you, Meidias, and which you accuse them of saying about you, you deserved your bad reputation. After all, you were doing an injustice to

---

[195] A scholion on the passage identifies Cratinus as the cavalry leader (*Hipparch*) on the expedition to Euboea. He may be the same person who moved several decrees in this period (*IG* ii² 109B, line 8; 134, line 6; 172, lines 3–4).

[196] I.e., the strait separating Euboea from Attica.

[197] There were ten cavalry units in the Athenian army, one for each tribe. When cavalry was needed on an expedition, a lottery was conducted to determine which units would serve. See MacDowell 1990: 351.

[198] The term used here is *astrabēs*, which was a saddle with a high back placed on a mule or donkey. A scholion says it was popular with women, and so Demosthenes may be trying to make Meidias look effeminate. Some manuscripts read "Argoura" instead of *argura* ("silver"), but this reading is unlikely.

[199] Lit. "the collectors of the one-fiftieth duty." The Athenians levied a duty of two percent on all imports and exports (for the similar tax on grain, see E. M. Harris 1999). Because Meidias was not equipped for battle, these officials thought that he had gone abroad to trade and confiscated his property when he did not declare it for import duties.

[200] Archetion is otherwise unknown.

them, these men here and to the entire city and covering them with shame. Yet if some people were trumping up false charges against you when you were innocent, and the rest of the soldiers were not criticizing them but rejoicing at your misfortune, then it is obvious that they thought that you deserved such a reputation for the other events in your life. In that case, you should have acted with greater moderation, not slandered them. [135] You threaten everyone; you harass everyone. You think that other people should consider whatever you want, but you yourself do not consider how you can avoid causing grief to other people. Indeed, the greatest and most shocking indication of his insolence, in my opinion at least, is the large number of men that, you filthy creature, you attacked all at once when you came forward. Who else would not have recoiled at the thought of acting this way?

[136] Now, when everyone else in the world is on trial, men of the court, I see them charged with one or two offenses, but they have an inexhaustible supply of arguments: "Which of you is aware that I have ever done something like this? Which of you has seen me doing things like this? It is not true—no, these men are telling lies about me out of personal malice: I am the victim of false testimony" and so on. For this man, however, it is just the opposite. [137] I believe that all of you know about his character, his brutal nature, and his arrogance, and I think some of you have been astonished for a long time by what you see for yourselves, not what you have just now heard from me. I also see that many of his victims are not willing to testify about all the wrongs that they suffered because they dread this man's violence, his tendency to meddle, and the resources, which make this despicable man here strong and intimidating. [138] When a man's evil and abusive nature is supported by power and wealth, this acts as a bulwark protecting against sudden attack. Should he be stripped of his possessions, he would perhaps not commit outrage, or, if he does after all, he will count less than the lowest in your eyes. In vain he will insult and scream, but he will be punished just like the rest of us if he becomes abusive. [139] As it is, I think Polyeuctus, Timocrates, and the swarthy Euctemon have acted as his shields.[201] These are the

---

[201] Polyeuctus was a politician who later in 347/6 moved a rider in a decree of honors for the rulers of the Bosporus; see Rhodes and Osborne 2003: no. 64,

sort of hirelings who surround him, and there are others in addition to these, an organized gang[202] of witnesses, who do not make trouble for you openly but very easily nod in silent approval at his lies. By the gods, they will not gain anything in my opinion from this man. But there are some, men of Athens, who are adept at being corrupted by the rich, following them around and testifying for them. [140] Each of the rest of you, I think, who lives as he can on his own resources, finds all this terrifying. For this reason, stand united! Each of you is rather weak in some way, whether in respect to friends, property, or something else, but standing united, you are stronger than each of them and will put a stop to their insolence.

[141] Perhaps you will be confronted with some argument like this: "Why is it then that so-and-so has been the victim of this or that crime and not punished me?" or "What in fact about this person?" perhaps naming again someone else that he has injured. I think you all know the reasons why each of these men refrained from trying to help himself. For example, lack of time, an unwillingness to get involved, lack of eloquence, shortage of funds; thousands of things are responsible. [142] Yet in my opinion, this man should not make these arguments, but either he should demonstrate to you that he has not committed any of the crimes that I have charged him with or, if he cannot, then this is all the more reason for putting him to death. If someone is so powerful that by tactics like this he can deprive each of us one by one of the right to obtain justice from him, it is the duty of all men to punish him for everyone's sake now that he has been caught, because he is the common enemy of our political system.

[143] There is a story told about Alcibiades, who lived during that

---

lines 65–66. Timocrates was the father of Polyeuctus and associated with Androtion. See Dem. 24.6, 13, 173, 177, 187. See Davies 1971: 513–514. For Euctemon, see 103.

[202] Demosthenes uses the word *hetaireia*, which denotes a band of companions linked together by close personal ties. This relationship was important during the Homeric period and remained so in the Macedonian kingdom. It came to be viewed with suspicion in democratic Athens, where the term was associated with tyrants and plots to overthrow the government (see Lys. 12.55; Hyp. 4.8; Thuc. 3.82.6, 8.48.3). For the *hetairoi* of the tyrant Hermias of Atarneus, see Tod 1947: no. 165, lines 10–11, 20–21, 25.

period of prosperity that the city once enjoyed a long time ago.[203]
Think about the number and extent of his services to the city, then
how your ancestors treated him when he decided to become offensive and insolent. Of course, I have not mentioned this story because
I want to compare Meidias to Alcibiades—I am not that foolish or
deranged—but so that you know, men of Athens, and understand
that there is not, nor will there be anything, not family, not wealth,
not power, that you, the majority, ought to tolerate if insolence is
added to it. [**144**] According to the story, men of Athens, that man
was descended from the Alcmeonids on his father's side[204] —they say
that this family fought on the side of the people and were driven into
exile by the tyrants,[205] and then after borrowing money from Delphi,
liberated the city and drove the sons of Peisistratus into exile.[206] On
his mother's side, he was descended from Hipponicus[207] and that family performed many great services for the people. [**145**] These were
not his only distinctions, but he himself also took up arms on behalf
of the people, twice on Samos, and a third time in the city itself,[208]

---

[203] On Demosthenes' portrayal of Alcibiades, see Gribble 1999: 32–33,
142–143.

[204] It was not Alcibiades' father but his mother who was an Alcmeonid (Lys.
14.39; Plut. *Alcibiades* 1.1).

[205] According to Herodotus (1.64.3), the Alcmeonids went into exile when Peisistratus gained power for the third and final time around 546. For the chronology,
see Rhodes 1981: 191–199. Some scholars believe that Cleisthenes, the leading
member of the Alcmeonid family, was Archon during the tyranny in 525/4, but
this is not certain. See Dillon 2006.

[206] This version of the story is similar to that found in Isocrates (15.232). According to Herodotus (5.62–63), however, the Alcmeonids obtained the contract
to rebuild the temple of Apollo at Delphi and used their own money to make it
more beautiful than the contract required by using Parian marble instead of lime-
stone. Herodotus also reports that they bribed the priestess to convince the Spartans to liberate Athens. For discussion, see Rhodes 1981: 236–237.

[207] Hipponicus was not Alcibiades' father but father-in-law (Isoc. 16.31; Plut.
Alcibiades 8.2). Hipponicus was a wealthy Athenian who belonged to the Kerykes,
which had special ties to the Mysteries at Eleusis, and was a general in 426/5
(Thuc. 3.91.4). On his family, see Davies 1971: 254–270.

[208] Alcibiades is known to have fought at Potidaea and Delium (Plato
Symposion 219e, 221a; Plut. *Alcibiades* 7) and served as general in Sicily (Thuc.

and showed his goodwill to his fatherland by risking his life, not by spending money and making speeches. His horses competed at the Olympic games and won victories and crowns,[209] and he appears to have been an outstanding general and the most talented speaker of all, as they say.[210] [**146**] But just the same, your ancestors in his time did not allow him to treat them with insolence for any of these reasons, but cast him out and made him an exile.[211] Even then, when the Spartans grew powerful, they endured the fortification of Deceleia[212] against themselves and the capture of the ships[213] and everything, for they considered it more noble to suffer any loss whatever against their will rather than willingly allow themselves to be the victims of his insolent abuse. [**147**] And yet what act of insolence did that man commit that equals the crime that this man has been proven to have done? He hit Taureas in the face when he was chorus leader.[214] But let that go: he

---

6.48–50). Later, he commanded the Athenian fleet in the eastern Aegean from 411 to 407 and was elected general while on Samos and at Athens. There is no indication, however, that he ever fought on Samos or in Athens.

[209] Alcibiades entered seven chariots at the Olympic games of 416 and won first, second, and fifth prizes (Thuc. 6.16.2).

[210] For Alcibiades' talent as a speaker, see Plut. *Alcibiades* 10.4: "and that he was a powerful speaker, not only do the comic poets testify, but also the most powerful of orators himself, who says in his speech *Against Meidias* that Alcibiades was a most able speaker in addition to his other gifts. And if we are to trust Theophrastus, the most versatile and learned of the philosophers, Alcibiades was of all men the most capable of discovering and understanding what was required in a given case. But since he strove to find not only the proper thing to say, but also the proper words and phrases with which to say it, and since in this last regard he was not a man of large resources, he would often stumble in the midst of his speech, come to a stop, and pause a while, a particular phrase eluding him. Then he would resume, and proceed with all the caution in the world." (trans. Perrin).

[211] Alcibiades was summoned to stand trial but fled to Sparta. He was then condemned *in absentia* (Thuc. 6.53, 61).

[212] The Spartans seized the town of Deceleia in 413 and occupied it until the end of the Peloponnesian War (Thuc. 7.19). Demosthenes neglects to mention that Alcibiades advised the Spartans to take the town (Thuc. 6.91.6).

[213] An allusion to the Athenian defeat at Aegospotami in 405.

[214] According to [And.] 4.20–21, Alcibiades and Taureas were competing against each other as producers of boys' choruses at the Dionysia. When

did this to a chorus leader when he too was a chorus leader without even breaking this law (the law was not yet passed). He imprisoned Agatharchus the painter.[215] Yes, so the story goes. But after catching him in some offense as they say. This is not even worth criticizing. He mutilated the Herms.[216] For all acts of impiety, I think it is right to feel the same amount of anger. But the complete destruction of holy objects is different from mutilating Herms. Certainly this man has been convicted of the former offense.

[**148**] Indeed, let us make a comparison: who is this man and what drove him to behave in this way? Do not think it noble, righteous, or pious for you, who are the descendants of men like this, to catch a man who is wicked, violent, and abusive, a nobody descended from nobodies, and then consider him deserving of pardon, indulgence, or gratitude. For what reason? For his service as general? Even as an individual soldier, this man is worthless, to say nothing about him as a leader of others. But what about his speeches? In his public speeches he has never had anything useful to say, and in private he insults everyone. [**149**] By Zeus, because of his family! Who among you does not know about this man's unspeakable birth, like something out of a tragedy? By coincidence, two utterly dissimilar things happened at his birth: the woman who was actually his mother, the woman who bore him, was the most sensible person in the entire world, and the

---

Alcibiades beat and chased away Taureas, the audience sided with Taureas by applauding his chorus. Despite their reaction, the judges awarded the prize to Alcibiades, partly out of fear, partly out of a desire to win his favor. This version is probably no more than an elaboration of Demosthenes' brief allusion, not an independent source. Plut. *Alcibiades* 16.4 probably draws on this spurious speech for the incidents about Taureas and Agatharchus.

[215] Agatharchus was a famous painter from Samos, who decorated buildings on the Acropolis (Plut. *Pericles* 13.2). Demosthenes does not say why Alcibiades imprisoned Agatharchus; a scholion on the passage plausibly suggests that Alcibiades caught him seducing his concubine. For the right to imprison a seducer, see [Dem.] 59.65–66. This is a more likely explanation than the story found in [And.] 4.17 that Alcibiades kept him imprisoned to force him to paint his house.

[216] According to contemporary sources (And. 1.11; Thuc. 6.28), Alcibiades was charged only with parodying the Mysteries, not with mutilating the Herms. Demosthenes may have altered events to make Alcibiades' crime similar to that of Meidias.

woman who pretended to be his mother and passed him off as her own was the most foolish of all women.[217] This is the proof: the former sold him the minute he was born, the latter paid for him when she could have bought a better one at the same price. [150] In fact, this is the means by which he gained control of property that did not belong to him and acquired a country that has the best reputation for following the laws when managing its affairs.[218] In my opinion, he finds it impossible to put up with these laws or even to follow them in any way. Instead, the truly barbarian, god-forsaken side of his nature exerts its influence through sheer force and makes it obvious that he treats the privileges he now enjoys as if they did not really belong to him—which in fact they do not.

[151] Although this disgusting, shameless man has done so many things like this throughout his life, some men who have dealt with him have approached me, judges, and advised me to settle with him and let this present case drop. When they did not persuade me, they did not claim that this man has not done many terrible things and should not pay whatever penalty he deserves for what he has done, but resorted to the following argument: "He has been convicted, and the vote was against him. What penalty do you expect the court to assess for him? Don't you see that he is rich and will mention his trierarchies and liturgies? Watch out lest he asks for lenient treatment with these tactics and has a good laugh at your expense when he pays a fine that is smaller than the amount he is offering to give you."[219] [152] First of all, I do not consider you capable of anything undignified, nor do I assume that you will assess the penalty for this man at anything less than what

---

[217] Demosthenes insinuates that Meidias' mother was a barbarian who sold him to an Athenian woman, who raised him as her own son. As a result, he became a citizen and was able to inherit her husband's property. This story is merely slander; there is no reason to accept it as true. For the view that barbarians sell their children, see Herod. 5.6.1.

[218] The Athenians believed that their democracy upheld the rule of law while oligarchy and tyranny were ruled by violence and the whim of those in power. See Aes. 1.4–6, 3.6.

[219] The imaginary interlocutor predicts that Meidias, if convicted, will propose a small fine at the assessment of the penalty (*timesis*) and that the court will vote for this fine instead of Demosthenes' proposal to put him to death.

is required to make him stop his outrages when he pays it. This penalty is most certainly death and, if not, confiscation of all his property.[220] Next, this is what I think about this man's liturgies, trierarchies, and arguments like this: [153] if performing liturgies amounts to this, men of Athens, declaring before you at every meeting of the Assembly and everywhere, "We are the men who perform liturgies,[221] we are the men who advance you money for the property tax,[222] we are the rich"—if performing liturgies amounts to saying things like this, I agree that Meidias is the most distinguished man of all in the city. He certainly is annoying when he says these things at every meeting of the Assembly in his tedious and boorish way. [154] But if you consider what it truly is to perform liturgies, I will tell you. In fact, see how fairly I am going to examine him by comparing him with myself.[223] This man, men of Athens, is perhaps about fifty years old or a little younger, but he has not performed any more liturgies than I have at age thirty-two.[224] In fact, the minute I came of age, I served as trierarch during

---

[220] This passage reveals that the speech was composed for delivery at the first part of a *graphe* procedure, in which the court considered only the guilt of the defendant. It also indicates that the assessment of the penalty lay in the future because Demosthenes does not make a specific proposal for a penalty at this point. See E. M. Harris 1989: 125–126.

[221] Men were probably assigned liturgies as the need arose and not from a permanent list. See MacDowell 1986.

[222] In 378/7 the wealthiest Athenians who paid the *eisphora* were divided into symmories (*FGrHist* 328 F41). Either at that time or in the late 370s, the three hundred richest members of the symmories were required to advance to the state the entire sum due from the symmories and then collected this from the other members. On these *proeispherontes*, see Wallace (1989), who argues that they "were never a standing college but were always newly appointed when an *eisphora* was required."

[223] Because a trial in Athens aimed at determining whether or not the defendant had broken the law and was not a contest in which the reputations of both litigants were judged on the basis of their generosity (*pace* Ober 1989: 226–230 and Cohen 1995: 112–113), accusers normally do not consider it relevant to mention their own public services. See, for example, Dem. 54.44. Demosthenes mentions his own liturgies here only for comparative purposes and argues that Meidias' own record should not affect the court's judgment.

[224] Demosthenes was born in 385/4 (Dem. 30.15, 17) and was actually about 38

the period when we served as trierarchs in pairs, paid all the expenses out of our own pockets, and hired crews for the ships by ourselves.[225] [**155**] This man, on the other hand, when he was the same age as I am now, had not yet begun to perform liturgies, but participated in this activity only when you created the system of twelve hundred contributors.[226] These men here collect a talent from the contributors, then hire out the trierarchies for a talent; the city provides the crews and supplies the equipment. As a result, some of them can actually spend nothing, giving the impression that they have performed liturgies and gaining an exemption from other liturgies.[227] [**156**] What else is there? This man once served as producer for tragedies, when I was a producer for *aulos* players at the men's competition. Yet everyone is doubtless aware that the expense for the latter is much greater than that for the former.[228] Besides, I am now volunteering, but at that time he took the position as the result of a challenge to exchange property: no one deserves gratitude for this. What else is there? I gave a feast for my

---

at the time. He subtracts a few years from his true age to make his own contributions look more generous and those of Meidias, less impressive. See E. M. Harris 1989: 121–125. *Pace* MacDowell 1990: 370 and Dilts, there is no reason to question the text.

[225] For the joint trierarchy, see Gabrielsen 1994: 173–176.

[226] Around 358/7 a politician named Periander passed a reform of the trierarchy. Previously, wealthy men had been assigned singly or in pairs to serve as captains of a trireme and to contribute toward their expenses. This system proved too burdensome for the trierarchs and was replaced by one in which 1,200 *synteleis* (contributors) were grouped into twenty symmories (tax groups). These symmories raised money from the *synteleis*, which was given to men responsible for the triremes, who also made a contribution of their own. For Periander's reform, see Gabrielsen 1994: 182–199. Meidias is recorded as a trierarch in a naval list (*IG* ii² 1612, line 29). If the date of the list is earlier than 357/6, it would prove Demosthenes wrong, but it could be dated later.

[227] Demosthenes probably exaggerates by giving the impression that the trierarchs received all their money from the *synteleis* and equipment and wages for crews from the state and had enough money left over to hire men to perform their duties. For exemptions from liturgies, see Dem. 20.8.

[228] Demosthenes' statement is tendentious: producing a tragedy could be just as expensive as producing a dithyramb. See Wilson 2000: 93–95. The manuscripts add "for the *aulos* players," but MacDowell, followed by Dilts, deletes this word.

tribe and was a producer for the Panathenaea, but this man did neither. [**157**] I have been the leader of my symmory for ten years, as long as Phormio,[229] Lysitheides,[230] Callaeschrus,[231] and the wealthiest men. I pay the war tax not according to what I actually own (my guardians stole that from me) but according to what people assume my father left for me and what I deserved to receive when I came of age. I have made such contributions to you, but what about Meidias? Up to now he has not yet been the leader of his symmory although no one stole any of his inheritance; on the contrary, he has received a considerable amount from his father.

[**158**] What distinction, then, has this man achieved, what are his liturgies or his grand expenditures? I do not see anything one could consider aside from these: he has built a house at Eleusis, which is so large that it casts a shadow over all his neighbors; he drives his wife to the Mysteries and anywhere she wishes in a carriage drawn by white horses from Sicyon;[232] he swaggers around the marketplace, taking three or four attendants with him and calling out the names of chalices, drinking horns, and fine plates[233] so that bystanders hear him.

---

[229] This Phormio is probably the freedman who became a wealthy banker and an Athenian citizen. For his career, see Trevett 1992: 10–15, 42–48, 52–54, 58–61, 174–176.

[230] Lysitheides was from the deme of Cicynna and was awarded a gold crown for his public service (Isoc. 15.93–94). Accused of embezzlement in 335/4, he was acquitted (Dem. 24.11–13).

[231] Callaeschrus is a common name in fourth-century Athens. Davies 1971: 239 identifies him with a metic from Siphnos who was a trierarch in 366/5 (*IG* ii² 1609, line 27) and whose son served as trierarch several times.

[232] Sicyon had a reputation for fine horses: see Homer *Iliad* 23.293–300; Herod. 6.126.2; Pausanias 6.19.2, 10.7.6.

[233] A *rhyton* (drinking horn) was a type of cup that appeared in Greek art shortly after 480 BCE. There were three types: bent *rhyton*, horn *rhyton*, and animal-head *rhyton*. Horn *rhyta* were often made of gold and silver and might contain a drain hole (see Athenaeus 496e–497e with Hoffman 1961: plate 12.1). The *phiale* (fine plate) was a deep dish, which was often used for pouring libations, and was often made of precious metal. Both the *rhyton* and *phiale* were associated with Persian luxury (Herod. 9.80), and certain forms of the *rhyton* and the Achaemenid *phiale* derive from Persian prototypes. On the *rhyton*, see Hoffman 1961; on the *phiale*, see Strong 1966: 74–89.

[**159**] I do not know what benefit most of you derive from all these items that Meidias purchases for his personal luxury and extravagance. Yet I do see that the abusive treatment that these items encourage him to dole out on many of us ordinary people. You should not show any respect or admiration for things like this nor consider it a mark of his desire for honor if someone builds conspicuously or acquires many maidservants[234] or beautiful furnishings, but only if a man shows his distinction and pursuit of honor in those things in which all of you have a share. You will not find any of these traits in this man.

[**160**] But, by Zeus, he contributed a trireme![235] I know he will babble on about this and say, "I contributed a trireme to you." Respond in this way: if, men of Athens, he contributed this out of a desire for honor, feel the gratitude that is appropriate for such gifts and return the favor, but do not allow him to commit outrage. This right must not be conceded for any action or achievement. If it becomes clear that he did this out of cowardice or lack of courage, do not be taken in. How then will you know? I will tell you about this too; and because the story is brief, I will tell it from the beginning. [**161**] The first set of contributions you had were for Euboea.[236] Meidias was not among them, but I was, and the man who served with me as trierarch was Philinus, the son of Nicostratus.[237] There was a second set of contributions after this for Olynthus.[238] Meidias was not among them either. And yet, as someone out to win honor,

---

[234] A euphemism for female slaves.

[235] In addition to the regular liturgies and military duties citizens might also be called on to make voluntary contributions (*epidoseis*) of money or ships. On voluntary contributions, see Migeotte 1992.

[236] In 357 the Athenians helped the Euboeans to resist a Theban invasion by sending soldiers and ships and forced the Thebans to withdraw under a truce (Aes. 3.85; Diodorus 16.7.2). A treaty was then concluded between Euboea and Athens in 357/6; see Rhodes and Osborne 2003: no. 48.

[237] Philinus of Lakiadai is listed as trierarch with a man named Pheidippus around 358/7 (*IG* ii² 1611, line 363; 1612, line 282) and also with Demosthenes (*IG* ii² 1612, line 301). It is not known whether the latter trierarchy is identical to the one mentioned here.

[238] These contributions were probably for the expedition to defend Olynthus against Philip of Macedon in late 349 (*FGrHist* 328 F49).

he should certainly have put himself forward at every opportunity. Now, there has been this third set of contributions. At this point he contributed. How? When pledges to contribute were being made in the Council, he was present but did not contribute then. [**162**] Only when the news was announced that the soldiers at Tamynae were under siege,[239] and the Council passed a preliminary motion calling up the rest of the cavalry, to which this man belonged, to depart, then finally this man, afraid that he would be called for this service, at the next meeting of the Assembly even before the Proedroi took their seats, came forward and made his contribution. Why is it so obvious that he cannot deny that he did this to avoid military service and not out of desire for honor? Because of what he did next. [**163**] At first, as the meeting of the Assembly moved forward and speeches were made, when it seemed there was no need for the support of the cavalry, and the proposal to send them out had been shelved, he did not go aboard the ship that he contributed but sent out a resident alien, the Egyptian Pamphilus. He himself remained here and during the Dionysia did the things for which he is now on trial.

[**164**] When the general Phocion sent for the cavalry from Argoura as a relief force, and Meidias was caught playing tricks, then this cowardly and accursed man here deserted his post and embarked on the ship and did not go out with the cavalry that he had asked at your meeting to command. If there were any danger at sea, he would clearly have departed on land. [**165**] Niceratus, the son of Nicias,[240] an only son, childless and physically quite weak, certainly did not act this

---

[239] In early 348 the Athenians sent support to Plutarch of Eretria in his struggle against Callias of Chalcis (for the date, see Dem. 39.16). Phocion landed on the coast and led an Athenian force inland to Tamynae, where they were surrounded by local troops. It was probably at this point that Phocion asked for reinforcements. Before they could arrive, Phocion defeated the Euboeans, and his victory made the reinforcements unnecessary (see 163). After Phocion's departure, Molossus took over command and lost control of the island. On this campaign, see Aes. 2.169, 3.86–87; Plut. *Phocion* 12–13 with Tritle 1988: 76–88.

[240] Niceratus was the great-grandson of the famous general Nicias. Like his ancestor, he invested in the silver mines. He performed several trierarchies and held the post of Treasurer of the Military fund and several religious offices. On this career, see Davies 1971: 406–407.

way, nor did Euctemon, the son of Aesion,[241] nor did Euthydemus, the son of Stratocles.[242] Each of them willingly contributed a trireme and did not escape military service in this way. Instead, they provided to the city a seaworthy trireme as a favor and a gift and considered it right to perform their liturgies in person as the law commanded. [166] But not the cavalry leader Meidias. No, he deserted the post assigned to him by law, for which he deserves the city's punishment, and is going to number this in his list of benefactions! By the gods, a trierarchy like this? Is it correct to call it pursuit of honor rather than tax collecting, exacting the two-percent duty,[243] leaving one's post, desertion from the army, and all sorts of things like this? When he could not find any other way to make himself exempt from service in the cavalry, Meidias discovered this new fangled two-percent cavalry duty.[244] [167] Consider this point next. When all the other trierarchs who contributed provided escort when you sailed back from Styra, this man alone did not provide escort, but without a shred of concern for you he shipped stakes, livestock, and doorposts for himself and timber for his silver mills.[245] This disgusting man made his trierarchy into a way of doing business instead of service to the state. Very well, although you already know that most of what I say is true, I will also call witnesses for you.[246]

---

[241] Davies 1971: 5 suggests that Euctemon's father Aesion is to be identified with a trierarch of the same name in the 350s or an orator contemporary with Demosthenes (Plut. *Demosthenes* 11.4).

[242] Stratocles and his son Euthydemus performed a joint trierarchy in the 350s (*IG* ii² 1612, lines 137–138, 271–272). On their family, see Davies 1971: 495.

[243] The Athenians imposed a two-percent duty on all exports and imports. Those who won the auction to collect taxes were given an exemption from military duty (Dem. 59.27). Demosthenes "suggests that Meidias has found that, for avoiding military service, paying for a trireme is as effective as buying a tax-collection" (MacDowell 1990: 385).

[244] For a suggestion about this cavalry duty, see 173n.

[245] For Meidias' leases of mines, see *IG* ii² 1582, lines 44, 82.

[246] This document is a forgery. Pamphilus was not one of the trierarchs, who were all citizens (see Gabrielsen 1994: 61), but a metic whom Meidias sent out in his place. The demotic of Niceratus is also wrong (see *IG* ii² 1629, line 494–495; 2409, lines 21–22). See MacDowell 1990: 386.

[**168**] [*WITNESSES*]

We, Cleon of Sounion, Aristocles of Paiania, Pamphilus, Niceratus of Acherdous, Euctemon of Sphettus, happened to be trierarchs along with Meidias, who is now on trial by Demosthenes, for whom we are testifying, at the time when we sailed with the entire fleet from Styra. When the entire fleet was sailing in formation and the trierarchs received the order not to leave until we arrived here, Meidias fell behind the fleet and crammed his ship with wood, stakes, livestock, and other things, and docked in the Piraeus alone after two days and did not join the fleet with the rest of the trierarchs.

[**169**] If his public service and achievements were actually such as he will soon claim and boast about and not as I portray them, not even in this case would he rightly escape punishment for his acts of abuse because of his services. I am aware that many men have provided you with many benefits, not on the scale of Meidias' liturgies, but men who have won victories in naval battles, captured cities, or set up many fine battle trophies for the city. [**170**] Nevertheless, you have never given any of these men (nor should you) this award: the power for each of them to abuse their personal enemies whenever he wishes and in whatever way he can. Not even to Harmodius and Aristogeiton, who received the most important awards from you because they performed the most important deeds.[247] And you would not have put up with it if someone had written another clause on their *stele* giving them also "the power to abuse whomever they wish." In fact, they received these other awards precisely because they stopped people from committing abuse.

[**171**] I also wish to show you that he has already received adequate thanks not only for the public service that he has performed (which in fact was quite minor) but also for the greatest services so that you do not think you owe this despicable man anything. Men of Athens, you elected this man treasurer of the *Paralus*[248] (despite being the sort

---

[247] On Harmodius and Aristogeiton, see Dem. 20.18n.

[248] The *Paralus* was a sacred trireme (cf. 174), which performed special missions for the state such as reconnaissance (Thuc. 3.33.1) and transporting ambassadors

of person he is), and also cavalry leader[249] (although he was incapable
of riding through the marketplace during the procession), as well as
supervisor of the Mysteries,[250] officer in charge of rituals,[251] purchaser
of cattle,[252] and positions like these. [**172**] By the gods, do you think
that putting a good face on his natural spite, cowardice, and baseness

---

(*IG* ii[2] 213, lines 6–9; Arrian *Anabasis* 3.6.2; Aes. 3.162), but also served as a warship in the fleet (Thuc. 3.77.3; Xen. *Hellenica* 6.2.14). Unlike the crews of other
triremes, which might have slaves or foreigners among its rowers, the crew of the
Paralus were all free citizens and drawn from an association called the *Paraloi*, who
worshiped the hero Paralus in the sanctuary Paralion (*IG* ii[2] 1254; Thuc. 8.73.5–6).
Jordan 1975: 153–184 claims that there were many sacred ships in the fleet, but see
Rhodes 1981: 688. The treasurer of the ship was elected (*Ath. Pol.* 61.7) and received funds from the state (174). Jordan 1975: 181–183 argues that the treasurer of
the *Paralus* did not serve as its captain (for the trierarch of the *Paralus*, see Is. 5.6,
42; *IG* ii[2] 2966). MacDowell 1990: 388–389 points to 174, in which Demosthenes
says that the Athenians ordered Meidias to sail and argues that "such an order
could appropriately be given only to the commander of the ship." Whatever his
precise role, the position was very prestigious. See Jordan 1975: 183 for other men
in the position.

[249] The Athenians elected two cavalry leaders every year (*Ath. Pol.* 61.4). Their
duties were to train the cavalry, lead it in religious processions (Dem. 4.26; cf.
174), and command it in battle; see Bugh 1988: 54–61. On Meidias as cavalry commander, see Bugh 1988: 159–166.

[250] There were four supervisors (*epimeletai*) of the Mysteries at Eleusis: one
from the *genos* of the Eumolpidae, one from the *genos* of the Kerykes, and two
from among all the citizens; see *Ath. Pol.* 57.1. Along with the Basileus, they conducted the festival and had the power to impose fines up to a certain amount on
disorderly participants. If the fine was larger, they issued a summons and brought
the offenders to court. Failure on their part to punish the disorderly would result
in a penalty. On their duties, see Clinton 1980: 280–283.

[251] On this position, see 115n. Rosivach 1994: 109 argues that Demosthenes is
mistaken when he says that Meidias was elected to this office and that of purchaser
of cattle. Rosivach assumes however that Meidias was appointed to one of the two
boards mentioned at *Ath. Pol.* 54.6–7, which were selected by lot. But some boards
were elected; see *IG* ii[2] 410, line 23.

[252] These officials (*Boōnai*) purchased cattle for public sacrifice out of state
funds. They are attested for the Panathenaea (*IG* ii[2] 334, lines 17–18), Dionysia in
the Piraeus, Dionysia in the city, Asklepieia, and the sacrifice to Zeus the Savior
(*IG* ii[2] 1496, lines 70–71, 80–81, 88–89, 118–119, 133).

by your offices, honors, and elections is a small reward and expression of thanks? Indeed, if someone were to deprive him of these reasons for boasting such as "I was a cavalry leader, I have been treasurer of the *Paralus*," what would this man deserve? [**173**] No, you surely know that when he was treasurer of the *Paralus,* he stole more than five talents from the people of Cyzicus.[253] Then, to avoid punishment for this crime, he made the city an enemy of ours by shoving people around and harassing them in every way and by ripping up treaties, and then he kept the money for himself. After being elected cavalry leader, he impaired the cavalry's effectiveness by passing laws that he then turned around and denied passing.[254] [**174**] And he was treasurer of the *Paralus* at the time when you made your expedition to Euboea against the Thebans.[255] After being ordered to spend twelve talents belonging to the city when you asked him to sail and escort the soldiers, he did not assist them but arrived only after the treaty that Diocles concluded with the Thebans went into effect.[256] And when he sailed,

---

[253] Cyzicus was an ally of Athens in 363 when Timotheus brought help to the city during a siege (Diodorus Siculus 15.81.6; Nepos *Timotheus* 1.3). In 362/1 Cyzicus attacked Proconnesus, an Athenian ally, and with Byzantium and Calchedon was forcing merchant ships bound to Athens to unload grain in its port. A scholion on the passage states that during the Social War (357–355) the Athenians voted to permit privateering against enemy ships. Meidias fell upon some merchants of Cyzicus and seized their property as enemy goods. When the merchants came to Athens and protested that friendly relations existed between their cities, Meidias argued so forcefully that he convinced the Athenians not to return their property. Upon their return home, the merchants caused Cyzicus to revolt. As Gauthier 1972: 169–170 suggests, Demosthenes may take "la cause pour la conséquence"; it is possible that Meidias' action postdated the outbreak of hostilities and was thus legal.

[254] A scholion on this passage says that Meidias proposed that the city did not need cavalry because they had brought shame on it and suggests that he did this to avoid military service. Bugh 1988: 163 more plausibly connects these laws with the "new fangled two-percent cavalry duty" mentioned at 166 and suggests that "Meidias was implementing Xenophon's proposal that certain cavalrymen might wish to buy their way out of the cavalry (*Hipparch.* 9.5)."

[255] In 357; see 161n.

[256] This was the treaty concluded in 357/6; see 161 and the note there. For Diocles, see Rhodes and Osborne 2003: no. 48, line 23.

he was overtaken by one of the private triremes! This is how effectively he equipped the sacred trireme! Well, then, as cavalry leader, what else do you think he did? Purchase a horse? This wealthy and distinguished man did not buy a horse but led the procession on a horse owned by someone else, Philomelus of Paeania.[257] All the men in the cavalry know this. To show that I speak the truth about these matters, call the witnesses of these events too.

[*WITNESSES*]

[**175**] Now, I want to tell you how many people you have convicted after the assembly voted that they were guilty of an offense concerning the festival.[258] I also want to show you what they did and how great your anger was, so that you may compare their actions with those done by this man. First, then, to recall the most recent decisions first, the Assembly voted that Evander of Thespiae committed an offense concerning the Mysteries after Menippus, a man from Caria, brought a motion (*probole*) against him.[259] The law about the Mysteries is the same as the one about the Dionysia; the former was passed after the latter.[260] [**176**] What then had Evandrus done, men of Athens, when you voted against him? Listen to this: he had won a maritime suit against Menippus,[261] and because he was not able to catch him earlier

---

[257] Philomelus was a wealthy Athenian who performed many liturgies and was given a crown for his public service (Isoc. 15.94). For his career, see Davies 1971: 548–550.

[258] Demosthenes discusses these three precedents to show that others like Meidias who received adverse votes at the *probole* also received harsh punishments. The first two precedents are less relevant to Meidias' case, but the third is quite similar to it. For discussion, see E. M. Harris 2006b: 351–355.

[259] The Athenian courts were open to foreigners like Evander and Menippus and were not just a forum for élite competition among wealthy citizens (*pace* Ober 1989).

[260] At 8 and 10 Demosthenes discusses two laws about *probole* for the Dionysia. Their provisions may have been combined in the single law about the Mysteries.

[261] Before roughly 350 maritime suits (*dikai emporikai*) were brought before the Nautodikae by citizens (Lys. 17.5) and before the Polemarch or Xenodikae by

(so he said), he seized him when he was attending the Mysteries.[262]
You voted against him for this reason; there were no other additional
grounds. When he came to court, you wanted to punish him with
death,[263] but the man who brought the action was won over, and you
compelled him to forfeit the entire judgment that he had previously
won, which amounted to two talents, and assessed an additional payment for damages, which the man calculated that he had incurred by
staying for your vote.[264] [**177**] This one man paid such a large penalty
for breaking the law in a private dispute at which no abuse was involved. Rightly so. This is what you must protect: the laws and your
oath. When you judge cases, you hold these like a deposit from the
rest of us that you must keep safe for all those who come before you
with justice on their side. [**178**] There was another man you thought
committed an offense concerning the Dionysia, and you voted to censure him while he was serving as assistant [265] to his son, who was the
Archon, because he seized someone who was taking his seat and barred

foreigners; see MacDowell 1978: 221–223. Sometime before 342 (Dem. 7.12) these
suits were transferred to the Thesmothetae and became monthly suits (Dem.
33.23). Under the new procedure, defendants who lost a maritime suit could be
placed in prison until they paid (Dem. 33.1). Because Menippus remained at liberty after losing his case, Evander must have brought his case under the old
procedure.

[262] The Mysteries at Athens were celebrated twice a year. The Great Mysteries
at Eleusis took place from 15 to 23 Boedromion (September); the Little Mysteries
were held at Agrai in Anthesterion (February). See Mikalson 1975: 65, 120. All
those who spoke Greek were eligible for initiation (Isoc. 4.157). The law about the
Dionysia, which was the same as that for the Mysteries, made it illegal for creditors to seize debtors whose payments were overdue. See 10.

[263] Even though Demosthenes claims that the court wished to vote for the
death penalty, it could not have done so because this was a private case. See
E. M. Harris 2006b: 352–353. See next note.

[264] After receiving a favorable vote at the *probole*, Menippus must have brought
a private action (*pace* MacDowell 1990: 395) because he would not have been
awarded damages in a public suit (see 28).

[265] Each of the nine Archons had two assistants (*paredroi*). Like other magistrates, these assistants had to pass a scrutiny and to undergo an audit after their
term of office. See *Ath. Pol.* 56.1 with Rhodes 1981: 621–622.

him from the theater. This man was the father of the most respectable Charicleides, who was Archon.[266] [**179**] You thought the man who brought the *probole* had a very strong legal argument when he said, "If I took a seat, man, and if I did not obey your orders as you said I did, what power does the law grant you even if you are the Archon himself? The power to order your assistants to bar him, not to beat him yourself. Suppose I do not obey even in this case: impose a fine, do everything except lay a hand on me.[267] The laws have provided many remedies to prevent a person from suffering physical abuse." These are the arguments this man made, and you voted to censure. This man did not actually bring his case to court but died before that.

[**180**] The Assembly unanimously voted against another man for committing an offense concerning the festival, and you put this man to death, Ctesicles, I mean. For what reason? Because he carried a horse whip during the procession and, while drunk, used it to strike someone who was his enemy. You decided that he struck with intent to outrage not because of wine and had seized on the excuse of the procession and his drunkenness to treat free men like slaves.[268] [**181**] In comparison with all these cases, men of Athens, in which one man lost the award that he had won, and another was clearly punished with death, I am certain that you all would say that Meidias' actions were far more terrible. He was not marching in a procession nor had he won a judgment nor was he an assistant nor did he have any other excuse when he did things very different from what these men did.

[**182**] But I will pass over their cases. Yet when Pyrrhus, the Eteobutad,[269] men of Athens, was denounced for serving as judge

---

[266] Charicleides was Archon in the year 363/2.

[267] Magistrates had the power to impose fines up to a certain amount. See Rhodes 1981: 634–635.

[268] The *probole* was a separate and distinct procedure from the public action for *hybris* brought against Ctesicles in court. At the *probole* Ctesicles was censured for committing an offense against the festival; at the trial he was condemned for an act of *hybris* against his victim.

[269] The Eteobutadai were a famous *genos*, from whom the priestess of Athena Polias was selected (Aes. 2.147). On this *genos*, see Parker 1996: 290–293. This case shows that the Athenians did not take social status into account when judging cases.

when he owed money to the treasury, some of you thought that he must be put to death, and after being convicted in your court, he was executed. And yet he tried to receive his payment because of poverty, not to commit abuse. I could discuss many other people, some of whom were put to death, others who lost their rights for actions much less serious than these. Men of Athens, you assessed a penalty of ten talents for Smicrus [270] and another equal amount for Sciton [271] when they were judged to have proposed illegal decrees. You did not take pity on them or on their children, their friends, and their relatives, nor on anyone else who appeared on their behalf. [183] Now, certainly do not make your anger plain when someone proposes illegal decrees, but when someone does something illegal and does not just propose it, show your gentle side. There is no word or name that is as dangerous for the majority of you as the action of a man who abuses any of you, no matter who he might be. Well, then, do not create a precedent like this that will harm you, that when you catch an ordinary, common person guilty of some crime, you will show him no pity nor release him but either put him to death or take away his rights, but when someone who is rich commits abuse, you show sympathy. No, do not do that; it is not right. Make it plain that your anger is the same for all men.

[184] Now, there are some topics that I consider no less necessary to discuss before you than what has already been said. After discussing these additional topics and saying a few words about them, I will step down. [272] There is something, men of Athens, that contributes a great deal to the advantage held by guilty men: your gentle character. [273]

---

[270] There were several men with this name in fourth-century Athens, but it is impossible to know if this Smicrus is identical with any of them.

[271] Davies 1971: 489 suggests that this name has been corrupted from Scipon, who is attested as a contributor to the *eutaxia* liturgy around 330 (*IG* ii² 417, line 20).

[272] This section probably marks the start of the *epilogos*, the final part of the speech, which summarizes the main points and urges the judges to uphold their oath and to vote against the defendant. See Erbse 1956: 139. For a similar phrase, see Dem. 20.154.

[273] For the idea that the Athenians were gentle and mild, see Dem. 22.51, 24.51, 170, 190.

Listen to me as I tell you why you should certainly not give him any part of this at all. In my opinion, everyone in the world makes contributions during their entire life to a fund created for their own benefit, not only those funds that some people collect and administer but also other kinds of funds.[274] [185] For example, one of us is moderate and generous and takes pity on many people. It is right for this man to receive the same treatment from all men if he ever finds himself in need or on trial. Or here is another man, who shamelessly abuses many people, treating some like beggars, others like scum,[275] and still others as worthless. It is right for this man to receive the same kind of payments that he has paid out to others. Well, if it occurs to you to think about it, you will discover that Meidias has collected the latter type of fund, not the former.

[186] I am certainly aware that he will take his children and weep, utter many words full of humility, shedding tears and making himself as pitiful as he can.[276] In fact, the more he makes himself humble, the more you should hate him, men of Athens. Why? Because if he were completely incapable of any humility and was so violent and abusive in his past life, it would be right to let up a little on our anger because his nature and the circumstances made him this way. But if he knows how to behave with moderation when he wishes and has chosen to live his life in a way opposite to this, it is surely obvious that even if he succeeds in fooling you now, he will again turn into the same man whom you all know. [187] You should surely not pay attention to this nor consider his current predicament, which this man is fabricating to suit his own purposes, more reliable or trustworthy than his entire

---

[274] Demosthenes repeats a point made at 101. Some have taken this repetition as an indication that the text of the speech is an unrevised draft, but this kind of repetition is not unusual in Demosthenes (e.g., Dem. 18.1, 8). See E. M. Harris 1989) 127–128.

[275] The Greek word used here is *katharmata*. In the language of ritual, the word refers to a person or object that has brought about some calamity. For the afflicted community to be purified and saved, the person or object must be expelled. See Parker 1983: 258–259. In Demosthenes and elsewhere, however, "the word is just a general term of abuse, not to be taken literally" (MacDowell 1990: 400).

[276] On children pleading for leniency in court, cf. 99.

life, which is well known to you. I do not have children, and I cannot place them next to me while I lament and shed tears over all the abuse that I have suffered. For this reason, therefore, will I, the victim, come out worse than the guilty party in your court? No, do not let this happen. [**188**] But when this man takes his children and asks you to vote for them, imagine that I have taken the laws and the oath that you swore[277] and stand next to them, asking and pleading with each of you to vote for them. There are many reasons why it is more just for you to take their side than this man's. Men of Athens, you have sworn to obey the laws, and you enjoy equal rights because of the laws, and all the benefits that you enjoy exist because of the laws, not because of Meidias nor because of Meidias' children.

[**189**] Perhaps he will talk about me and say that "this man is a politician."[278] If being a politician means giving advice about what he thinks are your interests only as long as he does it without annoying or browbeating you in any way,[279] I would not avoid or deny this label. Yet if a politician is the sort of speaker whom you and I see shamelessly growing rich off of you, I would not be this person. Indeed, I have not taken anything from you at all, but apart from a very small amount, I have spent my entire fortune for your benefit. And yet even if I were the most immoral person in this group, it was his duty to punish me by following the laws, not to abuse me while I was performing a liturgy. [**190**] Furthermore, not even one of the men who speak in public is taking my side in this trial. And I am not blaming any of them because I have never in your presence made any proposal as a favor to them. I have resolved on my own both to speak and to do what I think

---

[277] MacDowell 1990: 401 and Dilts follow Dobree and delete the phrase "and the oath that you swore" on the grounds that this section is about the law and not the judicial oath. "But Demosthenes often adds additional points to his arguments. It is better to keep the text as an example of his fullness of style" (Gagarin, *per litteras*).

[278] Demosthenes uses the word *rhetor*, which literally means "speaker" but came to be used for those who regularly addressed the Council and Assembly and was thus equivalent to the modern term "politician." In the fourth century, the term acquired negative connotations not unlike those attached to our word "politician." See Hansen 1983.

[279] MacDowell 1990 rightly compares Dem. 19.206.

is in your interests.[280] But soon you will see all the politicians lining up in order next to him. Yet how is it right for him to throw the label of politician at me as an insult, then ask to be protected with the help of these politicians?

[191] Now maybe he will perhaps argue along these lines: everything that I am now saying has been thought out and prepared ahead.[281] I admit that I have thought about and practiced my speech to the best of my ability and would not deny it. Yes, and I would be a sorry person if I were to give no thought to what I was about to say to you after suffering and continuing to suffer wrongs like these. Really it is Meidias who has written my speech for me. [192] By providing the actions that have furnished the material for my arguments, he is the one who would most deservedly bear the blame for this, not the person who thought and worried about presenting a just case right now. Yes, I certainly agree that I am doing this, men of Athens. But Meidias has probably never thought about justice in his entire life. If it ever occurred to him to think about things like this even to a small degree, he would never have gone so far wrong about the matter.

[193] Now, I know that he will not hesitate to accuse both the people and the Assembly but will repeat these charges that he dared to make when the *probole* took place: the people who attended the Assembly were all those who stayed behind when they should have marched out and all those who left the forts deserted, and those who voted against

---

[280] Demosthenes echoes here the language of honorary decrees for outstanding politicians. See, for example, *IG* II² 223, lines 4–5, 11–14; Veligianni-Terzi 1997: 282–283.

[281] Demosthenes predicts that Meidias will criticize him for delivering a prepared speech from memory instead of speaking spontaneously. For this stock charge and a possible response to it, see Anaximenes *Ars Rhetorica* 36.39. His criticism is based on the view that an impromptu speech was more honest and sincere. Cf. Alcidamas *On the Sophists* 28: "The speech spoken straight from the heart on the spur of the moment is alive and lives and is in line with events and bears a resemblance to the truth." Written speeches were associated with the sophists and teachers of rhetoric, who had a reputation for deceit and trickery. Cf. the criticisms made by Aeschines (1.175) that Demosthenes is a sophist who uses his skills to distract judges from the main issue.

him were dancers²⁸² and foreigners²⁸³ and men like that. [**194**] He grew so arrogant and shameless, men of the court, as all you know who were there, that by insulting, threatening, and casting intimidating glances at the part of the Assembly that at any time erupts in protest, he thinks that he will intimidate the entire people. This is what I think also makes the tears that he sheds now seem ridiculous. [**195**] What are you saying, you disgusting individual? Will you ask these men to have pity on your children or yourself or to take your side after you publicly trampled on them in the mud? Will you be the only person in the world who has the greatest reputation for being stuffed with so much arrogance toward everyone that even those who have nothing to do with you get irritated when they see your pushiness, your shouting, the way you strut around with your entourage, your wealth, and your abuse—and then find yourself pitied the minute that you are on trial? [**196**] You would certainly have discovered a great source of power—or rather of deceit—if you are able to gain for yourself two things that are most completely at odds with one another: loathing for the way you live and pity for your hypocrisy. There is no way that pity is the appropriate response for you, not in any respect, but the opposite: hatred and loathing and anger. These are the responses that your actions deserve.

But I will go back to my earlier point that you will accuse the people and the Assembly. [**197**] When he does this, bear in mind, men of the court, that this man came before you in the Assembly and was making charges against the men who served with him in the cavalry when they crossed to Olynthus.²⁸⁴ Now, by contrast, he, who stayed behind, will make accusations against the people who served abroad. Do you then agree that you are the kind of men that Meidias describes no matter whether you remain here or serve abroad or, on the contrary, that his man is always and everywhere god-forsaken and disgusting? What should one call this man whom neither the cavalry, nor his fellow-

---

²⁸² Those dancing in choruses received exemption from military service. See 15 with note 56.

²⁸³ Demosthenes is pointing out that Meidias' statement is outrageous; foreigners were not permitted to vote in the Assembly.

²⁸⁴ See 16n.

officers, nor his friends can stand? [**198**] For my part, I swear by Zeus, Apollo, and Athena (I will say it whether it be better or not) that when this man was going around making up stories that I reached a settlement with him, some men who enjoyed talking with him grew clearly irritated. By Zeus, one cannot help but sympathize with them. This man is unbearable; he alone is rich; he alone is eloquent; in his eyes all people are scum, or beggars, and not even human beings. [**199**] What then do you think that a man who has reached this degree of arrogance will do now if he is acquitted? I will tell you from what you already know about him if you should consider the evidence of what happened after the vote. Who is there who after being censured for committing impiety concerning the festival, even if he faced no further trial or risk, would not slip away and act with restraint at least during the period before the trial, if not for all time? There is no one who would not. [**200**] But not Meidias. No, from that day on he talks and insults and shouts. There is an election for some office: Meidias of Anagyra has been nominated. He acts on behalf of Plutarch,[285] he knows secrets, the city is not big enough for him. All these things make it obvious that he is demonstrating nothing else than that "the vote of censure has not hurt me at all; I am not terrified or afraid of the upcoming trial." [**201**] Men of Athens, doesn't this man who considers it shameful to appear frightened of you and dashing to pay no attention to you at all, deserve to die ten times? He thinks you will not be able to control him. Rich, arrogant, full of himself, boisterous, violent, shameless, where will he be caught if he slips away now?

[**202**] But in my opinion, if for no other reason, he should rightly pay the greatest penalty at least for the public speeches he gives and for the times he chooses to give them. Doubtless you know that when some piece of good news is announced to the city, the kind of news that makes everyone rejoice, Meidias is never anywhere to be found

---

[285] I see no reason to believe that this phrase indicates that Meidias was "the official representative of Eretria" (MacDowell 1990: 5). Demosthenes is accusing Meidias of supporting Plutarch, who was responsible for the Athenian defeat at Euboea, and the charge is probably just slander. For a similar use of the same verb (*proxenei*), cf. Dem. 18.82 where he charges Aeschines with supporting the envoys of Clitarchus and Philistides and does not imply that he held an official position.

among those who share in the people's joy and join in their happiness.[286] [**203**] But if something unpleasant happens that none of the rest would wish, he has been the first to stand up and address the people, jumping on the opportunity and feeling exhilarated by the silence that you fall into when you are troubled by recent events. "This is the kind of people you are, men of Athens. You do not march out, and you do not think you have to contribute money. Are you then surprised if things are going badly for you? Do you think I am going to make a contribution and that you are going to get a part of it?[287] Do you think that I will serve as trierarch and that you will not get on board?" [**204**] By hurling this kind of abuse, he reveals during a crisis both the harsh side of his character and the malice for the rest of you that he keeps hidden inside himself. So you must interrupt him now, men of Athens, when he tries to trick and deceive you by lamenting and weeping and begging, answering him like this: "Such is the kind of person you are Meidias: you are abusive, and you do not want to keep your hands to yourself. Do you wonder that you are going to suffer a miserable fate, you miserable person? Why, do you think that we are going to put up with you when you beat us? That we will acquit you, and you will not stop?"

[**205**] The men who speak on his behalf will help him not so much out of a desire to do this man a favor as to insult me because of the personal enmity that this man claims exists between us (whether I agree or not) and vehemently but wrongly asserts.[288] Too much pros-

---

[286] Demosthenes (18.198) made the same charge against Aeschines in 330.

[287] MacDowell 1990: 408 detects an allusion to the Theoric Fund, but this is unlikely. Demosthenes is alluding to the property tax (*eisphora*), which was levied for military purposes, and is probably alluding to payment for military service.

[288] This entire section is aimed at Eubulus, who is named at 206. Eubulus was a prominent politician, and Demosthenes is clearly anxious not to offend him. As a public figure, Eubulus tried to remain above the fray but occasionally found it necessary to take sides and support his friends. This would explain why he did not support Meidias in the Assembly but spoke for him in court. Cf. his attitude toward Hegesilaus and Thrasybulus (Dem. 19.290). Despite the friction between them because of Meidias, there were no major disagreements between Eubulus and Demosthenes about foreign policy and public finances. Both supported the Theoric Fund and opposed Philip's aggression. See E. M. Harris 2006a: 133–134.

perity sometimes carries the risk of making people overbearing: yet
even despite the harm inflicted on me, I do not agree that this man
is my enemy. Even when I leave him alone, he does not leave me
alone but opposes me when others are on trial and now will step up
and demand that I be denied the protection of the laws available to
everyone. How is this man not overbearing and more powerful than
what is good for any of us. [206] Besides, men of Athens, Eubulus
was present in the theater and remained seated when the people voted
against Meidias. When this man called on him by name and im-
plored and beseeched him, as you know, he did not stand up. Indeed,
if he thought that the *probole* had been brought against an innocent
man, he should then perhaps have spoken at least in support of a
friend. But if he recognized his guilt at the time and for this reason
did not respond to his appeal, but now when he had clashed with me,
he is about to ask for his acquittal for this reason, it is not good for
you to grant him this favor.

[207] Do not let anyone in a democracy grow so powerful that his
support in court will cause one man to suffer outrage and another
to avoid punishment. No, if you wish to harm me, Eubulus—by the
gods, I do not know why—you are powerful and active in politics,
so punish me in whatever way you like in accordance with the laws.
But do not take away my right to punish him for the outrage that I
have suffered in violation of the laws. If you are at a loss about how to
harm me in that way, let it be an indication of my reasonable nature
that you have no reason to bring me to trial although you have no
trouble doing this to others.

[208] Well, now, I have learned that Philippides,[289] Mnesarchides,[290]
Diotimus of Euonymea,[291] and some wealthy trierarchs like them will

---

[289] Philippides, the son of Philomelus, came from Paiania, the same deme as
Demosthenes, with whom he served as trierarch (*IG* ii[2] 1613, lines 191–192). He
was wealthy and made many contributions to Athens, for which he was honored
in 293/2. Lewis 1955: 20 suggests that he was the defendant in Hyperides *Against
Philippides*. He served as joint trierarch with Demosthenes in the 350s (*IG* ii[2]
1613, lines 191–192).

[290] Mnesarchides served at least twice as a trierarch. See Davies 1971: 392–393.

[291] Diotimus made a fortune from silver mines and served as a trierarch. For his
family and career, see Davies 1971: 161–165.

ask for his acquittal and plead with you on his behalf, claiming that they deserve to receive this favor.[292] I would not say anything derogatory about these men; after all, that would be madness. But I will tell you what you should think about and consider when they make their request.[293] [209] Imagine a situation in which these men seize control of the government along with Meidias and men of his ilk (may this never happen, and it will not happen!),[294] and one of you, one of the many, the common people, were to do something wrong to one of these people, not the kind of things Meidias did to me, but something else, and he were to come into a court packed with these men. What sympathy or consideration do you think he would receive? Would they be quick to do him a favor? Surely not. Would they grant the request of one of the many? Wouldn't they instead say right away: "A piece of filth, a wretch; to abuse this man and still breathe? If he is allowed to live, he should be grateful." [210] If these men would treat you in this way, do not act any differently toward them; do not pay respect to their wealth or reputation, but to yourselves. These men possess many advantages, which no one prevents them from keeping. Well, do not let them prevent you from keeping the freedom from fear that the laws provide to us as our common property.

[211] Nothing terrible or pitiful will happen to Meidias if he retains an amount of property equal to what most of you have, men whom he now abuses and calls beggars, and is deprived of the remainder, which encourages him to commit outrage.[295] And they are surely not justified in asking you for the following: "Do not decide the case in

---

[292] Although it was acceptable for powerful men to use their influence during the assessment of the penalty, it was considered wrong for them to ask the court to acquit a guilty man as a favor to them. See Aes. 3.198 with Rubinstein 2000: 218–220.

[293] Some scholars find 208–210 unnecessary after the previous section, a sign that the speech was left unfinished. But see E. M. Harris 1989: 126–127.

[294] Demosthenes gives the impression that these men might attempt to set up an oligarchy, but there is no need to believe that they were hostile to democracy. Such charges were often made without any evidence; Demosthenes himself was accused of oligarchic tendencies.

[295] Here Demosthenes imagines that Meidias will be condemned to pay a fine as a penalty.

accordance with the laws, men of the court. Do not help the victim of terrible crimes, nor uphold your oath. Do us this favor."²⁹⁶ This is the request that they will make if they make any request about him, even if they do not use these words. [212] But because they are his friends and think it terrible if Meidias does not keep his wealth, and are exceedingly wealthy themselves, and that is fine, then let them give him money from their own resources so that you cast a just vote in the case for which you have come here under oath and that these men may do favors from their own funds and not at the expense of dishonoring you. But if these men who have money should not give up some of it, how would it be good for you to give up your oath?

[213] There are many rich men standing around him, men of Athens, who have gained a reputation for being important people because of their wealth and are going to beg you. Do not abandon me to any of them, men of Athens. Instead, just as each of them eagerly pursues his own private interest and that of Meidias, you should be eager to protect yourselves, the laws, and also me, who had sought refuge with you. Hold firm to the decision that you have now reached. [214] Certainly, men of Athens, if the people had heard what happened and had absolved Meidias at the time when the *probole* occurred, that would not have been equally terrible. One might find consolation in the fact that the outrage never occurred or that the offense did not concern the festival or many other things. [215] But now this would be the most terrible outcome of all for me if you are about to acquit him after you clearly were all so furious and bitter and angry when the offenses occurred that when Neoptolemus,²⁹⁷ Mnesarchides,²⁹⁸ Philippides,²⁹⁹

---

²⁹⁶ "Our hostile sources suggest that friends sometimes engaged in asking the judges to have mercy upon the defendant as a special favour due to themselves, but unfortunately there is no friendly evidence to be derived from defence speeches against which we might test this prosecution topos" (Rubinstein 2000: 163). Whatever friends might have said at trials, it is unlikely that they would have gone so far as to ask the judges to ignore the law. Such a request is never found in any speech given by or for a defendant. Instead, litigants always show respect for the law; see Carey 1996.

²⁹⁷ Neoptolemus was a wealthy Athenian who later received honors for his generosity (Dem. 18.114). For his property and career, see Davies 1971: 399–400.

²⁹⁸ For this man, see note 290.

²⁹⁹ For this man, see note 289.

and some other very rich man were imploring both me and you, you shouted not to let him go; then when Blepaeus the banker[300] came up to me, you shouted very loud, as if I were about to accept his money, which is usually what happens. [**216**] This made me so terrified of your protests, men of Athens, that I lost my cloak and was almost naked in my bare tunic when that man was trying to drag me as I was trying to get away. After that you came up to me and said things like this: "Make sure you pursue your case against the foul man and do not settle. The Athenians will keep an eye on what you are about to do." After his crime was condemned as abuse and after they made their decision sitting in judgment inside the shrine, I persevered and betrayed neither you nor myself. So, now you are going to acquit him! [**217**] Do not do it! That is really the height of shame. I do not deserve this from you—how could I, men of Athens, when I put a man on trial who both seems and is violent and abusive, who has done wrong by bullying at a public festival and made not only you witnesses of his outrage but also all the Greeks who were staying here?[301] The people heard what he has done. What then? The people voted against him and turned him over to you. [**218**] Your decision cannot remain hidden and unnoticed and what you have decided when the issue comes before you cannot escape scrutiny. No, if you punish him, you will gain a reputation for virtue and being fine, upstanding men who hate evil. Yet if you acquit, people will think you were overcome by some other motive. He is not on trial for a matter involving the state—his case is not like that of Aristophon,[302] who removed the charge against him by returning the crowns[303]—but for abuse, because he cannot do

---

[300] Blepaeus is also mentioned at Dem. 40.52 and appears as a contractor at Eleusis (*IG* ii² 1675, line 32).

[301] Foreigners were able to attend the Dionysia. Aristoph. *Acharnians* 502–506; Aes. 3.43.

[302] Aristophon was a famous politician who had one of the longest careers in Athenian politics. See *Against Leptines* 148.

[303] MacDowell 1990: 419–420 suggests that "Aristophon, holding a financial or religious office, was required to supply some crowns for a festival and failed to do so, and he was therefore accused by *probole* of committing an offense concerning the festival, but the charge was dropped when he delivered the crowns." It is equally possible that he may have prevented an adverse vote by returning the crowns before the Assembly met about the *probole*.

anything to undo what he has done. This being the case, is it better to punish him later or now? Now, I think. The verdict concerns the community and so do all the offenses for which he is now on trial.

[219] Besides, men of Athens, it was not just me whom this man was hitting and abusing intentionally in acting the way that he did, but all whom he thinks may be in a weaker position than I am to obtain justice for themselves. If it was not all of you who were beaten and humiliated while producing a chorus, you surely realize that all of you do not produce a chorus at the same time, and no one would be able to sling mud on all of you with just one hand. [220] But every time one victim does not obtain justice, each person must then expect to be the first to be wronged next and should not ignore such possibilities nor wait until it happens to him but take as many precautions as possible. Perhaps Meidias hates me, but there is someone else who hates each of you. Would you then allow this man, whoever it is who hates you, to have the power to do to each one of you the very things this man did to me? I do not think so. No, men of Athens, do not sacrifice me to him. [221] Look: immediately after the court recesses, each of you will go back home, one more quickly perhaps, another more leisurely, without worrying or turning around,[304] not afraid about whether he will encounter a friend or a foe, a man who is big or small, strong or weak, or anything like this. Why in the world is this so? Because he knows in his own mind, is confident, and trusts in our form of government that no one will drag him off or abuse him or beat him. [222] And so you yourselves walk around in complete security; will you walk away without guaranteeing this for me? After being the victim of these crimes, what are the odds that I will survive if you are going to pay no attention to me now? "Don't be afraid, by Zeus," someone might say, "You will not be treated with abuse any more." If so, will you show your anger then, after acquitting him now? No, men of the court, do not betray me, yourselves, or the laws.

[223] If you should be willing to consider and examine what makes those of you who judge cases at any time strong and gives them power over all the city's affairs, whether the city appoints two

---

[304] Or "going in a different direction" to avoid meeting someone (MacDowell).

hundred, or a thousand, or however many,[305] you would discover it is not because you judges are the only citizens who are drawn up in arms, nor because they are in the best physical shape and are the strongest, nor because you are the youngest in age, or anything like this, but because the laws are strong. [224] And what makes the laws strong?[306] Will they come running and be there to help someone if he is wronged and cries out? No: the laws are only written letters, and they could not do this. What then gives them strength? You do if you confirm them and make them valid each time someone asks. [225] One must therefore defend them just as the victim of injustice defends himself and treat offenses against the laws as threats to the community, no matter what someone is caught doing. Neither liturgies, nor pity, nor any man, nor any skill[307] should be found to allow someone who violates the laws to escape punishment.

[226] Those of you who attended the Dionysia hissed as he entered the theater and booed and made all those signs that revealed your hostility without having heard anything yet about him from me. Next, before his guilt was proved, you were angry and summoned the victim to take revenge and applauded when I brought the *probole* before the people. [227] He was found guilty; and the people, meeting in a holy place, passed a preliminary decision against him; and the other actions done by this foul man were examined; and you were chosen by lot to judge the case; and it is in your power to put an end to the matter with a single vote. Will you now hesitate to help me, to bring joy to the people, to teach discipline to others, and to enable you yourselves to

---

[305] On the number of judges serving in Athenian courts, see Rhodes 1981: 728–729.

[306] Ober 1989: 300 believes that the thrust of this passage is that "the authority of the laws rested immediately on the ability of the populace to exert moral pressure upon individuals who broke the laws." But the point is that the laws cannot have their deterrent effect and assure public security unless they are enforced by the courts imposing punishments on the guilty. *Pace* Ober, the passage has nothing to do with "moral pressure" by the entire people but with the rule of law enforced by the courts.

[307] Demosthenes here summarizes the various ways that Meidias will attempt to avoid punishment: his performance of liturgies (151–170), asking for pity (186–188), the support of powerful men (205–218), skill as a speaker (196).

live in complete security for the future by making this man an example for others?[308]

For all the reasons then that I have stated and above all for the sake of the god against whose festival this man was caught in an act of impiety, cast a vote that is holy and just and punish this man.

---

[308] On the use of punishment as a deterrent, see Saunders 1991: 120 with note 208.

22. AGAINST ANDROTION

INTRODUCTION

Androtion was a wealthy Athenian who was active in politics.[1] His father Andron was associated with prominent intellectuals in the late fifth century[2] and may have played a role in the Revolution of 411.[3] Two sources make Androtion a student of the orator Isocrates,[4] but in his *Antidosis*, Isocrates (15.93–94) does not list him among his pupils.[5] Androtion entered politics around 385; a decree of 378/7 reveals that he was a member of the Council and presided over a meeting of the Assembly during that year.[6] At one point he was elected to a special office that granted him the power to collect the arrears for the property tax (*eisphora*; 48); some scholars place this in the 370s, but it may have occurred later.[7] Sometime before 365/4 he passed a decree instructing the Treasurers of Athena to melt down dedications to make processional

---

[1]For the evidence about Androtion's career, see Harding 1976 and Harding 1994: 13–25, 53–59.

[2]Plato *Protagoras* 315c; *Gorgias* 487c.

[3]For Andron's actions in 411, [Plut.] *Moralia* 833d–f; Harpocration s.v. Andron. But Harding 1994: 15 argues that this may be Andron, son of Androcles, of Gargettos. The claims made by Demosthenes that Andron was a public debtor are probably just slander (33–34, 56, 68; Dem. 24.125, 168).

[4]Scholion to 22 and Zosimus *Life of Isocrates* 256.91 (Westerman).

[5]For doubts about Androtion's connection with Isocrates, see Harding 1994: 17–19.

[6]See *IG* ii[2] 61, lines 6–7.

[7]Moscati Castelnuovo 1980: 254–257 places it in the mid 370s; Harding 1976: 193 n. 54, places it during his service in the Council (356/5).

vessels.[8] Between 358/7 and 357/6 he served as garrison commander on the island of Andros. We owe our knowledge of this appointment to a decree from the city of Arcesine on the island, which praises him for his honesty and generosity in carrying out his duties.[9] The decree commends him for lending the city money and advancing money for soldiers' wages, both without charging interest, which saved the city 12 minas, and for ransoming prisoners captured by the enemy. In 346/5 he passed a decree granting honors to the sons of Leucon, the king of the Bosporus mentioned in *Against Leptines* (31–44).[10]

In 356/5 Androtion served in the Council for a second time.[11] After his term of office, Androtion proposed in the Assembly a decree of honors for the members of the Council in his year. Euctemon, whom Androtion had earlier removed from office (27, 48), took this opportunity to retaliate against his enemy and brought a public action against Androtion for proposing an illegal decree (*graphe paranomon*). He charged that the decree violated the law in three ways: first, the motion was introduced to the Assembly without prior consultation with the Council (5–7); second, the law forbade the Council to ask for an award unless it had triremes built during its term of office, and this Council had not done this (8); and third, Androtion did not have the right to propose a motion because he had been a prostitute and was also a public debtor (21–24, 33–34). Demosthenes wrote the speech for Diodorus, who appeared at the trial as a supporting speaker for the accuser (1). Diodorus also says that he bore a grudge against Androtion for bringing a charge of impiety against his uncle (2).

Diodorus begins his speech with a brief introduction: there is no need for him to present an elaborate prologue because he is speaking second, after the accuser Euctemon, who probably presented the main

---

[8]See 69–77 with *IG* ii[2] 216/7 and ii[2] 261 and the analysis of Lewis 1954: 41.

[9]Rhodes and Osborne 2003: no. 51.

[10]Rhodes and Osborne 2003: no. 64.

[11]Dionysius of Halicarnassus (*Letter to Ammaeus* I.4) dates *Against Androtion* to the archonship of Callistratus (355/4), which would place Androtion's service in the Council in the previous year (356/5). Lewis 1954: 43–44 argued that Androtion served in the Council in 359/8, but see Cawkwell 1962: 40–45. For men serving twice in the council, see Rhodes 1972: 242–243 and Hansen 2006: 27.

charges against Androtion.[12] Diodorus says a few words about his personal motive for attacking Androtion, who brought an unsuccessful charge of impiety against his uncle (1–3), then devotes almost all of his speech to anticipating the arguments that he expects Androtion and his supporters will present (4–78). He predicts that Androtion will claim that the law does not require a preliminary motion for decrees of praise for the Council and will cite many precedents for this practice. Diodorus replies that the law requiring a preliminary motion for all decrees of the Assembly allows for no exceptions and that the precedents do not overturn this rule (5–8). Androtion will argue that the Assembly can grant honors to the Council even if no triremes are built in the previous year; all the law forbids is that the Council ask for honors in such a case. Diodorus calls this argument specious: if the Council is not permitted to ask for honors when no triremes are built, the Assembly does not have the power to grant them (9–11). He then uses examples from Athenian history to show how the construction of triremes is vital to the city's security (12–16).

In reply to Androtion's claim that the failure to build triremes was not the Council's fault because the funds earmarked for this purpose were embezzled, Diodorus urges the court to reject all such excuses (17–20). Androtion will denounce the charge that he is a prostitute as vicious slander. If it is true, Euctemon should bring a public charge of prostitution (*graphe hetaireseos*), not a charge of passing an illegal decree. Diodorus dismisses this argument on the grounds that the law about illegal proposals allows accusers to bring charges about the proposer's personal life and that the lawgiver Solon deliberately provided several procedures for each offense, each adapted to the different abilities of individual accusers (25–32). Androtion will challenge his accusers to prove that he is a public debtor, but it is up to him to refute the charge (33–34). As for Androtion's argument that he is not defending himself, but the Council, Diodorus tells the court that a conviction will prevent the Council from falling into the hands of unscrupulous speakers (35–39). When Archetion, speaking in support

---

[12]Cf. the brief prologue to *Against Leptines*, in which Demosthenes was speaking third.

of Androtion, defends the Council, the court should recall the charges that he recently brought against this body (40–41).

In the final part of the speech, Diodorus replies to Androtion's explanation of the attack on him as retaliation for his success in collecting the arrears for the property tax (*eisphora*) and his supervision of the gods' treasures on the Acropolis (42–78). All Androtion collected was seven talents, and the methods that he used to collect this were brutal and violated the rights of average citizens (47–58). By contrast, Satyrus collected thirty-four talents without using any violence (63–64). When Androtion melted down crowns to make processional vessels, he committed impiety against the gods and destroyed memorials of the city's fame and good reputation (69–78).

The outcome of the trial is not known. Demosthenes' silence about the trial in his account of Androtion's activities in *Against Timocrates* may indicate that he was acquitted.[13] Even if he were convicted, his punishment was not severe: he was not executed, sent into exile, deprived of his rights as citizen, or given a fine so large that he could not pay it because he was still active in Athenian politics in 346 when he passed a decree in the Assembly.[14]

22. AGAINST ANDROTION

[1] I will try, if I can, to do the very same thing, men of the court, that Euctemon thought he should do after what he suffered from Androtion, namely, help the city and seek justice for himself. Although Euctemon endured many terrible insults in violation of all the laws, these happen to be less serious than the trouble Androtion has caused me. While Euctemon was the victim of a plot against his property and an attempt to have him unjustly thrown out of the office to which you appointed him,[15] no one on earth would have even received me, if you had been taken in by the charges Androtion fabricated against me. [2] He accused me of a crime that anyone would be reluctant to mention (unless he happened to be the same sort of person as this man), kill-

---

[13]Thus, Navarre and Orsini 1954: 9.

[14]See note 10 above.

[15]Diodorus alludes to Androtion having Euctemon removed from the office of Collector (*eispraktor*). See 48.

ing my own father. Then after trumping up a charge of impiety not against me but against my uncle for having associated with me when I was allegedly guilty of this crime, he brought him to trial. If that had resulted in his conviction, who would have suffered a more miserable fate at his hands than I? What friend or guest-friend would have been willing to come near me? What city on earth would have allowed me to live in its territory if I were thought to be guilty of such an act of impiety? Not even one. [3] When I was tried in your court on these charges, I was acquitted and not by a narrow margin but so decisively that this man here did not gain one-fifth of the votes.[16] With your help I will try to retaliate against him both now and for the future.

Although I still have many things to say about his private life, I will pass over them. As for the charges you will vote on now as well as the considerable damage this man has caused you during his public career, and in particular those matters that I think Euctemon neglected but it would be better for you to hear, these are the topics I will try briefly to discuss.[17]

[4] If I saw that he had a straightforward defense against the charges facing him, I would not mention them. But as it is, I know for certain that he has nothing straightforward or honest to say but will try to deceive you by inventing and slipping in dishonest arguments in reply to each charge. When it comes to public speaking, this man is a skilled practitioner and has devoted his whole life to this subject.[18] To make

---

[16]This incident is also alluded to at Dem. 24.7. There is no reason to doubt the verdict, which was presumably public knowledge, but there is reason to question the margin of Androtion's defeat, for which he provides no evidence at all. If an accuser failed to gain one-fifth of the votes in a public case, he incurred a fine of 1,000 drachmas and lost his right to bring any public charges in the future. See E. M. Harris 2006a: 405–422. But Demosthenes (24.14) states that Androtion later brought a *graphe paranomon* against Euctemon, which indicates he did not lose his right to bring public charges.

[17]Euctemon brought the formal charge against Androtion; Diodorus is acting as his *synegoros* or "supporting speaker." A litigant might ask someone to speak on his behalf for several reasons. On *synegoroi*, see Rubinstein 2000.

[18]The scholion says that Androtion was a student of Isocrates, who taught rhetoric, but modern scholars are divided about whether he actually studied with Isocrates. See the Introduction to this speech.

sure that you will not be misled and persuaded to cast a vote that violates your oath and to acquit this man, whom you should punish for many reasons, pay close attention to what I am going to say so that after you have heard me, you will have the information you need to evaluate each statement he will make.[19]

[5] He has one argument, which he thinks is ingenious, about his failure to obtain the Council's prior approval.[20] "There is a law," he says, "that if the Council appears to deserve an award for performing its duties, the Assembly may grant the award. The President asked this question," he says, "the Assembly cast its vote, and the motion was passed. In this case, there is no need for prior approval by the Council. These actions followed the law." My opinion is the very opposite, and I think you agree with me: one should introduce preliminary motions only about matters that the laws permit, because in regard to matters not covered by the laws, one should not even make a proposal to begin with, not even one. [6] Well, now, he contends that all the Councils that have ever received an award from you have received it in this way and there was never a preliminary motion passed for even one of them. I believe, no, I am certain, that he is not speaking the truth. But even if this sort of thing happened quite regularly, while the law says the opposite, this mistake must not be repeated now just because it has already been made several times in the past.[21] On the contrary,

---

[19]The speaker refers to the judicial oath, which bound the judges to vote on only the relevant issues and to decide the case in accordance with the laws and decrees of the Athenian people. Diodorus claims that Androtion will attempt to distract them with irrelevant arguments and thus cause them to violate their oath. On this requirement, see Rhodes 2004.

[20]No proposal could be passed by the Assembly unless it received prior consideration from the Council (*Ath. Pol.* 45.4). See Rhodes 1972: 52–81. In this case, however, there may have been an exception to the general rule. See the Introduction to this speech.

[21]Diodorus is arguing that the failure to obtain prior approval in the past does not justify Androtion's failure to obtain it in this case. Unlike the practice in Common Law, the decisions of an Athenian court did not create a binding precedent that all courts had to follow. In this respect, Diodorus' argument is sound, but he may be misrepresenting the speaker's point. On the use of precedents in Attic oratory, see E. M. Harris 2006b.

one ought to begin by insisting this be done as the law commands, starting with you. [7] So don't go and argue that is what has happened many times, but rather that this is the way it should happen. If there has ever been some violation of the laws, and you have followed this precedent, you do not deserve to be acquitted for this reason. Quite the opposite; there would be far more reason to convict you. If one of those previous offenders had been convicted, you would not have made this proposal. In the same way, if you are punished now, no one will make such a proposal in the future.

[8] Now as for the law that explicitly prohibits the Council that does not have triremes built from requesting an award, it is worth hearing the defense he will present and observing his shameless character from the arguments he attempts to use. "The law" he says, "does not allow the Council to request an award if it does not have triremes built. I agree. But nowhere," he says, "does it prevent the Assembly from granting one. If I gave an award in response to their request, I made an illegal proposal. Yet if I did not mention the ships in the entire proposal, but stated some other reasons for crowning the Council, how have I proposed an illegal motion?" [9] It is not difficult to give you the correct answer to this argument, namely, that those who preside over meetings of the Council and the President, who put the motion to a vote and supervised the voting, asked, "Who thinks the Council deserves an award for the way it has performed its duties and who does not?" Those who do not request nor consider themselves worthy to receive an award should not even have been asking the question in the first place. [10] Beyond this there are in addition the charges Meidias and several others made against the Council,[22] charges that made its members jump up and beg that the award not be taken away from them. You men who are judging the case do not need to learn about these events from me; you yourselves were there in the Assembly and witnessed them as they happened. When he says the Council did not make a request, therefore, give him this answer: the law does not permit even the Assembly to give it to them when they have not had triremes built, as I will now demonstrate. [11] This is the reason, men of Athens, why the law is expressed in this way: it is not

---

[22]For the career of Meidias, see the Introduction to the previous speech.

permitted for the Council that has not had triremes built to request an award so that there is no possibility for the Assembly to be persuaded or tricked. The man who established the law believed that the matter should not depend on the ability of speakers but that whatever could be found to be just and at the same time beneficial for the people should be prescribed by law. You did not have triremes built? Then do not ask for an award. When the law does not permit asking for one, how does it not definitely prevent giving one?

[12] It is certainly worth examining the following question too: why is it utterly impossible to request an award if the Council has performed all its other duties well, and no one has any charges to bring against it, yet has not had triremes built? You will find that this rule has been established as a safeguard to protect the people. I think that no one would answer by denying the advantages the city has received in the past or now possesses from having triremes—and the disadvantages (so that I may avoid mentioning something unpleasant)[23] it has incurred from not having them. [13] For instance, anyone could give many examples, both from the past and from recent events, but among those that are familiar to everyone from hearing about them, if you wish, there are the men who built the Propylaea[24] and the Parthenon[25] and decorated the rest of the temples with the spoils taken from the barbarians, achievements that rightly give us all a sense of pride. You certainly know this from hearing about it that after leaving the city and being shut off on Salamis, they saved all their own possessions and the city by winning the victory at sea because they had triremes. They were also responsible for bringing the rest of the Greeks many great benefits, the memory of which not even time can erase.[26]

---

[23]Diodorus is reluctant to offend his audience by reminding them of Athenian defeats.

[24]The Propylaea was a large complex of buildings placed at the entry to the Acropolis.

[25]The Parthenon was the temple of Athena Parthenos ("the Maiden") on the Acropolis. Fragments of an ancient commentary on *Against Androtion* have been preserved, which contain a discussion of this passage. For the text and commentary, see Gibson 2002: 178–179, 181–185.

[26]An allusion to the battle of Salamis in 480, when the Greeks defeated the Persian fleet off the coast of Attica after Athens had been occupied by the Persians.

[**14**] Very good, but these events are ancient and long past. As for
events that you have all seen, you know that recently you went to help
the Euboeans in just three days and sent the Thebans away under a
truce.[27] Would you have done this so quickly if you did not have new
ships in which you sailed to help them? No, you could not have. Anyone could list many other benefits that have accrued to the city from
keeping the fleet well equipped. [**15**] Good enough—and how many
disasters from having them poorly equipped? I will omit many examples, but during the Decelean War (I will remind you of one incident
from the distant past that all of you know better than I do), although
the city suffered many terrible defeats, they did not surrender in the
war until their fleet was lost.[28] Yet why do I need to discuss ancient
history? During the last war against the Spartans, you know what
state the city was in when you thought you would not be able to send
the fleet out.[29] You remember that even vetches were for sale.[30] But
when you did send the fleet out, you obtained the kind of peace you
wanted. [**16**] Because triremes had such a great impact in both cases,
you were therefore right, men of Athens, to impose this requirement
on the Council as a way of determining whether it should receive an
award or not. If the Council has conducted all the rest of its business
well, but has not had those things built that enabled us to acquire
our possessions in the first place and now to keep them safe, I mean
the triremes, they gain no advantage from the former. Securing the
safety of all the people's possessions has to be the main priority. This
man has certainly reached the point where he thinks he can make any
speech or proposal he wants, and as a result, he has made a proposal to

[27]In 357 the Athenians brought back the Euboeans from alliance with the
Thebans to alliance with themselves.

[28]The Decelean War began when the Spartans occupied the Attic town of
Deceleia in 413 (Thuc. 7.18–20). During the Spartan occupation of Deceleia, more
than 20,000 slaves deserted Athens (Thuc. 7.27.3–5). The Athenians lost their fleet
at the battle of Aegospotamoi in 405 (Xen. *Hellenica* 2.1.21–30). For the ancient
commentary on this passage, see Gibson 2002: 179, 187.

[29]According to a scholion on this passage, this war broke out over Corcyra.
This would identify the conflict with the one which broke out in 374 after the
Spartan attack on Corcyra (Xen. *Hellenica* 6.2).

[30]Normally, vetches were not considered fit for human consumption.

grant the award, although the Council has discharged its other duties in the way you are being told but has not had the triremes built! [**17**] He could not say that this decree does not violate the law— and you should not be led to believe it. But I hear that he will make some argument along the lines that the Council was not responsible for the ships not being built but rather that the Treasurer for the Trieropoioi[31] ran off with two and a half talents and that this was just a bit of bad luck.[32] First of all, I am amazed that he actually thought the Council deserved a crown for bad luck: I thought such honors were reserved for successes![33] Next, I want to make the following point to you. [**18**] I maintain that it is not right to make both arguments: on the one hand, that the award was not given in violation of the law, and on the other, that it was not the fault of the Council that there are no triremes.[34] If it is right to give the award even when the Council

[31]The Trieropoioi was a committee of the Council that was responsible for the construction of triremes. The treasurer of this committee is not mentioned in the Aristotelian *Constitution of the Athenians*. For discussion of the ancient commentary on this passage, see Gibson 2002: 179, 187–188.

[32]Aristotle, in his discussion of *epieikeia* in the *Rhetoric* (1.13.1374b), distinguishes among wrongful acts (*adikemata*) done with evil intent (*mochtheria*), errors (*hamartemata*), and misfortunes (*atychemata*), things that take place contrary to expectation. The last two deserve more lenient treatment because these actions are not committed with evil intent. This distinction was known to the orators; see Dem. 18.274. For a similar argument that a defendant should not be held responsible for events beyond his control, see [Dem.] 56.21. On *epieikeia*, see E. M. Harris 2004b.

[33]Diodorus misrepresents Androtion's argument: Androtion believes that the Council should not be deprived of honors for performing its other duties well because of its failure to have triremes constructed, something that was beyond its control. Diodorus claims that Androtion is asking the Assembly to grant the award for its lack of success.

[34]Diodorus criticizes Androtion for making points that rely on contradictory premises: his opponent claims that the law does allow the Council to receive an award even if it has not had triremes built (as long as it does not request it), yet at the same time he argues that even if the law does not permit an award to a Council that has not had triremes built, it should still receive an award because its failure was due to circumstances beyond its control. But it was not unusual for Athenian litigants (like modern lawyers) to employ several alternative lines of argument, and Diodorus' criticism misses the point.

has not had them built, then why is it necessary to produce a reason why they have not been built at all? But if it is not allowed, why was it right for them to receive it if he demonstrates that they have not been built because of this or that person? [**19**] Apart from this, in my opinion such arguments present you with a choice: either you decide that you should listen to excuses and arguments from men who are doing you wrong, or you should have ships. If you accept these arguments from this man, it will be obvious to all Councils that they must find a plausible excuse rather than have triremes built. In that case, money will be spent, but you will not have ships.[35] [**20**] Yet if, as the law states and your oath requires, you sternly and without exception throw out these excuses and make it clear that you have revoked the award because they have not had the triremes built, all Councils, men of Athens, will have ships built and turn them over to you when they have seen that in your eyes all things are less important than the law.[36] And that no one else in the world is responsible for the failure to have triremes built, I will clearly demonstrate to you: it was the Council itself that broke the law by voting to elect this man.[37]

[**21**] Next, he will certainly try to discuss the law about prostitu-

---

[35] Here Diodorus shifts from legal arguments to consideration of public interest: if the court allows the Council to present excuses, future Councils will have no incentive to have triremes constructed.

[36] Diodorus claims that the Judicial Oath required the court to apply the law strictly, without taking other factors into account. This narrow approach to the Judicial Oath was not universally followed. It was possible for judges to allow litigants to bring considerations of fairness (*epieikeia*) to bear in a case, provided that they were based on general principles implicit in the law code as a whole. On this topic, see E. M. Harris 2004a.

[37] As ancient scholars noted, the argument is elliptical and unclear. The problem is compounded by the two different readings that the manuscripts preserve (*autēn* vs. *autēi*). I have accepted Jurinus' emendation (*autē*), adopted by Dilts, and followed the explanation of Rhodes 1972: 121–122: "The boule can hardly have made the appointment without reference to the demos (given so excellent a reason for not crowning the boule, Demosthenes would surely devote more than one sentence to it); perhaps it was normal for a free election to be held under an open probouleuma, but on this occasion the boule had recommended a candidate for approval of the ecclesia." Diodorus' point would then be that the Council cannot blame its failure to have triremes built on the Treasurer, because they were the ones who elected the Treasurer in the first place.

tion[38] and allege that we are insulting him and making irrelevant slanders about him. He even says that if we really believed the charges were true, we should go before the Thesmothetae[39] so that we would have run the risk of the 1,000–drachma fine if our charges were found to be false, but now we are playing tricks by making baseless charges and slanders and causing you trouble because you are not here to judge these issues.[40] [22] In my opinion, however, you should place the following point first in your considerations, namely, that slander and allegation are a completely different matter from proof. An allegation is when someone makes a bare assertion without providing a reason to trust what he says; proof is when someone makes a statement and at the same time shows it to be true. Well, then, it is incumbent on men who are trying to prove something either to present evidence that will make their argument clear and convincing to you or to argue from reasonable likelihood or to provide witnesses.[41] In some cases, it is not possible to present you with eyewitnesses, but if someone furnishes any of these kinds of proof, you rightly conclude that in each case you have an adequate test of the truth. [23] We are basing our case not on arguments based on likelihood nor from circumstantial evidence but from someone whom this man is in a position to punish, a man who has provided a document containing the events of this person's life and who has made himself subject to legal action by providing this testimony.[42] Thus, when Androtion says that these charges are just

---

[38]There was a public action (*graphe*) against prostitution, which could be brought against men who addressed the Assembly after they had performed sex in return for payment. There was another procedure called the "scrutiny of public speakers" (*dokimasia tōn rhētorōn*), which could also be brought against those who violated the ban on male prostitutes addressing the Assembly (see Aes. 1.32–33). For a discussion of these two procedures, see MacDowell 2005.

[39]For the ancient commentary on this passage, see Gibson 2002: 179, 188–189.

[40]Litigants in private cases swore an oath to keep to the point (*Ath. Pol.* 67.1), and litigants in public cases probably did the same; see Rhodes 1981: 718–719. Androtion accuses Diodorus of violating this oath. See note 19.

[41]For a similar distinction between arguments based on evidence or witnesses and those based on probabilities, see Aes. 1.90–92.

[42]A witness who testified in court was subject to the private action for false testimony (*dike pseudomartyriōn*). Isaeus (11.46) states that if a witness in a

slander and allegation, consider that this is proof and that what he does counts as "slander and allegation." And when he says we should have brought a charge before the Thesmothetae, consider this point, that we will also do this, but now we are discussing the law in the appropriate manner. [24] If we were making these charges when you were on trial for some other offense, you would have a right to be angry. But because the trial now underway concerns an illegal proposal, and because the laws do not allow men who have lived such a life to put forward even lawful proposals, and finally because we are trying to show not only that he has moved an illegal decree but that he has lived in an illegal fashion, how is it not appropriate to discuss this law that applies to his actions?

[25] Next, you should also realize this: Solon, the man who established these laws and most of our others—a lawgiver who was nothing like this man—did not provide one single way for men who wished to punish criminals, but many. He understood, I think, this fact that all men in the city would not have similar abilities or talents or the same degree of confidence or self-restraint. If he were to enact such laws as were suitable for moderate men to pursue justice, he figured that many scoundrels would go scot-free. Yet if the system favored men who were bold and talented speakers, private citizens would not have the same opportunity to obtain justice as the former.[43] [26] He thought that no one should be deprived of the right to obtain justice in a way suited to his level of ability. How then will this come about? If he creates many legal procedures for proceeding against offenders, as, for example, in the case of theft.[44] You are strong and confident

---

case was convicted on this charge, the entire case was tried again, but see Harrison 1971: 192–197.

[43]Private citizens (*idiotai*) were those who did not hold public office or address the Assembly and were often contrasted with public speakers (*rhetores*), magistrates (*archontes*), and generals (*strategoi*). On the term *idiotes,* see Rubinstein 1998.

[44]This passage is misleading as a description of the Athenian legal system, for its gives the false impression that each offense in Athenian law could be prosecuted in several different ways (*pace* Osborne 1985, who takes the passage out of context). This was true for theft and for the bribery of officials (see Hansen 1991: 193–194) but not for all other kinds of offenses. Nor should one conclude from

in your own ability: arrest him[45] and risk a fine of 1,000 drachmas.[46] You are weaker: lead the magistrates to him, and they will do it.[47] You are also afraid of this: bring a public charge.[48] [27] You do not feel confident, and since you are poor, you would not be able to pay the fine of 1,000 drachmas;[49] bring a private action before the arbitrator,[50] and you will run no risk.[51] None of these procedures is the same. The situation is the same with cases of impiety: someone can make an arrest,[52] bring a public charge,[53] bring a private charge before the

---

this passage that the main reason for creating various types of procedures for one group of offenses was to provide different social classes with access to the legal system. There were often major substantive differences between legal procedures (see, for instance, Hyp. 4.5–6 and Dem. 54.17–19). For an analysis of this passage, see Carey 2004.

[45]One could arrest a thief and bring him to the Eleven. If he confessed his guilt, he was put to death; if he denied it, his case went to court (*Ath. Pol.* 52.1). But this procedure could be used only when the offender's guilt was "obvious" (*ep'autophōrōi*), that is, in highly incriminating circumstances. See E. M. Harris 2006a: 373–390.

[46]I.e., if one lost the case. For this penalty, see n. 16.

[47]In this procedure (*ephegēsis*) the accuser led the magistrates to the offender and had them arrest him. See Hansen 1976: 24–35.

[48]There is some debate about the public action for theft; it may have only been available in cases of embezzlement by public officials. See Carey 2004: 126.

[49]I.e., if you lost the case. For this penalty, see n. 16.

[50]All private actions for more than ten drachmas were first heard by a public arbitrator; see *Ath. Pol.* 53.4–5. If either litigant was dissatisfied with his judgment, he could appeal the decision to a popular court. See Harrison 1971: 66–68.

[51]Aside from forfeiting the fee paid for initiating the suit (*prytaneia*), a litigant in a private action did not risk a penalty for losing his case. See Harrison 1971: 92–94. Taylor, followed by Dilts, deletes the next three phrases: "You wish to do neither of these. You are reluctant to do even this. Then denounce him (i.e., to an official)."

[52]The procedure of arrest to the Eleven was limited to thieves, enslavers, and clothes snatchers; see E. M. Harris 2006a: 291–293. Because the person who stole sacred property could be classified as a thief, he was thus subject to *apagōgē* to the Eleven. See n. 45.

[53]The public charge for impiety is well attested; it was the charge brought against Socrates in 399 BCE (Plato *Euthyphro* 5c).

Eumolpidai,[54] or make a denunciation to the King.[55] And it is more or less the same for all other procedures. [28] Imagine if someone should not argue that he is not a criminal or that he has not committed impiety (or whatever charge he is on trial for) but should ask to be acquitted for the following reasons if he was arrested: he should ask to be acquitted because his opponent could have brought a private suit before an arbitrator or should have brought a public charge, or, if he was a defendant in a case before an arbitrator, he should ask to be acquitted because you should have arrested him so that you would have risked a fine of 1,000 drachmas. These would certainly be ridiculous arguments. The man who has not committed a crime should not argue about the procedure for prosecution but show that he is innocent. [29] In the same way, Androtion, do not think that it is right for you to avoid punishment just because we could have lodged an indictment with the Thesmothetae if you proposed decrees after having been a prostitute. On the contrary, show that you have not committed the offense or suffer the punishment for moving a decree when you are this sort of person (something you cannot do). If we do not have you punished in all the ways that the laws allow, be grateful for the opportunities we are passing up, but do not assume that because of this you do not deserve any punishment at all.

[30] It is also worthwhile to study Solon, men of Athens, the man who established the law, and to consider how much foresight he displayed for all the laws he included in our constitution and how much more concern he showed for this general aim than for the particular offense for which he might have enacted the law. In fact, one can see this in many instances, not least of all in the law that forbids prostitutes to speak and move proposals. He saw that many of you who have the right to speak in public do not make speeches, and so he did

---

[54]Some scholars think that Lys. 6.11–12 describes a private charge of impiety, but see E. M. Harris 2006a: 417. On the judicial competence of the Eumolpidai, see Parker 1996: 296.

[55]The procedure of "pointing out" (*phasis*) was normally used to denounce the possession of illegal items such as enemy property (e.g., Isoc. 17.42; Aristoph. *Acharnians* 819–820, 911–914), but a recent inscription reveals that it could also be used in cases of impiety (*Hesperia* 49, 1980, 263, lines 27–29). On this procedure, see MacDowell 1991.

not consider this a heavy penalty. If he really wished to punish these men, he would have had many harsher penalties to impose. [31] But this was not his main concern. Rather, he imposed these restrictions to protect you and your constitution. He realized, yes, he realized that out of all constitutions, the one that is most hostile to men who have lived a shameful life is the one that grants all men the right to criticize their vices. Which one is that? Democracy.[56] But Solon was aware of the danger that at some time in the future there might be a large group of men who were both eloquent and bold but also led lives full of vice and depravity. [32] These men might mislead the people and cause them to commit many mistakes; indeed, they might try to overthrow the democracy altogether. (In oligarchies, by contrast, it is not possible to criticize magistrates even if they have led lives more disgraceful than Androtion's.) Or they might try to corrupt the people so thoroughly that they would turn out very much like themselves. He therefore completely deprived such men of the right to speak on public issues so they would not trick the people and cause them to make mistakes. But this fine, upstanding man paid no attention to these laws; not only did he think he needed to speak and move proposals despite this prohibition but he also did so in defiance of the laws.

[33] Then there is the law that denies this man the right to speak and even to make proposals because his father owed money to the Treasury and did not pay it.[57] If he claims that we must report him for this,[58] you would reasonably make the same correct argument: we will do this later, not now by Zeus, when you are required to present an account of your other crimes, but when it is legally appropriate to do so. Right now we are proving that the law does not allow you to move proposals, not even those that other people have a right to propose. [34] Show then that your father did not owe money or that he got out of prison not by running away but by paying the debt. If you

---

[56]For the ancient commentary on this passage, see Gibson 2002: 179, 189.

[57]The law deprived those who owed money to the Treasury of certain rights such as addressing the Council and Assembly. See Hansen 1976: 67–72, 84–88, 92–98.

[58]The speaker refers to the procedure of *endeixis*, in which a citizen might report someone who was illegally exercising a right to a magistrate. For this procedure and its use against *atimoi*, see Hansen 1976: 9–23, 90–98.

cannot show this, you have moved a proposal when you had no right to because the law makes you the heir of your father's loss of rights, and you should not have spoken or made a proposal after losing your rights.[59] As for the laws that I attached to my indictment, I think you should reply with the arguments I have explained if he tries to deceive and distract you.[60]

[35] He also has some arguments about other topics that are well designed to trick you. It is better for you to hear about them in advance. He has one argument that goes like this: "Don't take an award away from five hundred of your fellow citizens nor cover them with disgrace. I am fighting for them, not for myself." If you were only about to take this away from them, but bring no other advantage to the city, I would not ask you to take the matter so seriously. But if by doing this you are going to encourage more than ten thousand other citizens[61] to live better lives, how much better is it to make so many men virtuous than to grant five hundred a favor that they do not deserve? [36] I can also say that the responsibility lies not even with the entire Council but with only a few who are responsible for the harm and with Androtion. Who suffers disgrace if he keeps silent and makes no proposal, and perhaps for the most part does not even enter the Council house, and then the Council does not receive its award? Certainly no one does, but only in the case in which someone makes a proposal and conducts public business and persuades the Council to follow his wishes. It is their fault that the Council's performance does not deserve an award. [37] But even granted that the trial for the most part pertains to the entire Council, consider how much more you will

---

[59]The Athenians, like the Romans, followed the principle of universal succession in laws about inheritance. This meant that the heir acquired all the rights and duties of the deceased. If the liabilities of an estate exceeded the assets, the heir was responsible for paying all outstanding debts (see Harrison 1968: 125–130). Since Androtion inherited his father's debt to the treasury, he did not have the right to make proposals in the Assembly.

[60]The speaker turns from Androtion to address the court.

[61]Navarre in Navarre and Orsini (1954) suggested emending the number "ten thousand" to "twenty thousand" because this was the traditional number of Athenian citizens, but Dilts does not adopt this emendation. See Aristoph. *Wasps* 709; [Dem.] 25.51.

gain by a conviction than by an acquittal. If you acquit, the Council house will fall into the hands of those who make speeches, but if you convict, into the hands of ordinary citizens.[62] When the majority of citizens has seen the Council lose its crown because of this dishonesty of those who make speeches, they will not let them take over public business but will themselves offer their best advice. If this will happen and you get rid of the usual gang of orators, you will see everything work as it should, men of Athens. If, then, on no other grounds, you should condemn them for this reason.

[38] Listen now to another point that should not escape you. Philip,[63] Antigenes, the clerk,[64] and several others who together with Androtion have the Council house under their control and are responsible for these problems, will come forward and speak on behalf of the Council.[65] You all must realize that although the ostensible reason for their support is to help the Council, in reality they will fight to defend themselves and the accounts they have to render for their activities.[66] [39] This is the situation. If you acquit them on this public charge, they will get off scot-free and probably none of them will receive any punishment. For who would vote against them after you had given a crown to the Council where they were in charge?[67] If you convict, you will first of all have voted in keeping with your oath, and second, you

---

[62]In 25 the term private citizen (*idiotes*) refers to citizens who do not hold office in contrast to magistrates. Here the term denotes ordinary citizens who are members of the Council, in contrast to politicians who frequently make speeches.

[63]Because neither their father's names nor their demes are given, it is impossible to know if this Philip and this Antigenes are identical with any of the many Athenians who bore these names during this period.

[64]This was probably the clerk in charge of financial administration (*antigrapheus tēs dioikēseōs*) and is probably to be identified with the official of the same name who gave an account of public revenues to the Assembly every prytany (Aes. 3.25). See Rhodes 1972: 237–239.

[65]Diodorus predicts that these men will address the court as supporting speakers. For their role, see n. 17.

[66]These are magistrates who will have to present their accounts to the Logistai after their term of office (*Ath. Pol.* 54.2). They are worried that they are more likely to be indicted for their crimes if the Council does not receive a crown.

[67]For the reluctance of the courts to convict men who have received a crown, see Aes. 3.9–10.

will catch each of these men when he renders his accounts and punish whoever you think has committed a crime and then acquit whoever has not. Do not listen to them as if they were speaking on behalf of the Council and the majority of its members, but show that you are angry with them for trying to deceive you in order to help themselves.

[40] I also believe that Archias of Cholargus[68] (this man was a member of the Council last year) will come forward posing as an honorable man to beg you, pleading on their behalf. I think you should listen to Archias in roughly the following way: ask him about the charges brought against the Council and whether he thinks they are valid or not. If he says they are valid, do not pay any more attention to his claim about being an honorable man; but if not, ask him, on the other hand, why he did not then pursue these charges when he claims to be an honorable man? [41] And if he says he voiced objections, but no one followed his advice, it is certainly strange for him now to speak in defense of the Council when it does not follow his excellent advice. If he says he was silent, how can he be innocent if, when given the chance to stop men who were about to do wrong, he did not stop them, but now has the audacity to say that men who have done so much harm must receive a crown?

[42] I think he will not avoid making use of this argument: that all this trouble has happened because of the money he recovered, which he will say he collected for your benefit from a few men who shamelessly failed to contribute a large sum of money. And he will accuse them (an easy task, in my opinion) and say that there will be complete immunity for any failure to pay property taxes[69] if you vote against him. [43] First of all, men of Athens, keep these points in mind: you have sworn not to judge this issue but to determine whether he proposed a legal decree.[70] Next, it is quite amazing for a man who is accusing some people of crimes against the city also to ask that he

---

[68]Archias the son of Acestorides is listed as a joint trierarch on the ship *Stephanousa* in the 330s (*IG* ii² 1624, line 93). Davies 1971: 73 suggests a connection to the Philaid family on the basis of his father's name. Archias appears to have earlier accused the Council of wrongdoing. Diodorus now accuses him of hypocrisy for defending the honorary decree for the Council.

[69]On the *eisphora*, see Dem. 21.153n.

[70]The speaker again reminds the judges about their oath, which required them to pay attention only to the subject of the indictment and to ignore irrelevant issues.

himself should not be punished for even greater crimes. It is certainly a greater crime to propose an illegal decree than to fail to pay the tax. [44] Not even if it was obvious that if this man were to be convicted, everyone would stop paying taxes or that no one would be willing to collect them, not even in this case should you acquit him. The reason is that out of the taxes levied since the archonship of Nausinicus,[71] perhaps three hundred talents or a little more, there were arrears of fourteen talents, out of which this man collected seven, but I give him credit for the entire sum. For those who contribute willingly you do not need Androtion, only for those who default.

[45] Now, you need to consider whether you value the constitution and the established laws and obedience to your oath as highly as this sum of money. If you are going to acquit a man who has obviously made an illegal proposal in this way, everyone will think you have chosen that sum of money over the laws and obedience to your oath, a sum not worth accepting even if someone should give it to you from his own funds, much to take on the condition of collecting it from others.[72] [46] So when he makes this argument, therefore, remember your oath and keep in mind the indictment: the issue now is not about collecting taxes but whether the laws should have authority. On this score—the way he will try to divert your attention from the law and the replies to the argument that you should keep in mind so as not to give in to his arguments—I still have many points that I could make, but because I think this is sufficient, I will omit them.

[47] I also wish to take a close look at the policies of this fine, upstanding man, which will reveal that he has not refrained from committing any of the most serious crimes. I will show that he is

---

[71]I.e., in the year 378/7. This probably refers not to the whole period from this year to the time of Androtion's activity but to a shorter period, possibly only to the introduction of the *proeisphora*. In this system, a group of the wealthiest Athenians were required to forward to the state the entire amount of the *eisphora*, then to collect it from those liable to the tax.

[72]The speaker uses an *a fortiori* argument: because the amount of tax was so small that it was not worth accepting, even if one contributed the money voluntarily, there was even less reason to have Androtion go around collecting it. For voluntary contributions to the state by individuals in Athens and other Greek *poleis*, see Dem. 21.160–162nn.

shameless, impudent, a thief, arrogant, in short suitable for anything except a political career in a democracy. Indeed, first let us examine the way he collected the money, the achievement that gives him the most pride; pay no attention to his boasting but look at what actually took place. [48] This man said that Euctemon was withholding your tax revenues and that he would prove it or pay the money out of his own pocket. On this pretext he abolished by decree an office filled by lot and wormed his way into the job of collecting taxes.[73] He made speeches in the Assembly on this topic, claiming that there was a choice of three options: melt down the sacred vessels into coins, or levy another property tax, or collect money from those who owe it. [49] When you reasonably chose to collect the money from those who owed it, once he had you bound to these promises, he took advantage of the situation at the time to gain power for himself. He did not think he was bound to follow the laws established for these activities, nor set up new ones if he considered these inadequate, but right in front of you proposed terrible illegal decrees,[74] adding a clause instructing the Eleven to follow him around,[75] which allowed him to make a profit and to steal much of your money. [50] Then he took them along with him and led them into the houses of you citizens. But as for Euctemon, from whom he said he would collect money or pay the taxes himself, he was able to prove none of the charges against him but collected the money from you, as if he were going about this not because of his hatred for Euctemon but out of his hatred for you.

---

[73]Diodorus charges that Androtion had a special position created for himself instead of getting elected to one that already existed. For the position that Euctemon held, see Dem. 24.159–160.

[74]The Athenians drew a strict distinction between laws (*nomoi*), which were general rules and valid for all time, and decrees (*psephismata*), which were orders dealing with particular situations. For the distinction, see Plato *Definitions* 415b and Hansen 1991: 171–174. Diodorus claims that Androtion should have proposed a law when he changed the way of collecting the arrears from the property tax and that his decrees were therefore illegal. But it may have been possible to create ad hoc appointments by decree. See Aes. 3.13.

[75]The Eleven functioned as a police force and supervised the prison at Athens (*Ath. Pol.* 52.1), but they were not the only officials who could enforce the law. See Harris 2007a.

[**51**] Let no one assume that I am saying that it was not necessary to collect from those who owed the money. It was necessary. But how? In the way the law commands[76] and for the benefit of other citizens. This is the democratic way.[77] But when so little money was collected in this way, the advantage you gained did not outweigh the damage you suffered by introducing such habits into our political life. If you wish to examine the reasons why someone would choose to live in a democracy rather than an oligarchy, you would find this one the most prominent: all things are kinder and gentler in a democracy. [**52**] Now, that this man became more abusive than any oligarchy anywhere you choose, I will pass over. But when in the past did the worst atrocities ever occur in our city? Under the Thirty, you would all say. But at that time, as one can hear, there was no one who lost hope of survival as long as he kept himself hidden inside his house.[78] Instead, we criticize the Thirty for arresting men unjustly in the Agora. Yet this man's brutality so far surpassed theirs that he made each man's own home his prison by bringing the Eleven into private houses—even though he was conducting public business in a democracy![79] [**53**] And yet, men of Athens, what do you think when a poor man—or even a rich man who has spent a lot and is perhaps likely to be short of money in some way—either goes up over the roof to reach his neighbors or slips under his bed to avoid being physically seized and dragged off to prison? Or when he suffers the kind of indignities appropriate for

---

[76]The nine Archons and the members of the Council were required to swear an oath that they would act in accordance with the laws (*Ath. Pol.* 55.5–Archons; Rhodes 1981: 194–Council). This requirement probably extended to other officials.

[77]The Athenians often claimed that democracy was the only form of government that lived up to the ideal of the rule of law. See Aes. 1.4–6, 3.6; Thuc. 2.37.

[78]To put Androtion's actions in the worst possible light, Diodorus makes the crimes of the Thirty appear less serious than they actually were. According to Lys. 12.8 the Thirty did break into the houses of metics (resident aliens) and arrest them there.

[79]Normally, a magistrate could not enter into a private house without a decree authorizing him to do so. See Dem. 18.132 with E. M. Harris 1995: 172.

slaves, not free men?[80] Or when his wife, whom he, a free man and citizen of Athens, has married in honorable wedlock, sees him in this position? And when Androtion is responsible for this situation, a man whose conduct and life do not allow him to bring an accusation for his own sake, much less for the city's?[81]

[54] And yet if someone were to ask him whether one owes the property tax from one's property or one's person, he would say "from one's property" if he were willing to speak the truth. It is from this that we pay our property tax. Then for what reason did you not take the opportunity to confiscate land or houses and report them[82] and instead insulted and put in prison citizens and unfortunate metics, whom you have treated in a more insulting way than your own slaves?[83] [55] Indeed, if you wish to examine the difference between a free man and a slave, you will find this the greatest distinction: the bodies of slaves are subject to punishment for all their crimes, but free men can keep theirs safe from harm even in the worst disasters. In general, it is right to punish the latter by taking their property. But he did the opposite: he inflicted punishment on their bodies as if they were slaves. [56] He treated you in such a shameless and greedy way that he thought it was all right for his own father, in prison for a public debt, to escape without either paying the money or submitting to trial and winning acquittal, yet for other citizens he has anyone unable to pay his tax dragged from his house into prison. Then, as if he had the power to do anything at all, he seized as payment for debts, Sinope and Phanostrate,[84] pros-

---

[80]One of the main differences between slaves and free men was that the former were subject to corporal punishment, while the latter were not. See 55.

[81]The speaker alludes to his charge that Androtion was a prostitute and thus did not have the right to bring public charges. For the law, see Aes. 1.19.

[82]If someone owed money to the Treasury, anyone could report his property, which was then confiscated and sold by the Poletai to pay the debt; see Harrison 1971: 211–217.

[83]In some circumstances men in debt to the Treasury could be put in prison; see Harrison 1971: 241–244. Androtion's decree seems to have made failure to pay the *eisphora* such a circumstance.

[84]Sinope and Phanostrate were famous prostitutes (Athenaeus 13.586a). Sinope was mentioned in several comedies of the period. In his work *On the*

titutes who certainly did not owe the property tax.⁸⁵ [**57**] And yet if some people think that those women are fit to receive such treatment, they would not think the means used are appropriate when some people are so arrogant when the opportunity presents itself that they walk into houses and carry off furniture belonging to men who owe nothing at all.⁸⁶ Anyone can see that many people are fit to receive this treatment or to have received it. But that is not what our laws say, nor the customs of our community, which you must uphold. Contained in them, on the contrary, are pity, forgiveness, all the qualities free men ought to possess. [**58**] Understandably, neither his nature nor his upbringing gave him a share of all these qualities: he put up with many insults and much abusive treatment because he spent his time not with men who cared about him but with those who could pay his fee! You should have unleashed your anger not on any citizen you encountered, nor on the comrades in your profession,⁸⁷ but on the man who raised you in this way.

[**59**] This man will not be able to deny his conduct was terrible and violated all the laws. He is so shameless that when he was devising ways to attack my charge against him before the trial, he dared to say in the Assembly that he made enemies for himself by fighting on your behalf and to protect you and that now he faced the ultimate danger. I want to show you, men of Athens, that he has never suffered the least harm nor is he about to suffer any for what he did on your behalf. In fact, he has suffered nothing for being loathsome and god-forsaken until today—but he will suffer if you do what is right. [**60**] Look at it in this way: what did this man promise and what did you vote for him to do? To collect money. To do anything beyond

---

Athenian Courtesans, Apollodorus says that Phanostrate was nicknamed "Louse-Gate" for picking lice from her body as she stood at her door while awaiting customers.

⁸⁵These women were probably slaves. As the property of their masters, slaves could be seized by creditors as payment for their masters' debts. See, for example, Dem. 53.20.

⁸⁶Diodorus makes a distinction between slaves, who are normally treated harshly because of their status, and free persons, who should not be deprived of their property without just cause.

⁸⁷I.e., prostitution.

this? Not a single thing. Come, let me remind you in detail about the way he collected money. This man collected thirty-four drachmas from Leptines of Koile[88] and seventy drachmas and a little more from Theoxenus of Alopeke[89] and from Callicrates, the son of Eupherus,[90] and the young son of Telestes[91] (I cannot remember his name). Out of just about all the men he collected money from (so as to avoid naming them one by one), I do not know if anyone owed more than a mina.[92] [**61**] Do you think he has gained the hatred and hostility of each of these men because of this property tax? Or does one hate him because he said in the Assembly, while all of you were listening, that this man was a slave and his parents were slaves and that he should pay the one-sixth tax along with the metics,[93] and another should pay it because the mother of his children was a whore,[94] yet another because his father was a prostitute, about still another that his mother was a whore, and about another that he was going to report all the property he stole from the beginning of his career, about another he said this or that, and about another he cast insults, some fit to be uttered, some not, and so on for everyone? [**62**] I know that although each of those who suffered from his drunken abuse considered the property tax a necessary expense, he found it difficult to endure the humiliation and contempt. I know this too: you elected this man to collect money, not to insult and reproach each man for his personal misfortunes. If the allegation were true, you should not mention them (many things do

---

[88]This man may be identical with the man Demosthenes prosecuted in his *Against Leptines*. See the Introduction to that speech.

[89]Nothing else is known about this man.

[90]This man is mentioned in naval records of *IG* ii² 1622, 165–184. For his family connections, see Davies 1971: 277–282.

[91]The name is rare in the fourth century, and this man may be identical with the Telestes found in a list of members of a *thiasos* from the same period (*IG* ii² 2342, line 5).

[92]A mina was one hundred drachmas.

[93]Slaves who were manumitted and remained in Athens became metics, who had to pay a supplement of one-sixth for the *eisphora*; see Whitehead 1977: 78–80.

[94]Most prostitutes were slaves and thus not citizens. If a child was the son of a slave, he could not become a citizen (*Ath. Pol.* 42.1).

not turn out for each of us exactly as he wishes); if you were inventing disasters that had nothing to do with them, do you not deserve to be punished in any way whatever?

[63] Here is another point that will show you in more detail that each person hates this man not because he collected money but for his insults and drunken abuse. Satyrus,[95] the Superintendent of the Dockyards, collected on your behalf not seven but thirty-four talents from these same men and used the money to provide equipment for ships sailing out to sea. And yet this man says he has no enemy because of this, and none of the men he collected from has any quarrel with him. And rightly so. In my opinion, this man was carrying out his assigned task, but you on the other hand gave full rein to your rashness and arrogance and thought it necessary to heap harsh, lying insults upon men who have spent much money on the city, men who are better than you and come from better families. [64] Should you next persuade these men[96] that you acted on their behalf and expect them to accept that your senseless and evil actions were deeds done for their benefit? No, it would be more just for them to hate you than to save you. The man who acts on behalf of the city should imitate its character. And you should protect such people, men of Athens, and hate people like this man. You may know the proverb, but I will still repeat it: the sort of men that you favor and protect are the kind of men you will appear to resemble.

[65] He has never done anything for your benefit, not even collecting taxes, as I will immediately make clear to you. Take two kinds of people: men who farm and are frugal but fall behind in paying taxes because they spend money on raising children or household expenses or other liturgies, and then men who steal money from those who wish to pay the tax and from our allies, then waste it. If someone asked him which group he thinks commits the greater crime against the city, he would certainly not be so bold (despite his utter shamelessness) as to claim that those who do not pay the tax on their own property commit a greater crime than men who steal public funds.

---

[95]We know of several men of this name in the mid fourth century, but since Diodorus does not give the name of his father or of his deme, it is impossible to know if this Satyrus can be identified with any of them.

[96]I.e., the judges.

[**66**] What is the reason why, you disgusting person, in the more than thirty years you have been in politics, when during this time many generals and many politicians have committed crimes against the state and been tried in this court, and some have been executed for their crimes and others have gone into exile,[97] you never stepped forward to prosecute any of them nor expressed your anger about the harm done to the city despite your eloquence and self-assurance, but only in this case where you had to mistreat so many people, you were the one who was clearly concerned?

[**67**] Do you want me to tell you the reason for this, men of Athens? Because some of these men [have a share in their crimes against you and steal from those they collect money from. They thus reap a profit from the city to satisfy their greedy habits in two ways. For it is not easier to be angry at many who commit small injustices than at the few who do great wrongs. Nor indeed is it more democratic to pay attention to the injustices of the many rather than those of the few. But this what I say is responsible.][98] He knows that he is one of the wrongdoers, but he thought you worthless. For this reason he treated you in this way. [**68**] If this were agreed to be a city of slaves rather than of men who deserve to rule others, you still would not, men of Athens, put up with the outrages he inflicts on metics and Athenians alike in the Agora: having them tied up, arresting them, shouting at meetings of the Assembly from the speaker's platform that men better than himself and from better families are slaves and the children of slaves, asking if the prison was built to no avail (I would agree because your father escaped from there after dancing in his chains during the procession at the Dionysia).[99] One could not list all the other acts of insolence he has committed—the number is so large. You should impose a penalty today for all his crimes and provide an example for others so they will show greater restraint. [**69**] "Yet, by

---

[97]This statement is not an exaggeration. Hansen (1975: 60) has shown that in the period 432–355, out of 160 Athenian generals attested in our sources, 33 were brought to trial, and many were convicted.

[98]This section is deleted by Butcher, followed by Dilts.

[99]According to a scholion on the passage, prisoners were allowed to join in the procession at the Dionysia. At 33 Diodorus claimed that Androtion's father was put in prison for his failure to pay a debt to the Treasury.

Zeus, this is the way he has acted during his political career, but there are other tasks he has managed well."[100] Far from it: in all the rest of his career he has acted toward you in such a way that the things you have heard about are the least reason to hate him. What do you want me to discuss? How he repaired processional vessels and melted down crowns, and his splendid production of plates?[101] For these actions by themselves, even if he happened to commit no other crime against the city, it will be obvious he deserves to die not once but three times; indeed he is guilty of temple robbery, impiety, theft, and all the most serious crimes. [70] I will not mention the many things that he said to deceive you. But he claimed the leaves on the crowns had fallen off and that they became rotten over time as if they fell off violets or roses, not made of gold, and persuaded you to melt them down.[102] Then for the property tax he added a clause that the public slave be present, as if indeed he were an honest citizen—even though everyone who paid the tax was about to act as an auditor of his accounts.[103] But for the crowns that he melted down, he did not add this same honest provision, but he acted as politician, goldsmith, treasurer, and auditor.[104]

[71] And yet if you asked that all the things you do for the city be placed in your hands, it would only make your embezzlement less conspicuous. As it is, in regard to the property tax, you stipulated that the city entrust its affairs not to you but to its slaves, which is the correct procedure. Yet when involved in some other task and handling sacred objects, some of which were dedicated even before our lifetime, you clearly do not include this safeguard that you included

---

[100]The speaker imagines an opponent making an objection.

[101]Androtion's decree about these dedications may be referred to at *IG* ii² 216, line 13 and 217, line 13.

[102]As D. Harris 1995: 33 notes, "Demosthenes makes the claim sound ridiculous; but there is one entry in the inventories which shows that wreaths did lose leaves from time to time." See *IG* ii² 1377, lines 22–24.

[103]Some public slaves acted as clerks. When Androtion drew up the decree granting him the power to collect arrears, he added a clause instructing one of these slaves to check his accounts. He did this as a way of assuring the Assembly of his honesty, but Diodorus dismisses the precaution as unnecessary because everyone who paid the tax could determine if his accounts were trustworthy.

[104]The Athenians generally did not allow someone to hold more than one position at once; Diodorus accuses Androtion of violating this rule.

for the property tax. Isn't the reason for doing this obvious? I think it is. [72] Consider then, men of Athens, how noble and admirable were the inscriptions he has forever destroyed and how terrible and sacrilegious what he has written in their place. I think you see written on the mounting underneath the crowns "From the allies for the people because of their nobility and justice," or "A prize of valor from the allies for Athena," and from individual cities, "From such and such for the people for saving them," such as "The Euboeans gave the people a crown for restoring their liberty," and again "From Conon from the naval battle against the Spartans."[105] Such were the phrases written on the crowns. [73] These phrases, which brought the city much admiration and honor, vanished when the crowns were melted down.[106] On the bowls that this whore had made in their place, has been written "[These were made][107] under the supervision of Androtion." The man whom the laws prohibit from entering temples for having prostituted his body has his name written on the bowls in our temples! Is there any similarity between this and the earlier inscriptions? Do they bring you the same honor? Certainly not. [[74] Anyone could see from this that they have committed three of the worst offenses: first, they robbed the goddess of her crowns; second, they destroyed the admiration won by the city for its accomplishments, which these crowns served to commemorate while they existed; and third, they deprived the dedicants of their not inconsiderable fame and their reputation for being willing to remember the favors they received. Having committed such a great number of misdeeds of this sort, they have come to this point where they are so arrogant and so obtuse that they refer to these actions as if they were examples of their splendid administration! As a result, one thinks you will acquit him because of this, another sits down next to him and is not overcome with shame for what he has done.][108] [75] He is not only so shameless about money but also so uncouth that he

---

[105]Conon commanded the Persian fleet during their naval victory over the Spartans at Cnidus in 394. See Dem. 20.68.

[106]Demosthenes makes the melting down of these dedications sound like a terrible crime, but it appears to have been a routine matter. See D. Harris 1995: 31–36.

[107]Some editors delete this.

[108]This section is repeated from Dem. 24.182. Most editors believe it is a later addition to the text and delete it because it appears out of place in this context.

does not realize that crowns are a mark of valor, while bowls and such things are a sign of wealth. Every crown, no matter how small, brings as much honor as a large one; chalices and censers, if their number exceeds the normal amount, rub off on their owners a certain reputation for wealth. But if a man takes pride in trifles, far from gaining honor through them he also appears lacking in taste. By destroying the objects that gave you your fame, he has cheapened the objects that constituted your wealth and made them unworthy of you. [76] He did not understand that the people have never been eager to acquire wealth but rather to acquire fame above anything else. Here is a proof: when the people had the most money of the Greeks, they spent it all on the pursuit of honor. When they paid the tax from their private property, they shunned no danger in their pursuit of fame. What they acquired from this effort is everlasting, both the memory of their deeds and the beauty of the dedications set up to commemorate them: the Propylaea, the Parthenon, the stoas, the shipsheds. Not two little jars, or even three or four gold ones, each weighing a few pounds, which you will propose to melt down whenever you see fit! [77] Not by imposing a tithe on themselves[109] nor by doubling the property tax (that is a curse we reserve for our enemies) did they make these dedications. They did not conduct their politics using advisors like you but by defeating their enemies and bringing unity to the city, a goal that every intelligent man would pray for, they have left behind immortal fame—and they banned from the Agora people who follow the sort of lifestyle you do! [78] You have progressed, men of Athens, to the point where you are so simple-minded and heedless that despite the examples in front of you, you do not follow them. Instead, you have Androtion to repair sacred vessels, Androtion, Earth and gods! What impiety do you think is greater than this? In my opinion, the man who enters temples, touches lustral water and sacred baskets, and intends to take responsibility for looking after the gods, should not only keep himself pure for a prescribed number of days but keep his entire life pure from the kind of activities that this man has practiced during his life.[110]

---

[109]During his rule, Peisistratus imposed a tithe on produce, which was abolished by the democracy. See Thuc. 6.54.5 and *Ath. Pol.* 16.4 with Rhodes 1981: 215.

[110]For the need to be morally pure when performing religious rites, see Parker 1983: 96–97.

BIBLIOGRAPHY FOR THIS VOLUME

Amandry, P., 1976: "Trépieds d'Athènes: I Dionysies," *Bulletin de Correspondence Hellénique* 100: 15–93.

Badian, E., 2000: "The Road to Prominence," in Worthington (2000): 9–44.

Bakewell, G., and J. Sickinger, 2003: *Gestures: Essays in Ancient History, Literature, and Philosophy Presented to Alan L. Boegehold*. London.

Boegehold, A., 1995: *The Lawcourts at Athens: Sites, Buildings, Equipment, Procedure, and Testimonia (The Athenian Agora XXVIII)*. Princeton.

Bosworth, A. B., 1988: *Conquest and Empire: The Reign of Alexander the Great*. Cambridge.

Bresson, A., 1993: "Emporion," in Bresson and Rouillard (1993): 163–226.

———, 2000: *La cité marchande*. Bordeaux.

Bresson, A., and P. Rouillard, eds., 1993: *L'emporion*. Paris.

Bugh, G., 1988: *The Horsemen of Athens*. Princeton.

Burke, E. M., 2002: "The Early Political Speeches of Demosthenes: Élite Bias in the Response to Economic Crisis," *Classical Antiquity* 21: 163–193.

Cairns, D., 1996: "*Hybris*, Dishonour, and Thinking Big," *Journal of Hellenic Studies* 116: 1–32.

Cairns, D. L. and R. A. Knox, eds., 2004: *Law, Rhetoric, and Comedy in Classical Athens: Essays in Honour of Douglas M. MacDowell*. Swansea.

Cantarella, E., ed., 2007: *Symposion 2005: Vorträge zur griechischen und hellenistischen Rechtsgeschichte*. Cologne.

Carey, C., 1995: "The Witness's *Exomosia* in Athenian Courts," *Classical Quarterly* 45: 114–119.

———, 1996: "*Nomos* in Attic Rhetoric and Oratory," *Journal of Hellenic Studies* 116: 33–46.

———, 2004: "Offence and Procedure in Athenian Law," in Harris and Rubinstein (2004): 111–136.

Cartledge, P., P. Millett, and S. Todd, eds., 1990: *Nomos: Essays in Athenian Law, Politics, and Society*. Cambridge.

Cartledge, P., P. Millett, and S. von Reden, eds., 1998: *Kosmos: Essays in Order, Conflict and Community in Classical Athens*. Cambridge.

Cawkwell, G. L., 1962: "Notes on the Social War," *Classica et Medievalia* 23: 34–49.

———, 1963: "Eubulus," *Journal of Hellenic Studies* 83: 47–67.

———, 1981: "Notes on the Failure of the Second Athenian Confederacy." *Journal of Hellenic Studies* 101: 40–55.

Chremmydas, C., 2005: *A Commentary on Demosthenes Against Leptines 1–105*. Dissertation, University of London.

Clinton, K., 1980: "A Law in the City Eleusinion concerning the Mysteries," *Hesperia* 49: 258–288.

Cohen, D., 1995: *Law, Violence, and Community in Classical Athens*. Cambridge.

Cooper, C., ed., 2006: *The Politics of Orality*. Leiden.

Culasso Gastaldi, E., 2004: *Le prossenie ateniesi del IV secolo a.C.: Gli onoratia siatici*. Alessandria.

Currie, B., 2005: *Pindar and the Cult of Heroes*. Oxford.

Davies, J. K., 1967: "Demosthenes on Liturgies: A Note," *Journal of Hellenic Studies* 87: 33–40.

———, 1971: *Athenian Propertied Families 600–300 B.C.* Oxford.

Dillon, M., 2006: "Was Cleisthenes or Pleisthenes Archon at Athens in 525 BC?" *Zeitschrift für Papyrologie und Epigraphik* 155: 91–107.

Dimakis, P., ed., 1981: *Symposion 1979: Vorträge zur griechischen und hellenistischen Rechtsgeschichte*. Cologne.

Dorjahn, A. P., 1935: "Anticipation of Arguments in Athenian Courts," *Transactions of the American Philological Association* 66: 275–295.

Dover, K. J., 1968: *Lysias and the Corpus Lysiacum*. Berkeley, CA.

Easterling, P., and E. Hall, eds., 2002: *Greek and Roman Actors: Aspects of an Ancient Profession*. Cambridge.

Erbse, H., 1956: "Über die Midiana des Demosthenes," *Hermes* 84: 135–151.

Faraguna, M., ed., 2007: Nomos Despotes: *Law and Legal Procedure in Ancient Greek Society*. Trieste.

Fisher, N. R. E., 1992: *Hybris*. Warminster.

————, 2001: *Aeschines: Against Timarchus*. Oxford.

————, 2003: "Let Envy Be Absent: Envy, Liturgies, and Reciprocity in Athens," in Konstan and Rutter (2003): 181–215.

Frye, R. N., 1972: "Gestures of deference to royalty in Ancient Iran," *Iranica Antiqua* 9: 102–107.

Gabrielsen, V., 1994: *Financing the Athenian Fleet: Public Taxation and Social Relations*. Baltimore.

Gagarin, M., ed., 1991: *Symposion 1990: Vorträge zur griechischen und hellenistischen Rechtsgeschichte*. Cologne.

Garnsey, P., 1988: *Famine and Food Supply in the Graeco-Roman World: Responses to Risk and Crisis*. Cambridge.

Gauthier, P., 1972: *Symbola: Les étrangers et la justice dans les cités grecques*. Nancy.

Gentili, B., and F. Perusino, eds., 2002: *Le orse di Brauron: Un rituale di iniziazione femminile nel santuario di Artemide*. Pisa.

Gibson, C., 2002: *Interpreting a Classic: Demosthenes and His Ancient Commentators*. Berkeley, CA.

Goldhill, S., and R. Osborne, eds., 1999: *Performance Culture and Athenian Democracy*. Cambridge.

Gribble, D., 1999: *Alcibiades and Athens: A Study in Literary Presentation*. Oxford.

Habicht, C., 1961: "Falsche Urkunden zur Geschichte Athens im Zeitalter der Perserkriege," *Hermes* 89: 1–35.

Hall, E., 1989: *Inventing the Barbarian*. Oxford.

Hansen, M. H., 1974: *The Sovereignty of the People's Court in Athens in the Fourth Century B.C.* Odense.

————, 1975: *Eisangelia: The Sovereignty of the People's Court in Athens in the Fourth Century B.C. and the Impeachment of Generals and Politicians*. Odense.

————, 1976: *Apagoge, Endeixis, and Ephegesis against Kakourgoi, Atimoi, and Pheugontes: A Study in the Athenian Administration of Justice in the Fourth Century B.C.* Odense.

————, 1978: "*Nomos* and *Psephisma* in Fourth-Century Athens," *Greek, Roman, and Byzantine Studies* 19: 315–330.

————, 1980: "Athenian *Nomothesia* in the Fourth Century B.C. and Demosthenes' Speech *Against Leptines*," *Classica et Medievalia* 32: 87–104.

————, 1981: "Two Notes on the Athenian *dikai emporikai*," in Dimakis 1981: 167–175.

————, 1983: "The Athenian 'Politicians': 403–322 B.C.," *Greek, Roman, and Byzantine Studies* 24: 33–56.

————, 1985: "Athenian *nomothesia*," *Greek, Roman, and Byzantine Studies* 26: 345–371.

————, 1991: *The Athenian Democracy in the Age of Demosthenes.* Oxford.

————, 2006: *Studies in the Population of Aigina, Athens and Eretria.* Copenhagen.

Harding, P., 1976: "Androtion's Political Career," *Historia* 25: 186–200.

————, 1994: *Androtion and the* Atthis. Oxford.

Harris, D., 1995: *The Treasures of the Parthenon and Erectheion.* Oxford.

Harris, E. M., 1989: "Demosthenes' Speech *Against Meidias*," *Harvard Studies in Classical Philology* 92: 117–136.

————, 1990: "The Constitution of the Five Thousand," *Harvard Studies in Classical Philology* 93: 243–280.

————, 1992: Review of MacDowell (1990). *Classical Philology* 87: 71–80.

————, 1994: "Law and Oratory," in Worthington (1994): 130–150.

————, 1995: *Aeschines and Athenian Politics.* New York.

————, 1999: "Notes on the New Grain-tax Law," *Zeitschrift für Papyrologie und Epigraphik* 128: 269–272.

————, 2000: "Open Texture in Athenian Law," *Dike* 3: 27–79.

————, 2004a: "More Thoughts on Open Texture in Athenian Law," in Leao, Rosetti, and Fialho (2004): 241–263.

————, 2004b: "Le rôle de *l'epieikeia* dans les tribunaux athéniens," *Revue historique de droit français et étranger* 82: 1–13.

————, 2005: "Feuding or the Rule of Law? The Nature of Litigation in Classical Athens," in Wallace and Gagarin (2005): 125–142.

————, 2006a: *Democracy and the Rule of Law in Classical Athens: Essays on Law, Society and Politics.* Cambridge.

————, 2006b: "Did the Athenian Courts Attempt to Achieve Consistency? Oral Tradition and Written Records in the Athenian Administration of Justice," in Cooper (2006): 343–370.

————, 2007a: "Who Enforced the Law in Classical Athens?" in Cantarella (2007): 159–176.

————, 2007b: "The Rule of Law in Athens: Reflections on the Judicial Oath," in Faraguna (2007b): 55–74.

Harris, E. M., and L. Rubinstein, eds., 2004: *The Law and the Courts in Ancient Greece.* London.

Harris, W. V., 1989: *Ancient Literacy.* Cambridge, MA.

Harrison, A. R. W., 1968: *The Law of Athens: The Family and Property.* Oxford.

————, 1971: *The Law of Athens: Procedure.* Oxford.

Harvey, D., 1966: "Literacy in the Athenian Democracy," *Revue des Études Grecques* 79: 585–635.

————, 1990: "The Sycophant and Sycophancy: Vexatious Redefinition?" in Cartledge, Millett, and Todd (1990): 103–121.

Henry, A. S., 1983: *Honours and Privileges in Athenian Decrees.* Hildesheim.

Herman, G., 1987: *Ritualised Friendship and the Greek City.* Cambridge.

Hesk, J., 2000: *Deception and Democracy in Classical Athens.* Cambridge.

Hoffman, H., 1961: "The Persian Origin of Attic Rhyta," *Antike Kunst* 4: 21–26.

Jordan, B., 1975: *The Athenian Navy in the Classical Period.* Berkeley, CA.

Knoepfler, D., 1981: "Argoura: Un toponyme eubéen dans la Midienne de Démosthène," *Bulletin de Correspondance Hellénique* 105: 289–329.

Konstan, D., 2000: "Pity and the Law in Greek Theory and Practice," *Dike* 3: 125–145.

Konstan, D., and K. Rutter, eds., 2003: *Envy, Spite and Jealousy: The Rivalrous Emotions in Ancient Greece.* Edinburgh.

Krentz, P., 1982: *The Thirty at Athens.* Ithaca, NY.

Kurihara, A., 2003: "Personal enmity as a Motivation in Forensic Speeches," *Classical Quarterly* 53: 464–477.

Lanni, A., 1997: "Spectator Sports or Serious Politics: οἱ περιεστη-κότες and the Athenian Lawcourts," *Journal of Hellenic Studies* 117: 183–189.

Leao, D., D. Rosetti, and M. Fialho, eds., 2004: *Nomos—estudos sobre direito antigo*, Coimbra.

Lewis, D. M., 1954: "Notes on Attic Inscriptions I," *Annual of the British School at Athens* 49: 17–50.

———, 1955: "Notes on Attic Inscriptions II," *Annual of the British School at Athens* 50: 1–36.

Loomis, W. T., 2003: "Slander at Athens: A Common Law Perspective," in Bakewell and Sickinger 2003: 287–300.

MacDowell, D. M., 1963: *Athenian Homicide Law in the Age of the Orators*. Manchester.

———, 1971: "The Chronology of Athenian Speeches and Legal Innovations in 401–398 B.C." *Revue Internationale des Droits d'Antiquité*[3] 18: 267–273.

———, 1975: "Law-making at Athens in the Fourth Century B.C.," *Journal of Hellenic Studies* 95: 62–74.

———, 1976: "*Hybris* in Athens," *Greece and Rome* 23: 14–31.

———, 1978: *The Law in Classical Athens*. London.

———, 1983: "Athenian laws about Bribery," *Revue Internationale des Droits d'Antiquité*[3] 30: 57–78.

———, 1986: "The Law of Periandros about Symmories," *Classical Quarterly* 36: 438–449.

———, 1989a: "Athenian Laws about Choruses," in Nieto 1989: 65–77.

———, 1989b: "The Authenticity of Demosthenes 29 (Against Aphobos III) as a Source of Information about Athenian Law," in Thür 1989: 253–262.

———, 1990: *Demosthenes: Against Meidias (Oration 21)*. Oxford.

———, 1991: "The Athenian Procedure of *phasis*," in Gagarin 1991: 187–198.

———, 2000: "Athenian Laws about Homosexuality," *Revue Internationale des Droits d'Antiquité*[3] 47: 13–27.

———, 2004: "Epikerdes of Kyrene and the Athenian Privilege of Ateleia," *Zeitschrift für Papyrologie und Epigraphik* 150: 127–133.

———, 2005: "The Athenian Procedure of *dokimasia* of Orators," in Wallace and Gagarin 2005: 79–88.

Makres, N., 1994: *The Institution of the Choregia in Classical Athens.* Dissertation, Oxford University.

McCabe, D. F., 1981: *The Prose-Rhythm of Demosthenes.* New York.

Meritt, B. D., 1970: "Ransom of Athenians by Epikerdes," *Hesperia* 39: 111–114.

Michell, H., 1952: *Sparta.* Cambridge.

Migeotte, L., 1992: *Les souscriptions publiques dans les cités grecques.* Geneva.

Mikalson, J., 1975: *The Sacred and Civil Calendar of the Athenian Year.* Princeton.

Moscati Castelnuovo, L., 1980: "La carriera politica dell'Attidografo Androzione," *Acme* 33: 251–278.

Naiden, F. S., 2004: "Supplication and the Law," in Harris and Rubinstein (2004): 71–91.

Navarre, O., and P. Orsini, 1954: *Démosthène: Plaidoyers politiques* I. Paris.

Nieto, F. J. F., ed., 1989: *Symposion 1982: Vorträge zur griechischen und hellenistischen Rechtsgeschichte.* Cologne.

Ober, J., 1989: *Mass and Elite in Democratic Athens.* Princeton.

Osborne, M. J., 1981–1983: *Naturalization in Athens.* 3 vols. Brussels.

Osborne, R. G., 1985: "Law in Action in Classical Athens," *Journal of Hellenic Studies* 105: 40–58.

Ostwald, M., 1955: "The Athenian Legislation against Tyranny and Subversion," *Transactions of the American Philological Association* 86: 103–128.

Parker, R., 1983: *Miasma: Pollution and Purification in Early Greek Religion.* Oxford.

———, 1996: *Athenian Religion: A History.* Oxford.

———, 2004: "What Are Sacred Laws?" in Harris and Rubinstein (2004): 57–70.

———, 2005: *Polytheism and Society at Athens.* Oxford.

Parkins, H., and C. Smith, eds., 1998: *Trade, Traders, and the Ancient City.* London.

Pouilloux, J., 1971: *Nouveau choix d'inscriptions grecques: Textes, traductions, commentaires.* Paris.

Pritchett, W. K., 1991: *The Greek State at War.* Vol. V. Berkeley, CA.

Rhodes, P. J., 1972: *The Athenian Boule*. Oxford.

————, 1981: *A Commentary on the Aristotelian* Athenaion Politeia. Oxford.

————, 1985: "*Nomothesia* in Fourth Century Athens," *Classical Quarterly* 35: 85–90.

————, 2004: "Keeping to the Point," in Harris and Rubinstein (2004): 137–158.

Rhodes, P. J., and R. Osborne, 2003: *Greek Historical Inscriptions 404–323 B.C.* Oxford.

Rickert, G., 1989: ΕΚΩΝ *and* ΑΚΩΝ *in Early Greek Thought*. Atlanta, GA.

Rosivach, V., 1994: *The System of Public Sacrifice in Fourth-Century Athens*. Atlanta, GA.

Rowe, G. O., 1995: "The Charge against Meidias," *Hermes* 122: 55–63.

Rubinstein, L., 1998: "The Political Perception of the *idiotes*," in Cartledge, Millett, and von Reden (1998): 125–143.

————, 2000: *Litigation and Cooperation: Supporting Speakers in the Courts of Classical Athens*. Stuttgart.

————, 2004: "Stirring up Dicastic Anger," in Cairns and Knox (2004): 187–203.

Sandys, J. E., 1890: *The Speech of Demosthenes Against the Law of Leptines*. Cambridge.

Saunders, T. J., 1991: *Plato's Penal Code: Tradition, Controversy, and Reform in Greek Penology*. Oxford.

Scafuro, A., 2004: "The Role of the Prosecutor and Athenian Legal Procedure," *Dike* 7: 113–133.

Schaefer, A., 1885–1887: *Demosthenes und seine Zeit.*[2] Leipzig.

Schmalz, G., 2006: "The Athenian Prytaneion Discovered?" *Hesperia* 75: 33–81.

Schmitt Pantel, P., 1992: *La cité au banquet: Histoire des repas publics dans les cités grecques*. Rome.

Seager, R., 1967: "Thrasybulus, Conon, and Athenian Imperialism, 396–386 B.C." *Journal of Hellenic Studies* 87: 95–115.

Sealey, R. 1993: *Demosthenes and His Time*. New York.

Strong, D. E., 1966: *Greek and Roman Silver Plate*. London.

Themelis, P., 2002: "Contribution to the Topography of the Sanctuary at Brauron," in Gentili and Perusino (2002): 103–116.

Thomas, R., 1989: *Oral Tradition and Written Record in Classical Athens*. Cambridge.

Threatte, L., 1996: *The Grammar of Attic Inscriptions II: Morphology*. Berlin.

Thür, G., ed., 1989: *Symposion 1985: Vorträge zur griechischen und hellenistischen Rechtsgeschichte*. Cologne.

Tod, M. N., 1947: *A Selection of Greek Historical Inscriptions II: From 403 to 323 BC*². Oxford.

Trevett, J., 1992: *Apollodoros the Son of Pasion*. Oxford.

Tritle, L. A., 1988: *Phocion the Good*. London.

Tulin, A., 1996: Dike Phonou: *The Right of Prosecution and Attic Homicide Procedure*. Stuttgart.

Veligianni-Terzi, C., 1997: *Wertbegriffe in den attischen Ehrendekreten der klassischen Zeit*. Stuttgart.

Vince, J. H., 1930: *Demosthenes: Volume I*. Cambridge, MA.

Walbank, M. B., 1990: "Notes on Attic Decrees," *Annual of the British School at Athens* 85: 435–447.

Wallace, R. W., 1989: "The Athenian *Proeispherontes*," *Hesperia* 58: 473–490.

Wallace, R. W. and M. Gagarin, eds., 2005: *Symposion 2001: Vorträge zur griechischen und hellenistischen Rechtsgeschichte*. Vienna.

Werner, R., 1955: "Die Dynastie der Spartokiden," *Historia* 4: 412–444.

Westlake, H. D., 1969: *Essays on the Greek Historians and Greek History*. Manchester.

Whitby, M., 1998: "The Grain Trade of Athens in the Fourth Century BC," in Parkins and Smith (1998): 102–128.

Whitehead, D., 1977: *The Ideology of the Athenian Metic*. Cambridge.

———, 1983: "Competitive Outlay and Community Profit: ΦΙΛΟΤΙΜΙΑ in Democratic Athens," *Classica et Medievalia* 34: 55–74.

———, 2000: *Hypereides*. Oxford.

Wilson, P., 1991: "Demosthenes 21 (*Against Meidias*): Democratic Abuse," *Proceedings of the Cambridge Philological Society* 37: 164–195.

———, 1999: "The Aulos in Athens," in Goldhill and Osborne (1999): 58–95.

————, 2000: *The Athenian Institution of the Khoregeia.* Cambridge.

————, 2002: "The Musicians among the Actors," in Easterling and Hall (2002): 39–68.

Worthington, I., ed., 1994: *Persuasion: Greek Rhetoric in Action.* London.

————, 2000: *Demosthenes: Statesman and Orator.* London.

INDEX